A HISTORY OF
HAMLET CRITICISM
1601-1821

A HISTORY OF

HAMLET CRITICISM

1601 - 1821

PAUL S. CONKLIN

New Mexico College of Agriculture
and Mechanic Arts

HUMANITIES PRESS

New York 1968

Reprinted 1967 By
Arrangement With The
Author's Son, Paul Conklin

Printed in U.S.A. by
NOBLE OFFSET PRINTERS, INC.
NEW YORK 3, N. Y.

TO

Laura Faville Conklin

Preface

THIS STUDY has grown out of work I did for my doctorate at the University of Minnesota between 1935 and 1937. In fact, at that time I presented a dissertation dealing with *Hamlet* criticism up to the year 1800. Since then I have revised and expanded the original material, increasing its content by at least one-third. In several respects I trust that the present work is a more mature and more seasoned treatment than it was possible for me to accomplish then.

I cannot with assurance claim that my completed study makes mention of every relevant document bearing on the subject. It is my feeling, however, that no item of genuine value in *Hamlet* criticism between 1601-1821 has been slighted or overlooked. Whether my conviction is or is not justified, others must judge.

No formal bibliography is appended here. My footnotes, often elaborated I fear to painful lengths, give the exact citations necessary for the purpose. Background material is noted, and modern critics insofar as they seem relevant to the context, are mentioned. More than this would seem to me mere scholarly impedimenta.

In a work of this type, it would be impossible to give mention to the many individuals who have helped me on with the project. I feel, constrained, nevertheless, to name several for whose assistance I am especially grateful. The late C. R. Baskervill of the University of Chicago, in whose classes my interest in Elizabethan studies was first awakened, is one. Then also, there is R. S. Crane, of the same university, who gave me in his seminars the most disciplined training in the science of bibliography that one might ask for. Finally, I must speak of E. E. Stoll of the University of Minnesota, of whose work on Shakespeare and other poets and dramatists I surely need say nothing. I owe to him a heavier debt of gratitude than I can ever hope to repay. During the years in which I have had this material before me, he has given me constant encouragement and invaluable criticism.

I must mention also, the generous way in which the attendants of such libraries as those at the University of Chicago, the University of Michigan, the Library of Congress, the Folger Library, Columbia, Yale and Harvard have seen to it that I have found in their archives the materials that I needed.

The following publishers and individuals have given me their kind permission to quote from materials in copyright, or of which they are the authorized publishers:

To J. M. Dent and Sons, London, for excerpts from the Waller and Glover edition of Wm. Hazlitt, 1903; E. P. Dutton, for a selection from Lamb's *Tales of Shakespeare* in the Everyman edition; The Macmillan Company and the Cambridge University Press, for material from *Reformer* No. 9, found in *The Early Life and Correspondence of Edmund Burke,* ed. Samuels, 1923; Methuen and Company, London, for excerpts from the *Works* of Charles Lamb, ed. E. V. Lucas, 1903; Oxford University Press, for quotations from Walter Raleigh's *Johnson on Shakespeare,* 1925, Johnson's *Rasselas,* ed. G. B. Hill, reprint, 1926, and *The Letters of John Keats,* ed. M. B. Forman, 1935; Presses Universitaires de France, Paris, for a quotation from Paul Van Tieghem's *La Poésie de la Nuit et des Tombeaux,* in *Le Préromantisme,* 1930; Charles Scribner's Sons, for an excerpt from G. C. D. Odell's *Shakespeare from Betterton to Irving,* 1920; Mr. E. L. McAdam, Jr., for a quotation from his unpublished Master's thesis, *The Shakespearian Criticism of Kames, Richardson, and Mackenzie,* the University of Minnesota, 1929; and Professor George W. Stone, Jr., for quotations from his doctoral dissertation, *Garrick's Handling of Shakespeare's Plays and his Influence upon the Changed Attitude of Shakespearian Criticism during the Eighteenth Century,* Harvard, 1937.

Hanover,   P. S. C.
April 18, 1947

Contents

Introduction

I N THIS STUDY my main object is to investigate the growth of
Hamlet criticism from its beginnings through the year 1821. I shall
concern myself primarily with the character of Hamlet himself, and
his place in the play. Other aspects of criticism are treated when they impinge, as they often do, upon this central problem. It need hardly be said
that the character of the hero is the point of major consideration in modern criticism of *Hamlet*. Sooner or later all roads lead to this focal issue.

Although it is in no sense my function to set forth here *my* conception
of Hamlet's character, the reader will find that as chronicler and historian I have almost of necessity taken sides. One can hardly make his
way through the endless mazes of this criticism, and achieve any clarity of
thought regarding it, unless he forms his own opinion on the issues involved. The exigencies of exposition demand some yardstick, some critical norm around which the various findings may be grouped. The use of
such a yardstick at least implies partisanship. Notwithstanding this fact,
these pages will record all shades of critical opinion. And the reader, in
case my analysis of the data displeases him, is free to form his own judgment. *Hamlet* criticism as described here is set forth chronologically in an
historical framework. The story of this critical opinion becomes partly an
account of certain dominant trends of thought, or ways of looking on life
that have had their vogue in these 220 years. Different periods have had
different standards of criticism. They have had their peculiar vocabular-
ies, sometimes for saying the same thing. At times one word (for example,
"melancholy") in two periods denotes two things. The climate of opinion,
to use Leslie Stephen's term, of the early Eighteenth Century is not that
of its close, or to look ahead, of the period of Coleridge. These various
fashions of thinking and feeling are reflected in the criticism of *Hamlet*.
My purpose is to set forth descriptively this panorama. Hence the word
"historical."

It will be well at once to make a definite distinction between *Hamlet*
the play as acted, and *Hamlet* the play as read. It is not always easy to determine which *Hamlet* is being discussed by a critic; but as far as possible
the differences between these two types of criticism must be noted. The
importance of this fact should become increasingly clear as I proceed.

The data to be examined may be divided into the following three groups:

1. The allusions to *Hamlet,* widely diversified in type, which are found all through the Seventeenth and Eighteenth centuries. These allusions are often the imaginative bits that have struck the mind of some later poet, dramatist, or other writer. They may concern themselves with some larger aspect of the play, the moralizing over a skull, for example. Or again they may involve that central image, the ghost in armour, which seems to have been an item of association never long absent from the popular mind. It is possible to sense in these allusions the inner quality of a period's approach to Hamlet, how it viewed him through its own special lenses. This general and widespread material is consciously critical in only a minor sense, if at all. However, for this very reason such gleanings are valuable, and form an excellent background against which to throw the more explicitly relevant materials to be found in groups 2 and 3.

2. Under this group comes comment that is definitely theatrical in quality, comment which sets forth Hamlet as an histrionic figure. Many times it is centered upon the reigning Hamlet—upon Betterton, Garrick, or Kemble, for example. Under this category come specific reviews of a theatrical performance, certain memoirs about or by actors, and lastly, a widely diffused literature written by anyone and everyone, involving the history of *Hamlet* on the stage. By its very nature, this comment is anything but philosophical or really critical. It has its eye on the object, or takes the less complicated "public-speaking" attitude toward the play. It often centers upon the casual or merely colorful. How could it be otherwise when it comes from the pens of writers so widely separated in culture and native endowment as Addison and a linen-draper's apprentice? In my study I shall segregate the presentation of this material, through the time of Garrick. Afterwards, the items that are first and last obviously theatrical in point of view are less easy to isolate, largely because of the fact that such a point of view was often lost, or compromised by other attitudes.

3. The last group includes the largest and most important body of critical material—that in which there is a conscious effort to set forth a critical philosophy, or a more or less comprehensive discussion of Hamlet's character. These writers are usually critics in a sense that is different from the writers in group 2. Still, while the writers of group 3 have the philosophical or critical point of view so often lacking in the theatrical commentators of group 2, at times they lack quite obviously or painfully any feeling for the play as a dramatic entity; or the theatrical sense they exhibit is

conspicuously inadequate; or, for other reasons to be pointed out later, they ignore the simplest fundamentals of historical criticism. For these various reasons, all involving an absent or imperfect theatrical sense, eighteenth-century criticism of *Hamlet* from the 1770's on, becomes increasingly complex.

The thoroughness with which the critics of this last group approach any study of Hamlet's character varies. Early discussions of the play did not look upon the hero's character as a subject needing much elaboration. The point of view in which such a consideration is important is seen only after 1770. Thus it is that we shall have to be satisfied with a few words from Dennis, a few paragraphs from Addison and Steele, a quick comment from William Guthrie, and all too little from Samuel Johnson. Others add equally meagre bits. What is more, the two earliest essays that deal exclusively with *Hamlet* offer little on his character.[1] One's main consolation lies in the fact that critical silences are often fairly eloquent evidence upon the issue under investigation.

In my descriptive analysis, I shall at times present a series of critical excerpts that fall rather consistently under one or other of the three divisions outlined. At other times it will be necessary to cross rapidly over the boundary lines of one type of material to that of another. No conception of "types" must tyrannize here. The important consideration is what the material means in the process of analyzing a certain period's interpretation of Hamlet. My research has led me to believe that the Seventeenth and Eighteenth Centuries, certainly up to 1770, had one fairly consistent interpretation, expressed of course in different terms at various times. There are, indeed, shades of emphasis appropriate to a period, and now and then there are notes of dissent or prophecy. But what is more remarkable is the uniformity in critical point of view, spoken of above.

One final remark. The picture that develops is one more individualized than can be expressed by such general terms as "heroic" or "unheroic"; strong or weak; resolute or irresolute. The picture, with its various shades of coloration and emphasis, this more or less "consistent" Hamlet who exists from the time of Shakespeare until about 1770 will then serve as a norm against which to place in contrast later interpretations.

1. *Some Remarks on the Tragedy of Hamlet,* 1736; and *Miscellaneous Observations on the Tragedy of Hamlet,* 1752.

PART ONE

The Seventeenth-Century Hamlet

1

The Seventeenth-Century Hamlet

HAMLET criticism must of course be set against the background
of Shakespeare criticism in general. The latter evolved as a diffused and scattered phenomenon that became slightly more
unified and concentrated toward the end of the Seventeenth Century;
and finally crystallized into a formal entity in the next century. Its beginnings are found in a thousand and one scattered allusions that go back to
the closing days of the Sixteenth Century—to men like Edmund Spenser
and Robert Greene.[1] It is not my task here to trace the rise of this general
body of ideas, interesting though such a task would be.[2] Of the early references specifically to Hamlet, some are too general to be of great value
in this study.[3] What is of value is fragmentary indeed. However, at times
even fragments tell much.

The seventeenth-century Hamlet can take on a distinctness of outline
only by an act of the imagination—by the use of the bits at our disposal
to discreet advantage, and by frequent comparison with the more plentiful materials of the Eighteenth Century. It is a commonplace of knowledge that this early period did not gather its impressions of Hamlet in
the study. Shakespeare's plays were not widely available in printed form
until long after the years we are now examining. Without doubt, there-

1. Spenser notices Shakespeare, many scholars believe, in his reference to Aetion, in
Colin Clout's come home again, a shepherd "whose muse . . . doth like himself heroi-
cally sound." Greene's notice of Shakespeare is the famous one in *The Groats-worth of
Wit.*

2. *The Shakespere Allusion Book* (London, 1932), Vol. I, gives an excellent collection of these critical beginnings. If one were mentioning landmarks, the list might
be made up somewhat as follows: It is Ben Jonson's verdict "That Shakespeare
wanted arte" that first strikes the neo-classical note which forms so conspicuous a
part of later judgments on Shakespeare. We find other such critical beginnings in
Margaret Cavendish's *Sociable Letters* (1664); Dryden's scattered essays and prefaces;
Rymer's *The Tragedies of the Last Age Considered* (1678); and his *A Short View of
Tragedy* (1693); the first efforts toward biography, such as Winstanley's passage in
"The Life of King Richard III" (in *England's Worthies,* 1684); John Aubrey's account
in the *Aubrey Manuscripts* (c. 1680); the dramatic miscellanies of Langbaine, 1691,
Gildon, 1698, and Downes (published 1708); and the moralistic fulminations of Col-
lier in his *Short View,* with the answers they provoked.

3. For example, Gabriel Harvey's reference, which is one of the earliest: "The
younger sort takes much delight in Shakespeare's Venus and Adonis; but his Lucrece,
and his tragedy of Hamlet, Prince of Demarke, have it in them to please the wiser
sort." (*Allusion Book,* I, 56.)

fore, the Seventeenth Century knew *Hamlet* almost wholly by "direct perspective." It knew the play, not as a book, but as a dramatic experience. Its prince was a histrionic one. Through the printed records of the period, in pieces of all kinds, drama, fiction, poetry or other forms difficult to classify, we find echoes of Hamlet's words. These widespread echoes have their genesis in the type of phrase or idea that would strike the popular imagination of the century by direct contagion, caught in the theatre. They contain a potent spark of Shakespeare's imagination, a spark that could continue to glow with life because it had made contact with the imagination of another. What a vivid imprint on the period some of Hamlet's experiences, articulate in his words, made! The telling witness of this fact is the record: Hamlet's meeting with his father's ghost;[4] his "hillo, ho, ho,"; his whimsical "truepenny"; his "hic and ubique"; his words at the time he spared the king at prayer, words that some eighteenth-century critics were to call "cruel"; fragments of his bantering cynicism with Ophelia; his indignant reproach of his mother; his "funeral baked meats"; his words to the players; his

> *undiscover'd country from whose bourn*
> *No traveller returns.*

his moralizing on a skull; all these phrases of Hamlet's, preserved in memory through some dynamic vigor they possess, reflecting as they do a hero whose dramatic qualities had gone home to the heart and the imagination, are echoed through the Seventeenth Century, but especially through its earlier years.

One of the simplest impressions to be gathered from all this is that the age, as well as succeeding ones, enjoyed an "eloquent" prince. Whatever else they found in him—heroism or caution, activity or procrastination—they did accept him as a talker. Many years later, a minor scholar of the early Nineteenth Century, himself under the sway of critical attitudes now outmoded, says of Hamlet's gift of speech:

I believe our gratification will be found to result chiefly from the inherent and overbearing energies of the writing; from sentiments naturally introduced, and

4. Possibly through association, the Seventeenth Century remembered with equal facility, phrases from the ghost as it talked to Hamlet. One such bit carries the image of the hair of a terror-stricken mortal, standing on end: "Like quills upon the fretful porpentine" (See *The Merry Divel of Edmonton,* 1617 edit., *Sign* A3ᵛ; and Edward Ward, *The London Spy, for the Month of May, 1699,* p. 15.) Another such phrase is the ghost's "glowworm's uneffectual fire." One example of its use is found in Glapthorne's (?) *The Lady Mother,* 1635. (See A. H. Bullen, *A Collection of Old English Plays,* London, 1883, II, 178.) It is worth notice here that the ghost's phrase is embedded in the one section of the play that rises above its comic context to the achievement of a genuinely poetic and tragic power.

happily expressed; from that kind of fascinating eloquence which charms us in the Eloisa of Rousseau, notwithstanding the egregious improprieties that are attached to that composition.[5]

Aside from the fact that Seymour goes on to find "improprieties" in *Hamlet* also, a blemish of which the Seventeenth Century surely was not conscious, one may agree with, and yet press further the evaluation of this critic. Yes, like later periods, the Seventeenth Century was impressed with Hamlet's eloquence, but found in him, not in his creator, "inherent and overbearing energies." Indeed, as any student who examines Elizabethan drama in its social setting realizes, the theatre-goer surely loved the mouth-filling flood of iambic pentameter through which the dramatic experience was expressed and realized. So, in very truth, he found this "eloquent prince" to his taste. But the words themselves were not his primary focus of interest. I have found no mention in seventeenth-century literature, although such a reaction to Hamlet occurs many times over in later years, of a talkative prince. In this early period his eloquence was taken for granted, as merely the vehicle through which Hamlet's dramatic picturesqueness, his sharp liveliness, his melodramatic color comes home to them. How natural this is when one considers the fact that the record comes not from the pens of critics, but from the direct experience of the theatre-goer, and that it is embodied in a thousand and one phrases remembered from the lips of Burbage and his successors in the role. Eloquence, yes, but eloquence that expresses the life experience of the most interesting and most highly dramatic character on the Elizabethan stage!

We may now attempt to build up in more specific detail a picture of Hamlet and his character as the Seventeenth Century found him noteworthy. The early prince was most decidedly a malcontent avenger who still kept the markings of his Kydian ancestry. The evidence is too unmistakable to be controverted. Especially is this true of the earlier century. Here Hamlet is in the main pictured and accepted as a more primitive, more direct, more "Kydian," less individualized phenomenon than in the eighteenth-century interpretation. He must have been far less of the finely tuned Danish prince of Garrick's representation, a prince upon whom every breath of emotion played as upon an Aeolian lyre. This earlier Hamlet was more purely a straightforward avenger. This period did not see the prince in isolation as a figure to psychologize or dissect—the fate he finally came to in the closing days of the next century. It saw him as a mortal upon whom the ghost of his murdered father had laid a

5. E. H. Seymour, *Remarks, critical, conjectural, and explanatory upon the Plays of Shakespeare,* (London, 1803), II, 204, ff.

terrible and terrifying command.[6] In connection with this play and its central theme, the ghost had a place in the imagination of the English people which it was not to lose for many a day. It was of course inevitable that the "Hamlet, revenge" motif made popular by the Kydian Hamlet[7] should be reinforced later by Shakespeare's play.

The unmixed and elemental quality of this central motif in Hamlet's character is made clear by the nature of the allusions and the situations of which they are a part. Also, the wide variety in these situations bears eloquent testimony to the fact that the hero's actions and words were so thoroughly a common possession of the people that memories of him and of them could be fitted into widely differing contexts.

In Sir Thos. Smith's *Voiage and Entertainment in Rushia*, 1605, a young "once hoped-for Prince" commits suicide with his mother, when he finds that his father had done the same thing. Another more legitimate heir was coming to take possession of the kingdom. The young man

must notoriously know . . . that his Sonne was setting . . . and that the right heire was . . . apparent: that his father's Empire and Gouernment, was but as the *Poeticall Furie in a Stage-action*, compleat yet with horrid and wofull Tragedies: a first, but no second to any *Hamlet*; and that now *Reuenge*, iust *Reuenge* was comming with his Sworde draune against him, his royall Mother and dearest Sister, to fill vp those Murdering Sceanes;[8]

From this terrible situation the young prince escapes by suicide, but he leaves behind him a manly note defending himself against any possible charge of cowardice for not living to defend himself.

Two other very early allusions are a part of situations comic in tone. In 1607 a character in *West-Ward Hoe* is discussing marital infidelity, and says: "let these husbands play mad *Hamlet;* and crie reuenge. . . ."[9] This simple verbal motif, corresponding to Hieronimo's "Vindicta," was apparently in the old Kydian play. From the same year, Fletcher's *Woman Hater* contains an exact verbal echo of words that pass between Hamlet and the ghost, words not found in Quarto I, and here set in an atmosphere of burlesque:

Lazerello: Let me not fall from my selfe; speake I am bound to heare.

6. The ghost has a place either explicitly or by implication in 23 of the allusions I have found. Doubtless there are others. It is safe to say that revenge, the ghost, and the hero of the play were connected in the popular mind as different angles of the same dramatic situation.

7. As has been often pointed out, both Thomas Lodge's *Wit's Miserie*, 1596 (p. 56) and Dekker's *Satiromastix* (*Sign.* G3ᵛ), probably performed in the early autumn of 1601, contain this verbal motif as an echo from the Kydian play.

8. *Sigs.* 14ᵛ and K.

9. *Sign.* H3.

Count: So art thou to reuenge, when thou shalt heare the fish head is gone, and we know not whither.[10]

A fourth echo more serious in quality than the two just given is found in Samuel Rowlands *The Night Raven* of 1620. Here a scrivener, robbed of both cloak and hat, says:

> I will not cry *Hamlet Reuenge* my greeues
> But I will cal *Hang-man Reuenge* on theeues.[11]

It is obvious that in three of these four references, the phraseology is primitive and Kydian in quality. The chances are, nevertheless, that all four are connected with Shakespeare's play. For one must remember that by 1605, the year of the earliest allusion here, *Hamlet* had been in performance at least three, and possibly four years. Thus the law of probability would sanction the view that Shakespeare's revenge play had merely made more proverbial still a "Hamlet, revenge" fixation which the popular mind already possessed.

It is possible, however, to find early allusions to Hamlet as revenger that reflect the Shakespearean prince and situation in contexts that have more of the spirit of the original than any I have yet given. In the first one, from Beaumont and Fletcher's *Four Playes, or Morall Representations, in One,* acted in 1608 (?), Perolet, a young and noble former suitor, comes back to rescue Gabriella from the foul clutches of an unworthy husband:

> *Gabriella:* Wee'll watch him till he wakes,
>   Then bind him, and torture him.
>
> *Perolet:*   'Tis nothing.
>   No, take him dead drunk now without repentance,
>   His leacherie inseam'd upon him.[12]

Here, as can be seen, in a quite different context, the prince whom the Eighteenth Century was to call "cruel," is reflected. In one other play from the next year, Armin's *The History of the Two Maids of Moreclacke,* we find allusions set in a dramatic situation that is much closer to Hamlet's own. Here, young Humil, in remorse over his mistake in having thought his mother adulterous, cries:

> Sir, for your wrongs, if you remit black torture, tis
> My hell, and I appeale to sterne rigor, O you sonnes,
> Whose true obedience shines in maiesty,
> While mine more ugly then is vulcans tithye,
> Smels ranker then despised Hemlocke.[13]

10. *Sign.* D2.
11. *Sign.* D2.
12. Ffffff 2ᵛ. (London, 1647).
13. *Sign.* E3. (Tudor Facsimile Text, 1913).

A little later, in much the same tone, he exclaims:

> was I bewitcht
> That thus at hud-man blind I dallied
> With her I honor'd?[14]

The references I have given, starting with that from Sir Thomas Smith in 1605, are of varying tone and quality, but all of them reflect some angle of a fairly simple revenge situation, and all of them seem to me indisputably Shakespearian in origin. Some of them are more Kydian in tone than are others. None is dated later than 1630.[15] Three others I have found are dated 1682, 1698, and 1700 respectively, and are reminiscences of Hamlet's triumphant "strucken deer" speech.[16] The conclusion I would draw is that as the century progressed, Hamlet the avenger lost most of the direct Kydian associations he possessed as a necessary ancestral heritage, and appeared thereafter exclusively in his Shakespearian setting.

To proceed, what other characteristics of this avenger are reflected or distorted in the literature of the Seventeenth Century? Hamlet was seen, first of all, most decidedly as a malcontent; and at times as "madd," either as a lover or as possessed with a madness that is quite primitive and realistic, with comic overtones.

The Elizabethans must have looked upon the malady of malcontentism as containing aspects that were close to real madness.[17] The views of the first thirty years of the century are, in reference to Hamlet's character, reminiscent of several conceptions. It is not always easy to disentangle the various strands of thought and attitude. However, there are a number of echoes of a malcontent Hamlet who seems far from unbalanced. He is a Hamlet whom we can know today if we rid our perceptions of

14. *Sign.* E3ᵛ.
15. One is tempted to add a bit from Ford as evidence here:
> let my hot hare have law ere he be hunted to his death, that, if it be possible, he may post to hell in the very act of his damnation. (*Tis Pity She's a Whore*, V, iv.)

The idea expressed in this passage is, however, too widespread to be referred with confidence to Hamlet.

16. Aphra Behn, *The City-Heiress, Sign.* A3; *Pendragon, or the Carpet Knight, His Kalendar,* in *Allusion Book,* II, 416; and Edward Ward, *the Metamorphosed Beau,* in G. Thorn-Drury, *Some seventeenth century allusions to Shakespeare . . .* (London, 1920), p. 48.

17. Hamlet as malcontent is best treated by E. E. Stoll in "Shakspere, Marston, and the Malcontent Type," *MP.,* 3, 281-303. A point of view that contrasts with that of Stoll is taken by O. J. Campbell in his "Jaques," (*The Huntington Library Bulletin,* No. 8, Oct. 1935, pp. 71-102.) I have received helpful suggestions also from F. J. Marston, *A Study of the Malcontent Types in the Dramas of Shakespeare and Marston,* (U. of Chicago Master's Thesis, 1926).

any sentimental coloring, and try to be imaginatively sympathetic with this earlier period. This Hamlet is masculine and primitive. He is melancholy, but his emotion is not of the graveyard type so common in the next century; nor is it similar to that century's "social tear." This malcontentism is often bitterly sarcastic, cynical, cruel and obscene. No matter what admirers of Shakespeare's Danish prince may say, these lines exist in *Hamlet*. And the Seventeenth Century, especially in its earlier years, liked this bitter prince. We have already seen this emotional tone in such lines as those quoted from Beaumont and Fletcher's *Four Playes,* and of course its potency animates the "strucken deer" references in spite of the fact that at times the original tone is weakened by a new situation, or new context.

Here it is necessary to reemphasize a point already made, but one which must be continually before us in examining this early evidence. It is often difficult to separate the voice of Shakespeare's Hamlet in his harsher moods from that of the earlier Kydian figure, whose actual words of course we do not have. One case in point involves the proverb-like sentence from Robert Armin, in 1608: "Ther are, as Hamlet saies, things cald whips in store."[18] Shakespeare's prince did not utter these words, although one feels he might well have done so. It happens, however, that Hieronimo of *The Spanish Tragedy,* in his ravings over his murdered son, does say:

> And there is Nemesis, and Furies,
> And things call'd whips,
> And they sometimes do meet with murderers;[19]

It would seem possible that the Kydian Hamlet also uttered this sentiment. Armin, in 1608, with Shakespeare's play and no other on the stage, must have been thinking in terms of the reigning Hamlet, but puts into his mouth the primitive sentiments of earlier prototypes of that prince. Even before 1608, however, Hamlet's words to Rosencrantz and Guildenstern in Act II, ii, are echoed by Peter Woodhouse in *The Flea,* 1605.[20] Ten years later, Alex Niccoles paraphrases words again that are authentically Shakespearian, and by their situation and tone connected with Hamlet, although actually spoken by the player-queen. A chaste wife is importuned to be unfaithful during the absence of her husband, but she says:

18. *A Nest of Ninnies, Simply of themselves without Compound, Sign.* G3ᵛ.

19. IV, iv, lines 40-42. The value of this evidence is somewhat qualified by the fact that these lines are part of additions found in the Quarto of 1602, additions ascribed, somewhat doubtfully, to Ben Jonson. These additions may quite possibly go back to a considerably earlier period.

20. *Democritus his Dreame, or, The Contention between the Elephant and the Flea* (ed. Grosart, Blackburn, 1877), p. 35.

> In second husband let me be acurst
> None weds the second, but who kils the first[21]

Then in 1637, we get an echo of Hamlet himself, this time in one of his explicitly acid moments, as he talks to his mother (III, iv, 92-3), from Shakerley Marmion. Here the sisters of Psyche are exhorting her to kill her serpent husband, and they commence by emphasizing her present degradation:

> Now if this uncouth life, and solitude
> Please you, then follow it, and be still stew'd
> In the ranke lust of a lascivious worme:[22]

Last of all, from the very close of the century, *Pendragon, or the Carpet Knight,* already quoted, reechoes Hamlet's cynical by-play with Polonius, involving the cloud, the camel and the whale.[23]

The period, however, took from Hamlet's words a tone that probes more sharply still to the very bottom of the prince's cynical, bitter, and often cruel imagination, a tone which gives what I might call the full depths of malcontentism; and the expression of this deeper phase is often mingled with a tendency which is most definitely the century's own: the "memento mori" complex of ideas and emotions. Nothing, of course, is more characteristic of the Seventeenth Century than this; and what is more, through an evolutionary process this tendency reappears as a very different thing in the next century, though as a melancholy more in harmony with eighteenth-century predilections and tastes. What is interesting for our special purposes is that both centuries fasten upon certain aspects of Hamlet's character as harmonious with their own special approach to melancholy thoughts and emotions.

Hamlet's speeches, skull in hand, in Act V, i, must be seen in the light of a large body of lugubrious writings in the early Seventeenth Century. These writings, mostly religious, have a morbid preoccupation with graveyards, skeletons, skulls, and the like. Such themes of course have come down throughout the whole history of Christianity. The theme of "memento-mori" was very popular from the late Fifteenth to the early Seventeenth Centuries,[24] in the pulpit, on tombstones, in popular art,

---

21. *A Discourse of Marriage and Wiving,* p. 40.
22. *A Morall Poem, Intituled the Legend of Cvpid and Psyche, Sign.* E4[V].
23. *Allusion Book,* II, 416.
24. A French critic says: "Le xv siècle est celui des Danses macabres dans l'art et dès thèmes macabres dans la poésie. C'est à la même inspiration que se rattachent les scènes du cimetière au cinquième acte de *Hamlet.* Mais, avec le triomphe de l'idéal classique en Europe, cette veine sépulcrale, tantôt pathétique et tantôt railleuse, ou tous les deux, à la fois, tarit complètement dans la littérature, et surtout dans la poésie, plus soucieuse de plaire que d'enseigner." (Paul Van Tieghem, *La Poésie de la Nuit. . . .* 1921; quoted here from reprint in *Le Préromantisme,* Paris, 1930, p. 7).

and in literature. In the late Elizabethan period, this macabre tendency was deepened by Puritan influence.[25]

It is thus easily seen why seventeenth-century writers fastened upon Hamlet's malcontent musings with a skull. As early as 1604, in Part I of *The Honest Whore,* a character picks up a skull and philosophizes in a Hamlet-like vein:

> What's here? *(takes the skull)*
> Perhaps this shrewd pate was mine enemy's.
> 'Las! say it were; I need not fear him now!
> For all his braves, his contumelious breath,
> His frowns, though dagger-pointed, all his plot,
> Though ne'er so mischievous, his Italian pills,
> His quarrels, and that common fence, his law, . . .[26]

In 1606, John Raynold's poem, *Dolarnys Primerose, or the first part of the passionate Hermit,* seems even more reminiscent of *Hamlet.* The old hermit, who is leading a solitary life because of disappointment in love, takes a skull in his hand:

> He held it still, in his sinister hand,
> He turn'd it soft, and stroakt it with the other,
> He smil'd on it, and oft demurely faund,
> As it had beene, the head of his owne brother:
>   Oft would h'have spoke, but something bred delay;
>   At length halfe weeping, these words did he say.
>
> This barren scull, that here you do behold,
> Why might it not, haue beene an Emperours head? . . .
>
> Why might not this, haue beene some lawiers pate
> The which sometimes, brib'd, brawl'd, and tooke a fee,
> And lawe exacted, to the highest rate?

25. Examples of typical memento-mori Puritan literature should include: an elegy published in three forms under the following titles: *A Buckler Against Fear of Death,* 1640; *Midnights, Meditations, and Death with Pious and Profitable Observations,* 1646; and *Death Dissected* . . . 1650. Henry Vaughan's *Charnel House* had the same inspiration.

A bibliography of works on seventeenth-century memento-mori literature should include: Paul Van Tieghem, *La Poésie de la Nuit et des tombeaux,* 1921; Amy Reed, *The Background of Gray's Elegy,* 1924; J. W. Draper, *The Funeral Elegy and the Rise of English Romanticism,* 1929; Theodore Spencer, *Death and Elizabethan Tragedy,* 1936; three articles by C. A. Moore, *MLN,* 40, 431, ff; *Studies in Phil.,* 22, 467, ff; and *MP,* 24, 321, ff.

As an example of how the memento-mori conception colored the "real life" of the period as well as its literature, one may cite the striking preparations for his death-made by John Donne: the charcoal fires, the urn and the winding sheet, described so well by Isaak Walton in *The Life of Dr. John Donne,* 1640.

26. Act IV, i, lines 63-69.

Why might not this, be such a one as he?
Your quirks, and quillets, now sir where be they,
Now he is mute, and not a word can say.[27]

To be mentioned also, are several "skull scenes" in two plays of Cyril Tourneur: *The Revenger's Tragedy,* 1607 (?), and *The Atheist's Tragedy,* 1611 (?).[28] In each case the situation and words are reminiscent of the similar scene in *Hamlet.* The same thing may be said of Act IV, iii, of Randolph's *Jealous Lovers,* 1632. For example, at one place a sexton says:

It had been a mighty favour once, to have kiss'd these lips that grin so. . . . Oh! if that Lady now could but behold this physnomie of hers in a looking-glasse, what a monster would she imagine herself! Will all her perrukes, tyres and dresses, with her chargeable teeth, with her cerusse and pomatum, and the benefit of her painter and doctor, make this idol up again?

> Paint Ladies while you live, and plaister fair
> But when the house is fallne 'tis past repair.[29]

The allusion just given is the latest full "skull speech" reminiscent of *Hamlet,* which I have found in the Seventeenth Century.[30] Definite echoes from *Hamlet* of the type I have been describing so far seem to grow less frequent after the 1730's. The reason for the disappearance of "skull speeches" from the literature of the time seems to be that the memento-mori motif, still found in such abundance, is expressed less often dramatically, the specific form which would link it most obviously with Hamlet's words.

The Seventeenth Century, at least in its first twenty years, gives evidence of another special aspect of its interest in Hamlet's character. His madness was a phenomenon of special interest. Madness itself is not incongruous with malcontent characteristics; in fact the malcontent was supposed to be suffering from a malady which hovered between melancholy and downright insanity. His sudden lapses from sense to nonsense, from an ordered contemplation to bitter and cunning cruelty, his railing at women, his obscenity, his meditations on suicide, his talking instead of acting, his overt impulses themselves, that at times seem the result of

27. *Sigs.* D4^v. and E.
28. For the first of these plays, see the opening speech of Vindice, Act I, i. It is less reminiscent of *Hamlet* than the skull scene in the second. For this, see *Sign.* H3^v, ff.
29. Pp. 60-61.
30. One other poem that echoes Hamlet's words in Act V, i, although not specifically a "skull poem", is found in John Weever's *Ancient Funerall Monuments,* 1631, pp. 492-3. One later century skull poem is mentioned by Amy Reed, *op. cit.,* p. 68: *The Counter-Turn,* "a sort of Hamlet-like meditation on the skull of a politician." This poem is by Nahum Tate.

hysteria,—all this is at moments a part of Hamlet's character and actions. Besides, there is the Hamlet who is mad from love, as Polonius interpreted him. The earlier Seventeenth Century must have liked both the mad lover and the malcontent, whose madness might take almost any incongruous form, including a type of insanity quite primitive and realistic.

First let us look at the mad lover: In 1604, Anthony Scoloker's cryptic poem on "Daiphantus in love" gives a description of a mad lover that adds explicit details of dress and action not found in *Hamlet*. Yet the author was quite definitely thinking of Shakespeare's prince as he wrote the poem. As well as other literary sources, *Hamlet* furnished him with a number of mental suggestions, and no doubt with the most important ones. Consequently it is fair to say that the strange Daiphantus gives a clue to Scoloker's attitude toward Hamlet. He may wish to tell us that this mad lover of his, who is dressed like Hamlet, acts and speaks like him also:

> His breath, he thinkes the smoke; his tongue a cole,
> Then calls for bottell-ale; to quench his thirst:
> Runs to his Inke-pot, drinkes, then stops the hole,
> And thus growes madder, then he was at first.
>> *Tasso,* he finds, by that of *Hamlet,* thinkes
>> Tearmes him a mad-man; than of his Inkhorne drinks.

He also:

> Calls Players fooles, the foole he iudgeth wisest,
> Will learne them Action out of *Chaucers* Pander:
> . . . .
>> Puts off his cloathes; his shirt he onely weares,
>> Much like mad-*Hamlet;* thus as Passion teares.[31]

In spite of Scoloker's full stop, the last phrase of the section just quoted is evidently meant to act as an introduction to the next stanza. The mad lover now starts to "tear a passion to tatters":

> Who calls me forth from my distracted thought?
> Oh *Serberus,* If thou, I prethy speke?
> Reuenge if thou? I was thy Riuall ought,
> In purple gores Ile make the ghosts to reake:
>> *Vitullia,* oh *Vitullia,* be thou still,
>> Ile haue reuenge, or harrow vp my will.[32]

The next stanzas are filled with a mad piling up of hyperbole that in

---

31. *Daiphantvs, or The Passions of Love, etc.* (reprint ed. Grosart, Manchester, 1880), *Sign.* E4ᵛ.
32. *Ibid., Sign.* E4ᵛ.

spots is distinctly reminiscent of the ranting of Laertes and Hamlet at the grave of Ophelia. In fact the poem as a whole is a fine example of a process that becomes common in the Eighteenth Century: striking suggestions that have their source in *Hamlet* undergo a period of incubation and change in another's mind and imagination, and then have their own peculiar manifestation. The interesting thing here is the nature of the suggestions taken from *Hamlet:* the mad lover, the revenge motif, the feverish hyperbole. These are quite evidently the real cue to Scoloker's interpretation of the character.

One fine passage depicting the love-mad Hamlet is at the same time a piece of more direct dramatic criticism. Notable also, is the fact that while the first excerpt seems to have comic overtones, this one is serious and elegiac in quality. It is a poem written to commemorate the death in 1618 of Richard Burbage, the first great actor in the role of Hamlet:

> hee's gone and with him what A world are dead.
> which he reuiu'd, to be reuiued soe,
> no more young Hamlett, ould Heironymoe
> kind Leer, the Greued Moore, and more beside,
> that liued in him; haue now for euer dy'de,
> oft haue I seene him, leap into the Graue
> suiting the person which he seem'd to haue
> of A sadd Louer with soe true an Eye
> that theer I would haue sworne, he meant to dye,
> oft haue I seene him, play this part in ieast,
> soe liuly, that Spectators, and the rest
> of his sad Crew, whilst he but seem'd to bleed,
> amazed, thought euen then hee dyed in deed.[33]

Three other passages that reflect Hamlet as mad are all comic in nature. In *Eastward Hoe*, 1605, "Hamlet, a foote man" enters in haste, and "Potkinne, a Tankerd-bearer" accosts him thus:

Sfoote *Hamlet:* are you madde? whether run you nowe, you should brushe vp my olde Mistresse?[34]

Again, in a "dialogue" written by Dekker, 1608, two London porters are portrayed at a piece of typical Elizabethan cony-catching in which a corpse has a leading role. A "counterfet mad man" comes running:

Sometimes would he [the other porter] ouertake him, and lay hands vppon him (like a Catch-pole) as if he had arrested him, but furious *Hamlet* woulde pres-

33. *Allusion Book*, I, 272. Except in one or two small details, one involving an obvious misprint ("smiting" for "suiting") I have copied this poem as given.
34. III, ii (see J. S. Farmer, ed., Tudor Facsimile text, 1914), *Sign.* **D.**

ently eyther breake loose like a Beare from the stake, or else so set his pawes on this dog that thus bayted him, that with tugging and tearing one anothers frockes off, they both looked like mad *Tom* of Bedlam. . . .

At length he came to the house where the deade man had bin lodged: from the dore would not this olde Ieronimo be driuen, that was his Inne, there he woulde lie, that was his Bedlam, and there or no where must his mad tricks be plaid.[35]

In 1609, Dekker published another book, this one on the Elizabethan underworld, and distinctly of a cony-catching type. In it a "mad Hamlet" rushes in, this time to disperse a crew of gypsies at their "massacre" of stolen sheep, pigs and poultry.[36]

The mad Hamlet must indeed have made a vivid impression on early audiences. Appealing as Shakespeare did so definitely to a popular audience, and using material that in origin was really primitive, it would seem probable that the madness was often played more realistically than the script itself justifies.[37] It is notable that of these last four excerpts, only in the one on Burbage is Hamlet treated sympathetically. The other three show a distinct tinge of burlesque. It is true also, that no one of the comic pieces is dated later than 1609. They thus are from the period when Shakespeare's *Hamlet* was still a comparatively new piece, even keeping in mind the faster tempo of Elizabethan dramatic history. The Eighteenth Century, and the early Ninteenth, satirized *Hamlet*, but not like this. It seems quite possible that the Elizabethan audience, close as it was to memories of an older, more primitive play, saw Hamlet's madness as at times a laughable matter. No doubt the madness of the Kydian Hamlet, like the madness of Hieronimo, had awakened in them this reaction. Kyd had intended that it should. And so when they saw the Shakespearian prince, aesthetically they were able to find in the play a more primitive irony, a closer juxtaposition of extremes than a modern audience could. Such an aesthetic reaction could be possible in a period that shows such readiness otherwise to transfer the mad Hamlet to a fully comic context. To laugh at the skillful deception of a tragic Hamlet who plays madness

35. *The Dead Terme. Or Westminister's Complaint for Long Vacations and short Termes, Sign.* G3.

36. *Lanthorne and Candle-light. Or, The Bell-Mans second Nights-Walke, Sign.* H2.

37. We can imagine that such comic interest could easily have been "bootlegged" into the play by actors who could not resist this excellent opportunity to make madness fully comic to an audience who had seen madness comic in other contexts; who indeed had memories of a more comic madness in earlier versions of the very play they were seeing, and who therefore might desire it in *this* play. And Shakespeare himself has Hamlet say to the players: "And let those that play your clowns speak no more than is set down for them; . . ."

so well, is at least a more comprehensible attitude than that of later critics who change the comic Shylock into a pathetic figure.[38]

If, in the picture of the seventeenth-century Hamlet as drawn so far, there is generally lacking an appreciation of his character that seems more congruous with our own, this very fact might be used by the historical critic as evidence that the findings in question may be authentic. For why should the seventeenth-century audience have had exactly the same aesthetic reactions to certain data that we have? Possibly too, the gulf between centuries is not such a yawning abyss as some might think it. Our data are at best fragmentary; we must not take too much for granted. It is significant that when the material of criticism becomes more plentiful, a Hamlet more congenial to us emerges. This would lead one to suspect that a more complete seventeenth-century picture, even in the early years, would produce a prince more like "ours."

To fill in the records, I shall set forth certain miscellaneous aspects of early *Hamlet* criticism. These bits too, if interpreted imaginatively, bring the prince of the period closer to that of later ones. Hamlet's "to be" soliloquy is echoed in 1616 by Beaumont and Fletcher;[39] in 1630 (?) by Heminge;[40] in 1636 by Dekker;[41] and in 1646 by Suckling.[42] Again, in 1612 and in 1638 we get probably the first examples of a habit that became common in the Eighteenth Century: the use of Hamlet's speech to the players as a model for the training of speakers. Heywood makes such a use of it in his *An Apology to Actors*, and Richard Brome in *The Antipodes*.[43] Another use of Hamlet's words, prophetic of a fairly widespread eighteenth-century practice is exemplified by Henry Tubbe, who makes certain expressions from the hero's impassioned description of his

38. Would not such a Hamlet be valid even today? Is it not more terrible to have a tragic hero at whom we at times must laugh? just as it is more terrible to have an Othello who can say:

Keep up your bright swords, for the dew will rust them

change into an Othello whose mind seethes with the obscene images of a searing jealousy? The Eighteenth Century with its horror at Hamlet's "brutality," and its sentimentalism, could never have appreciated such a prince. He would have been equally foreign to the aesthetic sensibilities of the Nineteenth.

For interesting suggestions, see John Corbin, *The Elizabethan Hamlet*, 1895. Part of what Corbin says, however, seems now outmoded.

39. *The Scorneful Ladie* (1625 edit.), *Sign.* C2.

40. *The Jewes Tragedy* (1662 edit.), lines 1141-1167.

41. *The Wonder of A Kingdome, Sign.* B3.

42. *Aglaura*, IV, i. See *Sign.* C4, after fifth title page in *Fragmenta Aurea*.

43. Heywood, *Sigs.* C3^v. and C4; Brome, *Works* (1873), III, 259-60. In a similar connection, see also three comedies of Thos. Middleton (*A Mad World, My Masters*, 1606; *The Mayor of Queensborough*, 1617-18; and *The Spanish Gypsy*, 1623), where the motif of the travelling players is touched upon. I am endebted to D. J. McGinn (*Shakespeare's Influence on the Drama of his Age, studied in Hamlet*, Rutgers, 1938, pp. 97-99) for this reference.

father (in the closet scene) the pattern for similar praise in an elegiac poem on Charles I.[44]

From many of the citations used during this first section of my study, it has been more than evident that the Seventeenth Century put Hamlet's words, or reminiscences of them, together with the actions they implied, into a variety of contexts, some of them far removed from their significance in the original. This may be said, even allowing for the fact that the term "significance of the original" is a relative thing, as well as being the very aesthetic entity that is the subject of this investigation. But, in spite of this fact of relative interpretation, we must contend that *Hamlet* the play has had certain fundamental meanings for all audiences in the English tradition who have seen it since it first appeared. With this understanding as groundwork, it will be well to bring more sharply into focus the tendency of the Seventeenth Century to depart often, and sometimes with startling completeness from Shakespeare's context. Then we may draw what conclusions seem best from this aesthetic phenomenon. Let me illustrate:

I have spoken of the use in this century of the "Hamlet, revenge" motif, as well as of reminiscences from scenes in which we see the avenging prince in "cruel" anticipation of his deed, or in connection with his adulterous mother. Connected with this complex of motifs is also the prince who in Act I swears Marcellus and Horatio to secrecy just as he is about to start his fated career. In a play acted in 1605 (?),[45] Fletcher offers a high burlesque of this moment in Hamlet's career, a burlesque that contains no hint whatever of the substance or emotional quality of the original. All of the dramatic tension gained by the impact the ghostly visitation has made on the agonized heart and imagination of Hamlet has evaporated. The new passage, although obviously an imitation of the first, is pure burlesque.

Or take another example. No words from Hamlet's tongue seem to contain more of the acidulous quality of his temperament as a malcontent than his famous:

> Thrift, thrift, Horatio! The funeral bak'd meats
> Did coldly furnish forth the marriage tables.

It is more than arresting then, to see how completely all of the quality of the original malcontent irony has disappeared from the adaptation of the idea found in two passages of *Eastward Hoe*,[46] only a few years after

44. *Allusion Book*, I, 517.
45. *The Woman's Prize, or The Tamer tamed* (1647), *Sign*, Qqqqq (r, v).
46. Tudor Facsimile, *Sigs*, B3ᵛ; and Dᵛ.

Hamlet appeared. Here again the words and idea are present in an utterly alien context.

My final example is in a way the most informative, the most relevant to our purpose. It comes from Heminge's *The Jewes Tragedy*, 1630 (?), a play that may never have been acted,[47] and already mentioned above in a cursory fashion. Here Eleazer, the Jewish rebel, speaks in long soliloquies that have an unmistakable reference back to Shakespeare's prince, even going so far as to give his ideas the garment of a "to be" soliloquy. And yet, although there is in notable degree in these utterances the tone and reflected personality of Hamlet, Eleazer is not even in a small way really like him. He has permitted his father, the High Priest, to be murdered so that he himself may take the seat of power. Thus his thoughts on filial duty are those of Hamlet in reverse. He is not an avenger, but like Hamlet he is visited by his father's ghost. Yet beyond this inverted likeness in situation, coupled with the tone of his voice and the cast of his phrases, there is between Hamlet and him no similarity. To make even more striking the difference, there is the fact that it is only at special moments of great stress, twice or three times in the play, he in this strangely inverted manner, borrows the tone of utterance, some of the phrases and the mannerism of Hamlet:

> To be, or not to be, I there's the doubt,
> For to be Sovereign by unlawful means,
> Is but to be a slave to base desire,
> And where's my honour then?
> What a strange buzzing of ambition
> Pursues my thirsty soul?
> O *Eleazer!* can thy traytor breast
> Give harbour to a thought of Paricide?
> It is thy father, O the sacred tye
> Of filial duty, how that awful name
> Affrighteth all my faculties with fear . . .
> With fear . . . of what? . . . with foolery by heaven;
> If there be ought within this awful name
> That can extort obedience from a son,
> 'Tis but the rotten Carcass, there's the thing
> That for to please its self, begets another,
> So does a beast, and yet 'twixt them we see
> An equal freedome of society:
> As for the nobler part of man we know
> That's of a higher birth, if it be so,
> Thus low my knee shall bend, but thou my heart
> Scorn to obey, remember where thou art:

47. See Alfred Harbage, *Cavalier Drama* (New York, 1936), pp. 128-29.

I am resolv'd, the times are bloody, and the peoples hearts
I hear, are bent on me: *Jehochanans* the man
That I must fairly close withall, this done,
We shall be strong for opposition.
Soft, here a comes.[48]

From these illustrations just given, of a use of Hamlet's words, together with the dramatic situations that go with them, so completely at variance with the original context and their commonly accepted interpretations, I would gain a rather important fact concerning the earlier century's attitude toward Hamlet.[49] Although its main interpretation of him as malcontent avenger, plus the corollary points of view already given, is clearly evident, the period went further than this. It was so familiar with the words and personality of the hero, these had already become such a commonplace possession, that it could disassociate him completely from his Shakesperian context; the period possessed him so thoroughly that it could even destroy his dramatic significance when it wished. Because this prince and his words already so colored the English imagination, were so intrinsically a part of the very commonplace of life, they could be used without relevance or real meaning in terms of the original. Such a phenomenon shows complete possession of an aesthetic entity. No figure in life or in art can more completely become a part of a people. Hamlet, even in the first thirty years of the Seventeenth Century had reached this position. Can the same be said of any other character in English literature? On the blasphemous tongue of everyday man, Deity achieves this possibly dubious distinction. But an imaginative figure from the world of art, seldom. Hamlet did.

As the century progresses, a more pronounced analytical spirit is in evidence,—although there are still imaginative echoes of motifs from the play. The latter appear throughout the century, though in diminishing numbers. As for the new rational spirit, it is seen first of all in certain isolated "theatrical notes"; these might be said to form at least the beginnings of formal *Hamlet* criticism, and exist side by side with the general critical beginnings of which I have already spoken.

One excellent theatrical note has already been given. I refer to that found in the elegiac poem written after the death of Burbage, describing the actor as a distracted lover leaping into Ophelia's grave. This, however,

48. 1662 edit., lines 1141-67.
49. D. J. McGinn, *op. cit.*, offers a considerable body of convincing evidence on the widespread influence of *Hamlet* in the first half of the Seventeenth Century. He furnishes a number of new allusions, not all of them, however, fully convincing. I am endebted to him for several items used in my treatment of these years.

is an isolated allusion. The others come after the Restoration. While the later references do not add definitely to a picture of Hamlet himself as interpreted in the later century, they do give one a feeling for the continuity of tradition, and a knowledge which will help him to make certain deductions concerning the point at issue. In three separate entries in his *Diary*, Samuel Pepys emphasizes the impression that Betterton in the role of Hamlet had made on him.[50] Further emphasis on the importance of Betterton's Hamlet in the Restoration is to be had from the *Roscius Anglicanus* of John Downes, not published until 1708 but containing considerable material on theatrical matters from a time early in the Restoration period.[51] Downes makes the statement that Betterton was instructed in the role by Sir William Davenant, who had seen the part performed by an actor taught by Shakespeare himself; and "No succeeding Tragedy for several Years got more Reputation, or Money to the Company than this. . . ."[52]

There are, however, two comments which would tend to show that at times *Hamlet* was considered too old-fashioned for the new days. One is a remark from John Evelyn's *Memoirs and Diary:*

I saw Hamlet Prince of Denmark played, but now the old plays began to disgust this refined age, since his Majesties being so long abroad.[53]

The other is William Mountfort's remark in 1691, to the effect that the town was "thronging" to other lighter forms of amusement, and *Hamlet* will not "bring Charges."[54]

There is little more to add. Although nothing very illuminating for this study is involved, one may mention Jeremy Collier's *A Short View of the Immorality and Profaneness of the English Stage*, 1698; and J. Drake's *The Antient and Modern Stages Survey'd*, 1699. Drake feels called upon to defend Ophelia from Collier's aspersions. Also, he interprets the play as illustrating an "admirable distribution of Poetic Justice." Collier and Drake at least deserve mention as offering the nearest approach to a formal *Hamlet* criticism in the Seventeenth Century.[55]

50. See entries in *Diary* for Aug. 24, 1661; May 28, 1663; and Aug. 31, 1668.
51. Downes was familiar with the history of Davenant's theatre from the time of its opening in 1662. He acted as Bookkeeper and Prompter up to 1706. His account of the whole period, therefore, is that of an eyewitness.
52. Facsimile reprint (London, 1886), p. 21.
53. See entry for November 26, 1661.
54. *Greenwich-Park, Sign.* A2ᵛ.
55. The Shakespearian criticism of Collier, together with the answers it provoked can be found in excerpt form in the latter part of the *Allusion Book*, volume two.
Dryden, important as he is in the consideration of general critical beginnings, offers nothing specifically on *Hamlet*. One of the first critics to show any historical sense in *Hamlet* criticism is Gerard Langbaine. In a quaint "source comment" found

Let me gather up the threads of this discussion by presenting a summary of the findings so far. The evidence, fragmentary as it is, would lead me to speak of the Hamlet of this century as largely a phenomenon of "direct perspective," dramatically incarnated for them by Burbage and his successors. Hamlet was created for the stage, and there he remained for most of those who knew him during the first hundred years of his existence. Betterton, who first acted the role for Restoration audiences, closed his career in 1709. Englishmen for over forty-five years had seen him as the Danish prince. His acting is not described by a seventeenth-century critic,—or at least more specifically than Pepys does it. We must look to an eighteenth-century commentator for that.

The evidence at hand, however, gives a Hamlet who was an eloquent talker whose dramatic picturesqueness, liveliness and human quality made him the foremost character on the Elizabethan stage. He was, in addition, a malcontent avenger whose bitter and cynical words were stamped indelibly upon the memory of at least the first thirty years of the century. It is a reasonable supposition that the Hamlet of the rest of the century had less sharp contours. The Betterton prince as described by several critics of the early Eighteenth Century, to be quoted later, is a milder and more "humane" figure. Over a period of more than forty years Betterton may have changed his interpretation considerably, thus accommodating himself to the temper of different times. But it seems hardly possible, nevertheless, that the hero described by Steele and Cibber was basically different from Betterton's earlier portrayal.

Remembering Betterton, then, one must feel that in spite of the scanty evidence, it would be unfortunate to emphasize the sharp outlines of the seventeenth-century Hamlet. The milder aspects are implicit rather than explicit in the earlier interpretation. They were taken for granted. The people were merely more interested in Hamlet's sharp tongue and in his picturesque malcontent aspects; and because of this interest they spoke of them oftener, and used motifs from them in their writings. Furthermore, one must remember that even Hamlet's milder moments, as for example the mood of the "to be" soliloquy, can sometimes be interpreted as merely another aspect in the amazing transformation which the malcontent could quickly undergo.

Historically speaking, one sees how the Seventeenth Century viewed

---

in his *Account of the English Dramatick Poets,* 1691, he says: "I know not whether this Story be true or false; but I cannot find in the List given by Dr. *Heylin,* such a King of *Denmark,* as *Claudius.* All that I can inform the Reader, is the Names of those Authors that have written of the Affairs of *Denmark* and *Norway;* and must leave it to their further search: such are *Saxo-Grammaticus, Idacius, Crantzius, Pontanus,* etc. . . . (*Ibid.,* pp. 457-8).

Hamlet through the eyes of its favorite prepossessions,—with skull in hand, as mad lover (feigned, to be sure), and, in the earlier years at least, as a more primitive and Kydian avenger than we picture him. There is also evidence that at times early audiences may have found certain comic aspects in his behavior. One finds, furthermore, unmistakable proof of the fact that very early in this period Shakespeare's prince was accepted so completely by the English people as to become part and parcel of their imaginative processes; at times they use his words, actions and personality in ways that had little or no relevance and meaning in terms of the original.

I have spoken also of the diminishing number of general allusions, especially those of an imaginative cast, and of the increasingly evident rational spirit as seen in the first meager appearance of formal criticism, including a few brief theatrical notes. Beyond what I give here, my evidence will not permit me to go. We can be safe, however, in calling the seventeenth-century Hamlet primarily a bitterly eloquent and princely avenger. Such a description will keep him fairly close to his Elizabethan proportions; and I believe that for at least the first thirty years of the Seventeenth Century he kept such proportions.

PART TWO

The Eighteenth-Century Hamlet

2

Histrionic Tradition to the Retirement of Garrick

THE Eighteenth Century, as has been said before, saw the growth to considerable proportions of a formal body of critical dogmas on Shakespeare.[1] The first impetus came from Dryden, but genuine headway came only in the next century. As time passed, the volume of this critical current increased, and into it flowed the foreign streams of French and German criticism, to make up in the Nineteenth Century an ocean of print touching every conceivable phase of Shakespeare's art. In this general body of criticism, *Hamlet* at times played a modest part, but finally almost a predominant role.

As a background for the growth of Shakespearian criticism, and at times serving to color its texture and determine the direction of its growth, were certain social and cultural changes. One may speak of the enormous extension of the reading habit in England. This is the period when periodicals multiplied, when the novel was born, and when the reading public which these new literary vehicles encouraged, increased by leaps and bounds. Many new editions of Shakespeare appeared; the literature of his plays and the literature about them grew constantly. The radius of Shakespearian criticism was extending into France and Germany, and (of more immediate moment to our purpose) into Scotland. Furthermore, certain changes were working out in the English habit of thought and taste. The tide of sentimentalism and romanticism was mounting. All of these things had their influence on Shakespearian criticism. The effect on *Hamlet* might be set forth thus:

1. *Hamlet* criticism takes on a professional character

2. After 1770, the emphasis changes most noticeably from the spectator to the reader, and often not the English, but the Scotch or German reader. In other words, watching the play becomes an increasingly less important thing

3. *Hamlet* criticism, therefore, from the 1770's on, becomes largely the story

1. See Nichol Smith, *Shakespeare in the 18th Century* (Oxford, 1928); T. S. Eliot, "Shakespearian Criticism from Dryden to Coleridge," in H. Granville-Barker and G. B. Harrison, *A Companion to Shakespeare Studies*, 1934. For critical excerpts, see Nichol Smith, *18th Century Essays on Shakespeare* (Glasgow, 1903); and A. Ralli, *A History of Shakespearian Criticism* (2 v., Oxford, 1932).

of a departure from the direct perspective; and the task of this study a description and criticism of the new attitudes that arise[2]

The materials at hand for a study of the eighteenth-century Hamlet are
plentiful, and in their variety confusing. It will be helpful to start with
the more specific theatrical tradition. Although, as I have indicated in my
last paragraph, *Hamlet* criticism underwent important modifications in
the century, it started as a simple continuation of seventeenth-century
tendencies. And the center of vitality in *Hamlet* tradition at the beginning of the century, and through Garrick, was a most vigorous dramatic
—a theatrical—tradition. This cannot be denied. The evidence for such a
statement comes from both theatrical records and from a fairly voluminous general literature. *Hamlet* as a play kept the boards in fairly consistent fashion from the Restoration to Garrick's retirement.[3]

The point of departure, then, for my study here is this theatrical tradition. If it is possible to speak of a "real" eighteenth-century Hamlet, this
Danish prince of the theatre might well claim the honor. For is it not
sound criticism to insist that a dramatic entity can appear only in its
fullest reality when the written words and the situation, including the
character himself, are "given flesh" and being on the stage? Any number
in the Eighteenth Century, high and low, educated and vulgar, give their
testimony to the fact that they knew *this* Hamlet. The list, among others,
includes Addison and Steele, Tony Aston, Cibber, Fielding, Mrs. Montagu, Francis Gentleman, Aaron Hill, and such foreigners as Abbé
Prévost, Voltaire and Lichtenberg—not to mention the recorded comments of any number of others who belong to the multitude itself,—forgotten actor, schoolboy and stage-struck apprentice.

2. For my focal idea here, the point of view around which I have built my descriptive account, I am endebted mainly to Mr. E. E. Stoll, particularly to his *Hamlet: An Historical and Comparative Study* (*Research Publications of the University of
Minn., Stud. in Lang. and Lit.,* No. 7, Mpls., 1919); and his chapter on Hamlet in *Art
and Artifice in Shakespeare* (Cambridge, 1933).

3. For the last 40 years of the 17th Century, and the first ten of the next, no exact
record of performances is available. Pepys, however, records them in 1661, 1663 and
1668. John Genest adds two more years in his *Some Account of the English Stage*
(Bath, 1832): 1662 and 1673. And indication of how incomplete Genest is can be seen
by the fact that he fails to record at all performances for the years Pepys gives. Some
weight can be paid to what Downes says in his *Roscius Anglicanus* concerning the
popularity of Betterton's Hamlet: *supra,* p. 24.

For the 18th Century, G. C. D. Odell in his *Shakespeare from Betterton to Irving*
(New York, 1920), I, 224 and 227, speaks of the play's vitality on the stage. From
1710 to 1742, it was acted in London every year but two; from 1742 to 1776 it was
acted every year at Drury Lane, and every year but two at Covent Garden. Shaftesbury in 1711 speaks of the play as "That Piece of his, which appears to have most
affected *English* Hearts, and has perhaps been oftenest acted of any which have come
upon our Stage, ..." (*Characteristics,* London, 1732 edit., I, 275-6).

Hamlet as a play was the common possession of all classes of the English public. The records give impressive testimony to this fact. As nowadays a youngster wishes to break into Hollywood, so, in the Eighteenth Century, most young fellows with stage ambitions wanted to play Hamlet! In his *Memoirs*, Tate Wilkinson speaks of acting Hamlet at Portsmouth in 1759.[4] There are also several accounts of the performance of the role by young Charles Holland at his first benefit: "He was a clerk . . . when the night came, his friends attended, and his native village was left almost literally empty."[5] Two accounts of Holland's début in the part seem to have been given mainly in order to describe the humorous incident that occurred when the young actor's hat blew off. John Bernard gives a delightful account of the first time he played the role at school.[6] Later he gives an amusing incident—of how an Irish churchyard was robbed of a skull for use as property in the play.[7] Another amusing account of Bernard's tells of how the actor Crawford, in a performance in which he found himself deserted by the musicians so dear to an Irishman's heart, came before the audience in his "Hamlet clothes," and played "Paddy O'Rafferty" to them on his fiddle.[8] Or one may mention the now-forgotten actor, "Mr. Frodsham," spoken of so contemptuously by Tate Wilkinson, whose extreme egotism led him to believe that his Hamlet was better than Garrick's![9] Yes, they all wanted to play Hamlet! Jackson tells of a provincial troupe in which there was a small rebellion because each of the actors wished the leading role: "one and all, with one voice, cry out, 'Hamlet or nothing!' " Thus, one winter, the troupe had six Hamlets but no one willing to take lesser roles. Finally the play had to be abandoned for the winter.[10]

The catholicity of appeal in Shakespeare's leading roles, including Hamlet, is given satirical treatment by Arthur Murphy in his *Apprentice*, a short play which treats flippantly, also, another contemporary fashion, the rage for Shakespeare allusions. One prologue used with the play, says in part:

4. (New York, 1790), II, 100-1.
5. John Jackson, *The History of the Scottish Stage* (Edinburgh, 1793), pp. 338-40.
6. *Retrospections of the Stage* (London, 1830), I, 4-8. The incident is dated about 1772.
7. *Ibid.*, I, 260-1.
8. *Ibid.*, pp. 297-8.
9. *Op. cit.*, IV, 36, ff.
10. *Op. cit.*, pp. 159, ff. It must not be supposed that the lesser roles in *Hamlet* were always despised. Wm. Cooke gives the Ghost as one of Barton Booth's leading roles (*Memoirs of Charles Macklin*, London, 1804, pp. 360 and 376). Wilks, too, was famous for the same part (*Ibid.*, p. 356). One performer has gone down in the records because he boasted that he had played with Garrick as the cock in *Hamlet*! (Cooke, *Memoirs of Samuel Foote*, London, 1805, III, 100.)

Our hero is a youth . . . whose stage struck mind
Nor *fate* could rule, nor his *indentures* bind.
A Place there is where such young *Quixotes* meet,
'Tis call'd the SPOUTING CLUB;—a glorious treat!
Where prentic'd kings—alarm the gaping street!
There *Brutus* starts and stares by midnight taper,
Who all the *day* enacts—a *woollen-draper.*
There *Hamlet's* Ghost stalks forth with doubl'd fist;
Cries out with hollow voice—*List, list, O list,*
And frightens *Denmark's* prince—a *young Tobacconist.*
The Spirit too, clear'd from his deadly white,
Rises—a *Haberdasher* to the fight!
But hark! I'm call'd,—be warn'd by what you see,
Oh! spout no more: *Farewell, remember me.*[11]

As a corollary fact that goes with the widespread appeal of *Hamlet* and
its central figure, there is the assumption that this stage tradition must
have involved a fairly settled interpretation of the focal dramatic situation and of the title role.[12] No other single characteristic is more typical
of popular art. A conception such as this becomes the common possession
of the age; it belongs to high and low. It becomes almost legendary, as, in
another literary medium, does the figure of King Arthur or Robin Hood;
or, in American fictional and dramatic history, the figure of "Uncle
Tom." One is well justified, then, in looking for such a settled tradition
concerning *Hamlet*; and to take absence of contradictory evidence as a
basis for assuming that the play follows this general rule. It is common
knowledge what happened when Garrick tried to change, not his interpretation of the leading role, but the grave-diggers scene and the fencing-
match between Hamlet and Laertes in the fifth act. In deference to
pseudo-classical prejudice, he omitted them both. The result that might
be expected followed. Tom Davies says: "The people soon called for

11. *Theatrical Bouquet* (London, 1780), pp. 172-3.
12. Thos. Wilkes in *A General View of the Stage* (London, 1759), speaks of the
fact that certain well known dramatic situations had settled interpretations; they
"have obtained all the perfection they are capable of, or at least [he thinks] that
custom has so far authenticated them as not now to be conveniently departed from.
Of this kind is that of Hamlet at the appearance of the ghost, and of Romeo in the
Tomb-scene, etc." (*Ibid.*, pp. 152-3.) Wilkes goes on a little later to illustrate this
point further by telling of the experience of a "young gentleman of genteel figure"
who tried to play Hamlet with certain innovations. The rash young gentleman's
friends turned out in large numbers to witness his performance, only to be much
disappointed; while the others in the audience accepted the entertainment as burlesque. (*Ibid.*, pp. 167-8.)
Tony Aston, a minor figure in the dramatic world of the early century, gives
testimony to the power of such a dramatic tradition when he remarks that in his
opinion a younger Hamlet than Betterton would have been more appropriate, but "no
one else could have pleas'd the Town, he was so rooted in their Opinion." (Hazelton
Spencer, *Shakespeare Improved,* Cambridge, Mass., 1927, p. 68)

Hamlet as it had been acted from time immemorial."[13] Another reveal-ing comment on Garrick's changes is: "No bribe but his own inimitable performance could have prevailed on an English audience to sit patiently and behold the martyrdom of their favorite author."[14]

We have examined the scattered but widespread testimony concerning the now-forgotten smaller figures in the eighteenth-century dramatic world of England, Scotland, and Ireland. There exist in addition rather ample records describing the performances of the Hamlets who led in the role. These include Betterton, who lived through most of the first decade; the minor Hamlets of Barton Booth, Wilks and Quinn; the great inter-pretation of Garrick; the less important one of Henderson; and finally, the late-century portrayal of Kemble. It is safe to conclude that the interpretations through Garrick's time should provide a descriptive ac-count of the traditional role. It was about the time of the death of Gar-rick that new forces somewhat altering the main lines of *Hamlet* criticism must be taken into account.

Coming from the late Seventeenth into the early Eighteenth Century is, for this study, like changing from a place of shadows into a lighted room. Where before it has been necessary to pick up a fragment here or there, with no detailed account to guide us, now it is possible to get in comfortable detail reactions to the performances of Betterton, Wilks, Garrick, Kemble, and the other Hamlets of the period. One link, how-ever, there is between the centuries, and that is Betterton. Over a span of years that was almost half a century, he acted Hamlet for the English people. It will be well, then, to remember that his Hamlet as seen by eighteenth-century men, must, with due allowance for any changes in interpretation over the years, and for the eighteenth-century vocabulary and point of view with which he is described, be also a portrayal that Pepys or Evelyn saw.

This, then—the eighteenth-century Hamlet—is the first one that can take on full outlines for us. His contours change somewhat, from actor to actor. In the changes can be found a register of the varying abilities of each, his emotional capacity and ability to read his "score"; and also the register of a changing zeitgeist. Eventually, after the seventies, come the changes in interpretation that were motivated by perusal of *Hamlet* in the study. One logical terminal point for such a critical tendency comes early in the Nineteenth Century with Lamb, who was willing to banish Hamlet from the actual stage completely. Lamb would make him an

13. *Dramatic Miscellanies* (2nd edit., London, 1785), III, 153.
14. *Biographia Dramatica* (London, 1812), II, 144. Another discussion of this point is to be found in Tate Wilkinson's *Memoirs*, IV, 260.

actor on the stage which a reader may set up in his imagination. He wished no other Hamlet!

Betterton's Hamlet, however, was of quite a different aesthetic species. He walked the boards as a creature of flesh and blood. His was not an interpretation overloaded with subtleties, but it was moving. Hardly a "glass of fashion" or a "mould of form" himself, he nevertheless offered a "sweet prince" who pleased many an audience. It is recorded of him that at first he played the role in the dress of a courtier of Charles II, and later with streaming shoulder-knots, cocked hat, and powdered wig.[15] As has been observed already, but on not too authentic evidence, his interpretation is said to have been the one approved by Shakespeare himself.[16]

In 1709, Steele in the *Tatler* says apropos of Betterton's last recorded performance in the role at the Haymarket:

> Had you been to-night at the play-house, you had seen the force of action in perfection: your admired Mr. Betterton behaved himself so well, that, though now about seventy, he acted youth; and by the prevalent power of proper manner, gesture, and voice, appeared through the whole drama a young man of great expectation, vivacity, and enterprise.[17]

The closing words of this description offer an illuminating contrast with some of the impressions of later periods. This is a Hamlet who conforms quite adequately to what the man in the street expects of a "hero."

In addition to his ability to portray a prince who possessed the proper qualifications for popular success, Betterton had genuine capacity to move even his more critical fellow actors. Barton Booth, who played the ghost opposite him, said: "When I acted the Ghost with Betterton, instead of my awing him, he terrified me. But divinity hung round that man!"[18] The most impressive account of Betterton's Hamlet, however, comes from the pen of another actor, Colley Cibber. What is more, he includes descriptive details not given by the others:

> You have seen a Hamlet, perhaps, who, on the first appearance of his father's spirit, has thrown himself into all the straining vociferation requisite to express rage and fury, and the house has thundered with applause, though the misguided actor was all the while, as Shakespeare terms it, *tearing a passion into rags.* I am the more bold to offer you this particular instance, because the late Mr. Addison, while I sat by him, to see this scene acted, made the same observation, asking me, with some surprise, if I thought *Hamlet* should be in so violent a passion with the *Ghost,* which, though it might have astonished, had not provoked him? For you may observe that in this beautiful speech, the

15. H. P. Phelps, *Hamlet from the Actor's Standpoint* (New York, 1890), pp. 5-6.
16. Downes, *op. cit.,* p. 21.
17. *Tatler 71* (ed. Chalmers, London, 1822), II, 177-8. Steele speaks here in the person of "Mr. Greenhat."
18. Quoted from Hazelton Spencer, *Shakespeare Improved,* p. 10.

passion never rises beyond an almost breathless astonishment, or an impatience, limited by filial reverence, to inquire into the suspected wrongs that may have raised him from his peaceful tomb, and a desire to know what a spirit so seemingly distressed might wish or enjoin a sorrowful son to execute, towards his future quiet in the grave. This was the light into which Betterton threw this scene, which he opened with a pause of mute amazement; then rising slowly to a solemn, trembling voice, he made the *Ghost* equally terrible to the spectator as to himself, and in the descriptive part of the natural emotions which the ghastly vision gave him, the boldness of his expostulation was still governed by decency, and manly but not braving; his voice never rising into that seeming outrage or wild defiance of what he naturally revered. But, alas! to preserve this medium, between mouthing and meaning too little,—to keep the attention more pleasingly awake by a tempered spirit, than by mere vehemence of voice,— is, of all the master-strokes of an actor the most difficult to reach. In this none yet have equalled Betterton.[19]

Cibber's description contains a good portion of what may be termed the "orthodox interpretation" of Hamlet in this period. Other more subtle touches were to be added later in the century, to modify Betterton's rather simple portrayal. However its essential outlines persisted: a mortal man visited by the supernatural, which enjoined revenge upon him as a sacred duty; the terror, coupled with a determination to get at the truth; the "sorrowful son," filled with "filial reverence." These are notes in the interpretation that persisted through the time of Garrick. Some of Betterton's straightforward manliness was tempered, and new notes were added. The rest persisted.

During the years between the passing of Betterton and the rise of Garrick, many actors took the role. Of these, only Robert Wilks and Barton Booth deserve any detailed mention. Wilks was evidently the more successful of the two. Although not a worthy successor to Betterton, he received at least a critical attention not bestowed upon Booth, or upon his now forgotten competitors in the part.[20]

Two facts concerning the role as played in this period stand out from contemporary histrionic criticism. Hamlet is a part that consistently demands, from an actor, extreme versatility: he must be both thoughtful and carefree, tender and brutal, delicate and bawdy—with a change from mood to mood that is lightning-like in rapidity. When a lesser artist tries the part, the inevitable result is that he can capture some of the moods, but not all. In attempting the others, he is apt to fail lamentably. So it is that Aaron Hill, a critic of the period we are now in, speaks of the fact

19. *An Apology for the Life of Mr. Colley Cibber* (London, 1822), pp. 89-90.
20. A list of these minor actors would include: John Thurmond, George Powell, Thomas Elrington, Lacy Ryan, Henri Giffard, John Mills, Milward, Dennis Delane, and William Havard (W. Widmann, *Hamlets Bühnenlaufbahn*, 1601-1877, Leipzig, 1931, p. 39).

that contemporary theater-goers had seen only "Half a Prince Hamlet." Wilks could play the "gay half" and Booth the "solemn."[21] Together, they would make an effective Hamlet:

IN *This,* then, the Double Capacity, of *Mr.* WILKS, and *Mr.* BOOTH, shou'd *unite,* in ONE Actor.—The First cou'd be *wanton;* but, He was *wanton* without *Weight:*—The Second cou'd be *Weighty:* but, He was *Weighty,* without *Easiness.*—*Mr. Wilks* had a Spirit, that ran away with his Body: *Mr. Booth* had a Body, that dragg'd too heavy, on his Spirit.—When the One was *most* delightful, He seem'd animated, without *Purpose:* When the Other was most strong, He gave IMPRESSION, without *Briskness.*[22]

Of Wilks we have another interesting comment that brings to light a different type of blemish that the interpretation of a less gifted actor may possess. Wilks could not capture completely the imagination of the listener. He gave a performance in which one noticed the externalities, the speeches, the gestures. The eloquence which is always a part of every Hamlet became less a matter of the perfect expression of an inner vitality of spirit than with Betterton; it took on the character of stage business. This is the impression one gathers from a contemporary account.[23] The quality of externality seen in such an actor as Wilks, however, emphasizes anew the very presence of the eloquence that is always implicit in Hamlet's character. Unless an actor has an adequate imagination and emotional power, the eloquence becomes an outer thing, a matter of elocution and gesture, not the full voice of something within. Betterton could carry the part. Wilks couldn't.

It is Aaron Hill who sets forth a critical specification of what his age should demand from an actor in the role. He does it in the same essay in which he comments upon the failure of both Wilks and Booth. This is the Hamlet whom he would wish to see:

THE characteristic Distinction, that *marks* the Temper of *Hamlet,* is a *pensive,* yet *genteel,* HUMANITY.—He is, by *Nature,* of a *melancholy Cast:* but, His polite Education has illuminated the *Sable;* and, like the Sun, through a *wet* MAY *Morning,* mix'd a *Gleam,* with his *Sadness.*—When he *grieves,* he is never *Sullen:* When He *trifles,* he is never *light.*—When, *alone,* He is *seriously solid:* When in Company, *designedly flexible.*—He *assumes,* what he pleases: but he *is,* what He ought to be;— the Lamenter of his murder'd *Father:*—the Discerner of his *Mother's* Levity: and the Suspecter of his *Uncle's* Baseness.

21. From his words, one judges that Hill had never seen Booth in the role.
22. *The Prompter,* No. 100 (October 24, 1735).
23. I have not been able to trace the ultimate source of this account. My source is a note by Edmund Bellchambers at the end of his edition of Cibber's *Apology,* 1822, pp. 513-14. It is possible that my analysis of Wilks' performance may be too harsh, for Bellchambers adds, "Wilks, indeed, was so successful in his representation of this part, that "Hamlet" was frequently chosen, as a favourite play, to open the season with."

How *weigh'd,* then, and *significant,* should he be found in his *Looks,* and his *Actions!*—When He counterfeits Distraction with *Ophelia,* and perceives that she is *observing* him, All his Air is as light, and as empty of Purpose, as if *really* as *mad,* as He designs She should *think* him.—But, no sooner has he declin'd himself from the Glances of HER Eye—than His OWN gives us Marks, of his *Pity,* and his *Prudence.*—The WILDNESS He but *affects,* quits his Air in a Moment, and a touching Sensation of SORROW *paints* his *Soul,* in his *Gesture:* which again, the next Moment, He transforms into *Wantonness,* in the very Instant of Time, while He *returns* toward the Lady.[24]

There are several new notes here: the "humanity," the "melancholy cast," the intense mobility of spirit, with its roving quickness and intellectuality, its sensitivity. This is a Hamlet who retains all of the old cleverness of the malcontent, without his acid maliciousness or cynicism. This is an eighteenth-century Hamlet. Hill shows himself here a critic who can get almost a complete reading from the score offered by Shakespeare. As we have seen, however, there was no actor in 1735 who could interpret fully Hill's reading. Indeed, one feels that Betterton himself could not have satisfied Hill completely; Betterton was not so subtle as this. No wonder a Wilks or a Booth could not succeed. One wonders what Hill thought of Garrick.

With the exception of Quinn, whom Garrick supplanted, there was no other important portrayer of the role before him. Quinn need not be discussed, as his performance of the part hardly merits attention.[25]

Much may of course be said concerning the Garrick Hamlet. From any one of a number of sources it is possible to gather detailed information on the man, his art, and his particular importance in this study.[26] I shall restrict myself here to the characteristic features of his portrayal of the role. He seems to have taken the more robust Hamlet of Betterton and subtilized it, made it more "feeling," more sentimental, more "delicate." The melancholy asked for by Aaron Hill was more in evidence. This melancholy was a meditative thing, with little bitterness in it. It was gentle and "philosophical"—in the full eighteenth-century tradition as it

24. *Op. cit.*

25. One critic says of Quinn's Hamlet: "As to Quinn, he was in such a rage at his father's ghost, that he was more than half afraid he would have killed it, instead of filial reverence, terror at beholding the awful and beloved shade, compassion for its mortal and then wretched fate—he stamped and raved at it." From *Reformer* No. 9, March 24-1747-48. (Quoted in *Early Life and Correspondence of Edmund Burke,* ed. Samuels, Cambridge, 1923, p. 174.)

26. Practically every set of "memoirs" written by an eighteenth-century actor or about actors, dwells voluminously on Garrick. The incidental literature of the times is fairly crowded with references to Garrick and his acting. For more formal accounts, there is the contemporary biography of Thomas Davies, first edition, 1780. Other valuable records are Arthur Murphy's *The Life of David Garrick, Esq.,* (2 V.) 1801; and Percy Fitzgerald's *The Life of David Garrick,* 1868.

is seen in graveyard poetry, having as one of its ingredients a rationalistic playing with one's own emotions—half thought and half feeling—a psychological inversion whereby the contemplator gains pleasure out of pain. This is the type of musing on death and the after life that one sees, for example, in Young's *Night Thoughts*.[27] Garrick's interpretation of the famous "to be" soliloquy seems to have owed its popularity to the fact that it fitted in so well with eighteenth-century predilections for melancholy and gentle scepticism.[28] Garrick knew how to fit the temper of his age.

Enough has been said to indicate that Garrick made himself a splen-

27. It would make a fascinating side study to record the many cases in which motifs from *Hamlet* are echoed in Eighteenth Century poetry of a melancholy or grave-yard cast. For example, William Broome in 1729, echoes Hamlet's expression, "ponderous and marble jaws" in his *Melancholy: An Ode:*

> Open thy marble jaws, O tomb
> Thou earth, conceal me in thy womb!
> And you, ye worms, this frame confound;
> Ye brother reptiles of the ground!
>
> (quoted by Reed, *Op. cit.*, p. 104)

Grainger's *Solitude* contains a distinct echo of Hamlet's words to his father (Act I, v, lines 58-63):

> Save me! what's yon shrouded shade,
> That wanders in the dark-brown glade?
> It beckons me!—vain fears adieu,
> Mysterious ghost, I follow you.
> Ah me! too well that gait I know,
> My youth's first friend, my manhood's woe!
>
> (Dodsley's *Collection*, London, 1770, IV, 234)

Other examples, less definite, are Thomas Warton's *Pleasures of Melancholy,* line 47, ff.; Blair's *The Grave,* which Miss Reed (*Op. cit.*, p. 191) says is reminiscent of the grave-diggers scene; and Mallet's *William and Margaret,* also mentioned by Miss Reed.

28. That such an interest in the "to be" soliloquy was very real in the century is attested in various places. Both Mrs. Elizabeth Montagu and James Boswell discuss it. Mrs. Montagu's analysis puts the interpretation in a most typical eighteenth-century manner:

> Every possible sentiment is caught by this great genius; every shade of passion, every gradation of thought is marked. In the famous soliloquy, "To be or not to be?" how naturally do all the questions arise! and how finely are those circumstances set forth which are most grievous to the discontented mind. The insolence of office, the rich man's contumely, the law's delay, the thousand scorns that patient merit from the unworthy takes, these are the grievances a splenetic mind complains of; it is not the anguish or the fear of bodily diseases that prompts the desperate hand of self-murder, it is gloomy pride and discontent at the offences offered by fellow creatures that drives the soul to sullen desperation. (From a letter to Lord Lyttleton: *The Letters of Mrs. Elizabeth Montagu,* London, 1813, IV, 299 ff.)

Boswell gives expression to a more specific angle of eighteenth-century interest in

didly adequate mouthpiece for Hamlet's eloquence. He had the inner energy to carry it completely. The inner force seeks expression in words. Shakespeare furnishes the words for any actor who can take them as his own. Garrick could accomplish this miracle.

Finally, it should be said that with the greater delicacy that Hamlet put on in Garrick's interpretation, there was, paradoxically, no sense of a prince who could not act, or who was unmanly. "The progress of his impassioned sensation" became the "action"! There is, to be sure, a touch of sentimentalism in the picture, but it remains a mere ingredient in the whole. It doesn't dominate. Melancholy is there, as Aaron Hill would have it; but, though it may be a malady like the malcontentism of earlier days, it does not paralyse initiative or dissolve resolution.

It will be profitable to get the testimony of one who really witnessed Garrick's acting. Tom Davies says:

When Mr. Garrick first saw the Ghost, the terror he seemed to be impressed with, was instantaneously communicated to the audience; his expostulations with the vision though warm and importunate, were restrained by filial awe. The progress of his impassioned sensation, till the Ghost beckoned him to retire with him, was accompanied with terror and respect. His determination to obey the repeated invitation of the Ghost, by action, to withdraw, was vehemently resolute; his following him, awful and tremendous. . . . The soliloquies of Hamlet are distinguished by peculiar and pathetic feelings of the mind; all the varieties

---

the "to be" soliloquy; he takes up the subject of suicide. In his *Hypochondriak* 51 (Dec. 1781) he calls the soliloquy "a capital piece of philosophical reasoning" which "everybody recollects, and which cannot be answered unless one had an undoubted intimation from the world of spirits. . . ." (Quoted from 1928 edition, arranged by Margery Bailey, Stanford Calif., 1928, II, 139.)

Possibly the piece which exhibits most characteristically what an eighteenth-century approach to the "to be" soliloquy could be, is a poem of William Hamilton's: *A Soliloquy—In Imitation of Hamlet*. I shall quote the concluding lines only, where Hamlet is given some delightfully pious advice:

> Then Hamlet, cease; thy rash resolves forego
> God, nature, reason, all will have it so;
> Learn by this sacred horror, well supprest,
> Each fatal purpose in the traitor's breast.
> This damps revenge with salutary fear,
> And stops ambition in its wild career,
> Till virtue for itself begin to move,
> And servile fear exalt to filial love.
> Then in thy breast let calmer passions rise,
> Pleas'd with thy lot on earth, absolve the skies.
> The ills of life see friendship can divide;
> See angels warring on the good man's side.
> Alone to virtue happiness is given,
> On earth self-satisfy'd, and crown'd in heaven.
>> (Quoted from *A Complete Edition of the Poets of Great Britain*, Edinburgh, 1794, IX, 431.)

of sentiment, impressed with passion, were delivered by Garrick with singular exertion.[29]

This illuminating account, combined with hints from Fitzgerald, who gathered his material from many contemporary sources, allows one to see the central details of Garrick's portrayal. He seems to have made the character his own through a progressively effective interpretation. The main secret of his dramatic effectiveness here lies in the fact that he saw the whole play in terms of action! Hamlet's every thought was registered on Garrick's wonderfully mobile face; every gesture and movement were vital action.[30] Hamlet's following the ghost had as great a dramatic value for the spectators as they could find, for example, in the meeting of Hotspur and Prince Hal on the battlefield at Shrewsbury. What is more, this portrayal had other qualities not possible in a play where the "action" is carried out on an orthodox level. The "progress of impassioned sensation" wore as its characteristic garment melancholy, expressed at this period in terms of a delicate eighteenth-century meditativeness. There was no hint of a madness akin to Bedlam, or reminiscent of the cruder exhibitions that Elizabethans might have applauded.

It remains for me to call attention to one comment that contains at least a small hint of another type of Danish prince. This is found in Thomas Wilkes' *A General View of the Stage* of 1759. Wilkes is discussing Garrick's Hamlet:

The author has drawn this prince of a reserved cautious turn, arising from a melancholy stamped on him by his father's untimely death, and some consequent misfortunes. The passions whereby he is actuated do not, except in a few places, rise to any height; and to distinguish his feigned madness from his real provocation, is a master-piece which he hits off admirably. His manner of receiving his father's ghost on its first entrance has a fine mixture of astonishment, deference, and resolution; . . .[31]

In the hands of future closet critics, this "reserved, cautious turn" of Hamlet's was to become a devastating thing. Before the century is over, it will bear all of the aspects of a genuine "tragic flaw."[32] With Wilkes,

29. *Memoirs of the Life of David Garrick* (London, 1808), I, 64-5.

30. There is eloquent testimony to the extent of Garrick's achievement in making Hamlet's total *experience* a dramatic thing. The ghost scene illustrates this well. Such a scene would in any event be "dramatic"; but Garrick succeeded in giving a histrionic value to every shred of Hamlet's experience in the scene. In connection with it one remembers Partridge as described by Fielding in *Tom Jones* (Mod. Lib. edit., pp. 737-40); or the vivid account given by Lichtenberg, who saw the play on a visit to England. The latter is quoted by Fitzgerald (*op. cit.*, p. 258). For original, see *Vermischte Schriften* (1844), III, 209-10.

31. Pp. 249-50.

32. Possibly a close reading of Cibber's words on Betterton (*supra*, p. 34) or

however, there is a mere suggestion of such a thing, a suggestion that received its full negation in the last sentence of the paragraph I have just quoted.

One other minor note of dissent is recorded by Fitzgerald. It seems that some spectators thought Garrick too rough and violent in his treatment of Ophelia.[33] This would offer a clue that Garrick was not blind to the biting "malcontent" quality of many of Hamlet's words to Ophelia. However, the prevailing impression seems to have been in agreement with the opinion of Wilkes, that Garrick showed Hamlet's "real tenderness for Ophelia" and his "ineffectual endeavors to hide it."[34]

The full outlines of the eighteenth-century Hamlet of the stage are now before us. Garrick it surely was who fixed the century's orthodox picture of the Danish prince.[35] This picture held until the last quarter of the century, at least.[36] In this period he wore a characteristic mental and emotional garb in which "humanity" and "melancholy" were the chief ingredients. His madness, here, never put on a comic tinge—it would have taken a primitive sense of humor not possessed by the Eighteenth Century to have allowed such a thing as that—his madness was made artistic and intellectual. His "filial reverence" and "awe" were emphasized. Under Garrick, his every sensation took its place as part of the action. He was meditative with an eighteenth-century rationalistic touch. For a century that produced deism and Hume's scepticism, he talked most appropriately of life after death, and suicide. In spite of his "caution," he was still a

---

Aaron Hill (*supra*, p. 36) might cause some careful critics to see in these earlier interpretations a hint of what becomes later a "tragic flaw." Both critics imply that Hamlet has a thorough control over the extent to which he will allow himself to feel. Hill calls this characteristic "prudence." Later century critics were not so charitable. However, before these earlier simple suggestions can take on an uglier note, a number of complexities of interpretation that could develop only with time and a changing zeitgeist, must be taken into account.

33. It is true that the general charge of Hamlet's "cruelty" had been voiced before 1759. We hear it first, however, in a form that precludes its discussion here as part of the "dramatic" picture. As set forth by Hanmer in 1736, it is distinctly closet criticism. I cannot find evidence that would lead me to believe that Hamlet's "cruelty" was in this period (or possibly in any later period!) a theatrical problem. As described by the closet critics, I shall treat it later.

34. *Op. cit.*, pp. 249-50.

35. Of the many minor actors who played the role of Hamlet during the Garrick period, one may mention the following: Thomas Sheridan, Cashell, Furnival, Banbury, Goodfellow, Lee, Barry, Murphy, Holland, Mossop, Fleetwood, Ross, William Powel, Lewis, Cautherley, and Smith (Widmann, *op. cit.*, p. 45).

36. It is interesting that Murphy in *The Life of David Garrick, Esq.* (London, 1801, I, 45 ff.), interprets Garrick's portrayal of Hamlet in terms of a new point of view. Garrick for him made Hamlet a prince of "irresolute temper." Would Murphy have seen Garrick's prince in this light in 1759, or in 1770? It is notable that in the earlier periods no dramatic critic with a fully theatrical point of view, did so!

fairly heroic prince. And notwithstanding a few doubts to the contrary, he was "tender" to Ophelia.

I have said enough already to indicate the immense importance of Garrick in fixing the interpretation of Hamlet in eighteenth-century histrionic tradition. This importance can hardly be overemphasized. Besides the widespread notice taken of his Hamlet in other forms of the literature in the period, he was even made the prototype of a fictional hero, appearing as "Mr. Ranger," in Edward Kimber's novel.[37] What is more, it is surely true that he had a most potent secondary influence in shaping the tone and even the content of formal criticism during his long and distinguished career. One discerning present-day critic speaks of that change in the Eighteenth Century which

abandoned the neo-classical standards one and all and built up a new dramatic criticism which centered about the pole of character delineation rather than of plot structure, which treated Shakespeare's characters as living beings with lives of their own, and which found that the dramatist not only chronicled the stages of all life, but was also the profoundest of moral philosophers.[38]

Of this change in critical point of view toward Shakespeare so far as it effects *Hamlet,* I shall speak in some detail later. Suffice it to say here that Mr. Stone feels that Garrick was a definite influence in the movement. He

presented a new type of acting,—a natural realistic type which showed a psychological understanding of character,—that made a great impression upon his audiences and which was diametrically opposed to the declamatory style which possessed the stage in 1740.[39]

If this is true of Garrick's service to the Shakespearian stage in general, it is surely doubly true of his service to the histrionic tradition of *Hamlet,* for here he gave his finest and most famous character delineation.

But Garrick, according to the same critic, did even more:

Without Garrick, or some actor of equal intelligence, enthusiasm, ability, and Shakespearian interests, Shakespeare would have been the plaything of the closet and of the academician in the Eighteenth Century.[40]

I feel that this generous evaluation of Garrick is not exaggerated, and that again, it has an added relevance as applied to *Hamlet.* In fact, it was Hamlet, as we shall see later, who was the foremost victim of closet

37. For comment and quotation, see R. G. Noyes, "Shakespeare in the Eighteenth Century Novel," *ELH,* 11, 225.

38. Geo. W. Stone, Jr., *Garrick's Handling of Shakespeare's Plays and his Influence upon the Changed Attitude of Shakespearian Criticism during the Eighteenth Century* (Harvard doctoral dissertation, 1937), p. 489.

39. *Ibid.,* p. 490.

40. *Ibid.,* p. 494.

criticism, and it is surely significant that the ravages of that movement set in with an accelerated tempo in the very decade that saw Garrick's retirement from the stage.

In spite of any changes in the outline of his character as interpreted over a century and three-quarters, a histrionic Hamlet was the common possession of the English public. Through all of his evolutions, including interpretations by a series of fine actors, he was an active prince with a task on his hands, a task which in due time he carried out successfully.

It is sound criticism, I believe, not to regard overseriously the rather distinct difference in outline between the Hamlet of 1610, and the prince of the time of Garrick. In spite of the fact that the lusty avenger with comic possibilities, or the malcontent in memento-mori background may seem sharply distinguished from the gentle prince of Garrick's day, the difference may well be more apparent than real. For the earlier period our data are at best fragmentary; for the later years, abundant. Such a fact alone must keep us from too dogmatic generalization.

It is safe to insist that the *Hamlet* stage tradition which we have seen in broken glimpses, would form a unity if our evidence were more complete. Seventeenth and Eighteenth Centuries would blend into each other. It cannot be otherwise, for such is the nature of the historical development of art. Unity is to be found in the midst of diversity. Seventeenth-century habits of thought are a correlative of the more simple, harsher interpretation which Shakespeare's lines justify. Eighteenth-century rationalism and sentimentalism must be seen as the correlative of a different, more "human" Hamlet. But the later conception grew from the earlier one; and underneath the difference there was a common denominator, a dramatic substratum that did not change. True it is that eighteenth-century men in increasing numbers read *Hamlet* in their studies, but their impressions gained there were always subject to modification and correction. A more potent Hamlet than any who could be met with in the study, still held the stage at Drury Lane and Covent Garden, and was seen not infrequently at a dozen and one provincial theatres in England, Scotland, and Ireland.

3

English Tradition, as Presented in Formal Criticism, to 1770

THE MORE PERVASIVE UNDRAMATIC ASPECTS

EIGHTEENTH-CENTURY *HAMLET* criticism must of course be seen against the background of ideas that form the animating nucleus for neo-classical dramatic theory. This body of ideas was the result of an evolutionary process that gained its impetus from the Italian and the French theorists of the Renaissance. Much of what I choose to call the undramatic aspects of this *Hamlet* criticism was motivated by an important neo-classical dogma: the emphasis upon truth as the final justification of art, thus giving to drama for example, primarily a didactic function,[1] a function that encouraged the negation of any really dramatic point of view. With this dogma there was often combined the important corollary that truth may be wrapped seductively in words and rhetorical "ornament," thus to wing it on its way to the imagination and understanding.[2]

It was inevitable that Shakespeare's *Hamlet*, with its splendid solilo-

---

1. Poetry, with drama as one of its major genres, must have first and foremost an "ethical and civilizing" function. Pleasure was distinctly secondary in importance. Aristotle's "katharsis" was given a didactic interpretation. See J. E. Spingarn, *A History of Literary Criticism in the Renaissance. . . .* (New York, 1908), p. 75. In the hands of such eighteenth-century critics as Shaftesbury and Reynolds, beauty and truth are identified as finally one and the same. Great art gives the highest beauty and the highest knowledge. Poet and philosopher are one (Shaftesbury, *The Moralists,* part III, section 2). Reynolds' ideas on the same subject are best set forth in his *Seventh Discourse.*

2. All of the features that are responsible for the emotional appeal of literary art: imagery, rhythm, metaphor, simile, etc., are accepted as secondary instruments, useful in bringing about the primary purpose. The poet, to paraphrase Minturno, may be defined as a good man skilled in language and imitation. (Spingarn, *op. cit.,* pp. 53-4) This aesthetic position is implicit in such leading critics as Johnson and Reynolds. Literary beauty becomes almost wholly a matter of "ornament." The neo-classical dogma of "ornament" is partly an outgrowth of Locke's psychology. The aesthetic implication is that there are only a limited number of images from nature that are available for the poet's use. His task then, is to combine and embellish. For later poets, who come after everything has been said, all that can be possible is a new variation of, and embellishment of, old themes. One may see the working out of this whole aesthetic position in Johnson's "Life of Pope" or Reynolds' *Seventh Discourse.*

quies, its fine quotable passages, its hero so directly concerned with moral problems that strike at the very heart of life, should at times be fastened upon by this didactic moralizing century, and given an undramatic interpretation. Shaftesbury's famous words on *Hamlet* and its hero are of such a nature:

That Piece of his, which appears to have most affected *English* Hearts, and has perhaps been oftenest acted of any which have come upon our Stage, is almost one continu'd *Moral*; A Series of deep Reflections, drawn from *one Mouth*, upon the Subject of *one* single Accident and Calamity, naturally fitted to move Horror and Compassion. It may be properly said of this Play, if I mistake not, that it has only ONE *Character* or *principal Part*. It contains no Adoration or Flattery of the *Sex*: no ranting at *the Gods*: no blustring *Heroism*: nor any thing of that curious mixture of *the Fierce* and *Tender*, which makes the hinge of modern Tragedy, and nicely varies it between the Points of *Love* and *Honour*.[3]

In this paragraph Shaftesbury has not forgotten the fact that he is discussing a play; however, the net result of his appraisal of *Hamlet* is to reduce its main character to a mouthpiece for a "series of deep reflections." In other words, the Hamlet that is important to Shaftsbury is a perpetually soliloquizing Hamlet! He is the utterer of great and permanent truths of deep moral import. It is because of his facility in the expression of such truths that he became, in eighteenth-century eyes, "virtuous" and "good." The theatrical criticism of this century, previously discussed, does not emphasize such aspects of Hamlet's character. It is true that Garrick portrayed a Danish prince who could certainly be called "virtuous" and "good." Such adjectives, however, seldom come to the lips—or the pens—of those who describe Garrick's portrayal. These qualities were implicit rather than explicit in the Garrick Hamlet, as they were in the other theatrical Hamlets of earlier date. In other words, "goodness" and "virtue" were Hamlet's possessions acquired in a type of criticism that was definitely undramatic.

Originating, then, in a critical impetus that seems to start in the library rather than in the theatre, there was a most definite eighteenth-century habit to dwell upon Hamlet's words because they exhibited virtue, wisdom, and beauty. Often the passages in which these qualities were found, are labelled as "beauties."[4] The effect is to set forth a prince

---

3. *Characteristics* (London, 1732 edit.,) I, 275-6.
4. The "Beauties-Faults" type of criticism is a distinct eighteenth-century genre. It can be said to owe its origin, partly to the separatist tendency which I have traced in my discussion—a tendency that reduced a dramatic texture to a "series of deep reflections"; and partly to another neo-classical habit, the pointing out in Shakespeare of a number of "defects", most of them violations of decorum. The "beauty-blemish

isolated from his proper dramatic context, a prince who is a compound
of Confucius, Solomon, and a twentieth-century Sunday School teacher.[5]

Connected very definitely with the growing tendency to enjoy *Hamlet*
in the study, and gaining a good share of its impetus from the didactic
turn of mind, was the widespread taste for quotation from Shakespeare.
Hamlet's eloquence made him an ideal victim for such a practice.[6] There
was also the custom, begun as will be remembered in the Seventeenth
Century,[7] of using Hamlet's words to the players as a lesson in public
speaking and histrionics. Good eighteenth-century examples of such a
use are *Tatler* 35, and Charles Gildon's *The Life of Mr. Thomas Better-*

---

cant" as one writer calls it, is plainly evident in Dryden and Dennis, for example; and
many traces of it are found throughout the Eighteenth Century. For a short discussion,
see Aisso Bosker, *Literary Criticism in the Age of Johnson* (The Hague, 1930),
pp. 18-19; and R. W. Babcock, *The Genesis of Shakespeare Idolatry* (Chapel Hill,
1931), p. 240, note.

5. Hamlet's words find a place, of course, in such a work as Dodd's *The Beauties
of Shakespeare*, 1752, and reprinted in 1757, 1780, 1782, etc.; C. Taylor's *The Beauties
of Shakespeare*, 1778, 1783, 1792; and *The Beauties of Shakespeare*, Dublin, 1783. Of
a somewhat different turn, but definitely related to this school of criticism, is Mrs.
Griffith's *The Morality of Shakespeare's Drama*, 1775, in which Hamlet's words do
their part in helping to establish Mrs. Griffith's edifying thesis. An early nineteenth-
century example is C. Lofft's *Aphorisms from Shakespeare*, 1812.

6. His words were used for any and every purpose. The list of those who use them
includes, among others, Samuel Foote, Tate Wilkinson, Mrs. Montagu, James Boswell,
Robert Burns, Colley Cibber, and J. G. Cooper. The allusion habit in general is ridi-
culed by Murphy in *The Apprentice*, which he makes a tissue of allusions from Shakespeare. To show the widespread nature of this habit of quotation, Boswell quotes a
contemporary advertisement used by a butcher of more than common literary pre-
tensions, one who speaks of the easing of the present exorbitant prices for meat as the
"Consummation devoutly to be wished." (*Hypochondriack* 22, Bailey edit., I, 275).

Mrs. Elizabeth Montagu's voluminous letters contain a number of allusions from
Hamlet's speeches. Her general attitude is well illustrated in a letter to her sister on a
family disappointment. Here Hamlet is indeed reduced to an undramatic type form.
He becomes the "good Mr. Hamlet", with the right bit of wisdom on his lips, to be
relevant in the present distressing situation (*Elizabeth Montagu The Queen of the
Blue-Stockings*, London, 1906, II, 20).

Of all who quoted Hamlet often, it is probably Burns who does it most felici-
tously. Quotation with him, while remaining a polite accomplishment, was also the
very expression of his thought and emotion. It is moving indeed to read such words
as the following, penned in June 1796, shortly before his death:

> . . . I may see you on Saturday, but I will not be at the Bell.—Why should
> I? "Man delights not me, nor woman either!" Can you supply me with the
> Song, "Let us all be unhappy together"—Do, if you can, and oblige
>
> le pauvre miserable, R. B.
>
> (J. D. Ferguson, ed., *The Letters of Robert Burns*,
> Oxford, 1931, II, 323)

7. *Supra*, p. 20.

ton.[8] Other special purposes for which Hamlet's words were found useful were in eulogy or dedication,[9] biography,[10] and light parody.[11]

Formal Criticism: Major Aspects—to 1770

It is now possible to turn from the minor phases of eighteenth-century criticism which reduce Hamlet from Danish prince to "good Mr. Hamlet," the mouthpiece for clichés and "ultimate truths," to the more important aspects of the subject.

What function may dramatic criticism fulfill in any period, no matter what drama is being examined? In answer to this important question, it seems reasonable to say that any critical attitude comprises some combination or negation of two approaches toward the aesthetic data making up the play. The data may be examined:

1. with reference to their Absolute (immediate) significance

2. with reference to their Relative (historical) significance[12]

8. Pp. 70 and 81.

9. Colley Cibber uses Hamlet's fervent words in praise of his father for an eulogy of Wilks (*Apology, op cit.,* pp. 423-4); an unknown poet turns Hamlet's "What a piece of work is man!" into praise of Shakespeare himself (Dodsley's *Collection,* VI, 276); and Corbyn Morris closes his dedication of an essay to the Earl of Orford with these words:

> And when your *last Hour* shall come, which *Heaven* yet long suspend, this *aking* NATION shall, with one *joint Sigh,* lament her loss, and pay the grateful Tear to the Memory of WALPOLE; crying, like *Hamlet,* o'er his Father,
>> *He was a Man, take him for all in all,*
>> *We ne'er shall look upon his like again.*

(from *An Essay towards fixing the True Standards of Wit, Humour, Raillery, Satire, and Ridicule. . . .* London, 1744, pp. xxxiii and xxxiv.

10. See William Cooke, *Memoirs of Charles Macklin,* p. 345.

11. Besides Murphy's *The Apprentice,* already referred to in other connections, one good example provides a parody of the "to be" soliloquy, that starts:

> To print, or not to print—that is the question

(Dodsley's *Collection,* V, 82-3.)

12. The following may be listed as some of the items for analysis:

> 1. under Absolute (with the critic seeing the data in terms of their universal significance: (a) medium used-words; (b) art and artifice in play; (c) larger questions bound up in meaning of tragedy and art; (d) the play staged; (e) the audience.
> 2. under Relative: (a) emendation; (b) dramatic conventions of time of writing; (c) dramatic intentions of playwright; (d) sources; (e) the particular audience for whom play was written; (f) particular aesthetic formulas influential at time; (g) other dramas of period; (h) dramatic history of play through successive periods.

On the face of it, it would not seem possible for any really fruitful criticism to limit itself to merely one of these significances; or to a single aspect of one of them. It would not be possible, that is, unless the critic wishes to be a pure impressionist; or unless he ignores completely the integrity of the genre he is examining, and takes a romantic attitude toward his material, or simplifies it until it loses all except one narrow range of interest, as happens for those who see dramatic material merely as "beauties" or axioms. The "undramatic" pitfalls are part of the inevitable danger that exists because it is necessary for one who wishes to be more than a "theatrical" critic, to examine the play in his study. He is forced to go to the library for the leisure as well as the material necessary if he wishes to pass careful judgment upon the aesthetic data. When there, he may fall victim to the "reader's attitude." Intellectually (or otherwise), he may never return to the theatre. He may accept interpretations of the play not possible on the stage. Or he may see the play in sections, rather than as a whole. The list may be prolonged. The history of *Hamlet* criticism offers an excellent illustration of critics who take partial attitudes, as well as of critics who accept the major heresies,— the Richardsons, and Mackenzies, and Goethes.

It is possible, I believe, to label the ruling criticism or aesthetic formulas of any period by an analysis of what combination of absolute and relative judgment it accepts. The neo-classical doctrine, if one may dare to describe in terms of unity a tissue of tendencies, may best be classified as a static or partially historical criticism, distinctly colored by the special prejudices of the age. It was built upon a narrow interpretation of Aristotle's *Poetics,* combined with the use of other classical authorities such as Horace and Seneca. This involved a marked warping of certain features of the *Poetics,* and a definite misunderstanding of others. One of the main contributions of modern critical scholarship has been the description and analysis of neo-classicism,[13] and the development subsequently of a more objective and valid form of historical criticism.

Blended with the various strands of neo-classicism, there is a strain that

13. The special features of neo-classical doctrine that impinge directly upon a consideration of *Hamlet* are: (a) the didactic impulse, with its complex philosophical and critical origin, (b) the identification of truth and beauty, (c) the doctrine of the three unities, (d) the rigid separation of comedy and tragedy, (e) poetic justice, and (f) decorum.

For neo-classical origins, see J. E. Spingarn, *op. cit.;* George Saintsbury, *History of Criticism and Literary Taste in Europe;* Aisso Bosker, *op. cit.;* S. H. Butcher, *Aristotle's Theory of Poetry and Fine Art* (new edit., London, 1911), chapters 6 and 7. For general background of rationalism, see Leslie Stephen, *History of English Thought in the Eighteenth Century.*

For discussion of one of the key terms in the vocabulary of neo-classical criticism, see A. O. Lovejoy, "Nature as Aesthetic Norm", *MLN,* 42, 444-50.

has never been long absent from English habits of thought—a sturdy empiricism.[14] Such a tendency accounts for some of the surprisingly acute things said by critics whose observations are otherwise of more limited quality. Looked at from the point of view of historical criticism, it may be said, on one hand, that *Hamlet* criticism gives evidence of a gradual loss of feeling for the Elizabethan background of the play, and on the other hand, a sharpened perception of this background. Paradoxically enough one critic, the author of the 1736 *Remarks*, exhibits in a single piece the two tendencies of which I have spoken. Furthermore he combines these with other seemingly discordant notes. He is a good example of the type of mind that seems so typically English, a mind that may be termed synthetic rather than analytic in its critical approach. On the other hand, any one critic may take such a position concerning his data as to label himself as the exponent of one special position in neo-classical thought; he may thus exhibit flagrantly some specialized point of view. As the Eighteenth Century progressed, *Hamlet* criticism passed through many a change. Finally its most important coloring was given it by several gifted critics whose central method involves a highly partial application of the "reader's attitude"; a negation of practically all of the characteristics that form the portrait of the traditional Hamlet described in an earlier section of this study.

Up to the time of Dr. Johnson's *Edition* of Shakespeare, the references to characters are, with a few exceptions, casual and conventional. How many an eighteenth-century critic, using a ready-made and traditional formula, thinks he has done his duty on the subject by saying that a certain character is "true to Nature"! Theoretically, the aesthetics of this period would seem to make possible a realistic study of dramatic character. Practically, such is not the case. The neo-classical "truth to nature," set as it is in its dogmatizing, moralizing, generalizing context, did not lend itself to any straightforward appreciation of Shakespeare's characters. Even Dr. Johnson, whose notes on Shakespearian characters are freshly and vigorously expressed, was not the pioneer that at least one important critic has called him.[15] Rather than being the first in a new criticism that regarded character as of chief interest in any study of drama, he is the critic who expresses in its most definite and complete form, the doctrine of character generalization.

Hamlet of course had his part in the general criticism of Shakespeare extending from Margaret Cavendish in 1664, to Johnson in 1765; and

14. In fact, the neo-classical command, "Follow Nature" may be given an interpretation that encourages the empirical attitude. (*Ibid.*, pp. 447-49.)

15. D. Nichol Smith, *Shakespeare in the Eighteenth Century*, p. 78.

the burden of these critiques is that Shakespeare's characters are true to life, well distinguished and consistent, and "follow Nature." Other critics who strike one or more of these notes are Dryden, Nahum Tate, Dennis, Pope, Theobald, and Hanmer.[16]

In the early Eighteenth Century, however, Hamlet received even less attention than other characters. Caliban, Othello, and Desdemona were all given preference to the Prince of Denmark in the pages of formal criticism. Long before there is a good critical appreciation of Hamlet, John Hughes makes some fairly incisive and penetrating remarks on Othello and Iago.[17] Two years later, Theobald writes two periodical papers on *King Lear*,[18] and in 1735, there was an essay on Polonius in the *Prompter*.[19] These all antedate the *Remarks* of 1736, the first formal criticism of *Hamlet* that presents the prince as its exclusive subject.

The slightness of volume, however, in the data for which we are searching is not wholly discouraging as far as conclusions are concerned. It is possible to interpret what is found partly in the light of what is not said.[20] As a whole, it is necessary to treat silence on the part of a critic who discusses Hamlet, as acquiescence in the traditional conception as portrayed on the contemporary stage.

Steele's *Tatler* 106 offers the first eighteenth-century criticism of *Hamlet* that I have found. I have already spoken of the *Tatler* in connection with Betterton's last performance, and the use in one of its issues of the speech to the players. Here, however, is a comment that is closer to formal criticism. In discussing a "widow's chastity," Steele puts as a foil to so agreeable a subject a long passage in which Hamlet soliloquizes bitterly over his mother's hasty marriage. Then there is a long paragraph of comment upon his words. Here we see the usual picture of a distracted, agonizing son who possesses "true filial piety," and feels indignant rage at his mother's frailty, and a contempt for women in general.

Steele struck one new note.[21] That is his treatment of Hamlet's psy-

16. There are, to be sure, other minor notes. For example, Dryden and Rowe discuss Shakespeare's use of the "humour" type of character, as illustrated in Falstaff.

17. The *Guardian*, April 23, 1713. My remarks above should be qualified by adding that Hughes uses the "beauties-faults" approach to his subject.

18. The *Censor*, numbers 7 and 10. These are descriptive observations on beauties and morals.

19. May 27.

20. The conservative complacency with which the Eighteenth Century before 1770 must have viewed the play and its hero, can be illustrated by the good-humored satire of *Hamlet* commentators and editors, found in Fielding's *Covent Garden Journal* for April 18, 1752.

21. Here Steele anticipates the period when Hamlet will be looked upon as a specimen for psychological dissection. His comment is a distinct foreshadowing of a similar treatment of the same passage by Richardson in 1774, and Priestley in 1777.

chology as demonstrated in the use of time as a motif that shows the heightening passion:

> The circumstance of time I never could enough admire. The widowhood had lasted two months. This is his first reflection: but, as his indignation rises, he sinks to scarce two months: afterwards into a month; and at last, into a little month: but all this so naturally, that the reader accompanies him in the violence of his passion, and finds the time lessen insensibly, according to the different workings of his disdain.[22]

In *Spectator* 44, Addison deals with the general subject of the various methods of moving an audience to pity and terror. His comment is definitely theatrical in point of view, although not so in the narrower sense of the word. As is quite natural in connection with such a subject, he brings forth the ghost scene in the first act of *Hamlet*. The young prince is given his time-honored role, that of a mortal in sore distress visited most awfully by a supernatural summoner. What is more, Addison gains historical perspective by a comparison of Hamlet with the Orestes of Sophocles.

Nicholas Rowe had anticipated Addison, however, with a comparison in 1709, of *Hamlet* with the *Electra* of Sophocles. He goes further than Addison was to go. Hamlet, like Orestes, is an avenger. Also, in both plays a guilty mother appears. The difference lies in Hamlet's more humane actions. He does not kill his mother, as Orestes kills Clytemnestra. Rowe implies that Hamlet was capable of doing like Orestes. Each hero has the same piety towards his departed father, and a resolution to avenge his death. Each has the same abhorrence for his mother's guilt. Hamlet, however, was definitely restrained from taking his mother's life by the injunction of the Ghost:

> But howsoever thou pursu'st this Act,
> Taint not thy mind; nor let thy soul contrive
> Against thy mother ought[23]

Here Rowe is quoting the lines that the nineteenth-century Werder was to use as a key to the "Hamlet mystery." There is this difference, however; as yet there is no mystery. For Rowe, Orestes and Hamlet were definitely the same type of character. One hundred and fifty years later, Werder, like his fellow Germans, had lost the ability to see the play and its hero in such simple terms.

After Rowe, in 1711 came Dennis. His one contribution of interest to us is the statement that "young Hamlet," like a number of Shakespeare's

22. The *Tatler* (1822 edit.), II, 422.
23. "Some Account of the Life, etc. of Mr. William Shakespeare" (quoted from D. N. Smith, *Eighteenth Century Essays on Shakespeare*, pp. 18-20).

other characters, had no tragic fault; for his killing of the King was justi-fied by a call from Heaven.[24]

One characteristic is common to all of the pieces glanced at so far—those of Steele, Addison, Rowe, and Dennis. All are "critical" in a sense that separates them from those that set forth a more simple theatrical treatment. Addison and Rowe deliberately take Sophocles into account, and thus see Hamlet in terms of an avenging prototype. Both approach the play in terms of its main function—the awakening of pity and fear in the spectator. Rowe, however, looks upon Hamlet as a hero who can do this more adequately than Orestes because of his more humane actions. Steele examines Hamlet's mental processes much more closely than one could do it outside the leisure of a study. Dennis finds one point of in-terest in the play: the hero's undeserved fate. Here are four critics with pretty much the same interpretation of an heroic Hamlet, but each find-ing his own focal point of interest.

Proceeding chronologically, one may pass over Pope's *Edition* of 1725 as offering nothing that concerns this study, and stop for at least a mo-ment to glance at Lewis Theobald. Theobald was first of all an emen-dator.[25] He had a definite historical sense, as his interest in source ma-terial shows.[26] In the quality of this historical sense lie both his strength and his weakness as a critic of Hamlet's character. His attitude toward Hamlet must be gathered partly by implication. One may infer that he saw him as the usual heroic prince.[27] Theobald has the distinction, though, of being the first critic I have found to open up a characteristic vein of comment; there is much of it through the rest of the century. He criticizes adversely Hamlet's coarseness and obscenity, thus showing how thoroughly he was imbued with the neo-classical principle of decorum. How many a warm admirer of the "noble prince" was to distress himself over the same embarrassing matter! They were not historically minded

24. "On the Genius and Writings of Shakespeare," *Ibid.*, p. 29.

25. The line of emendators starts with Theobald, and among others, includes Hanmer, Warburton, Upton, the anonymous author of the *Observations* of 1752, Johnson, Steevens, Ritson, and Malone. By the end of the century the text of *Hamlet*, as of a number of other Shakespearian plays, was well established. It need hardly be added that a conclusion can never be written to such activities, as witness Dover Wil-son's recent interpretations of the text of *Hamlet*. The extent to which the craze for emendation was taken up by even the general reading public can be realized if one examines a file of the *Gentleman's Magazine* for the years 1765 on.

26. Theobald knows that *Hamlet's* "source" is Saxo Grammaticus. The only use he makes of such knowledge is to preen himself on his superiority over Pope—who didn't know it (*Works*, London, 1767, VIII, 103-4). He traces also the source of the grave digger's song to a poem of the Earl of Surrey (See preface to *Works*, I).

27. See his remarks on Horatio's words: "Of that I shall have also cause to speak" (*Works*, VIII, 244).

enough to realize that all clever malcontents—and Hamlet was that—must be accomplished in just this line of conversation. Theobald, however, is quite matter-of-fact in his treatment of the subject. Of remarks that Hamlet makes to Ophelia he says: "Hamlet is talking to her in such gross double *entendres,* that she is forc'd to parry them by indirect answers: . . ."[28]

This critic does not attempt to make the question of coarseness and obscenity an ethical one. For him it was purely a matter of taste. Even here, Hamlet was really not to blame. It wasn't his fault, it was Shakespeare's. Commenting upon the prince's brutal "Do you think I meant country matters," Theobald says: "But, indeed, if ever the Poet deserved Whipping for low and indecent Ribaldry, it was for this Passage; ill-tim'd in all its Circumstances, and unbefitting the Dignity of his Characters, as well as of his Audience."[29]

Such is the extent of Theobald's comment upon Hamlet. In 1736, three years after Theobald's *Edition* appeared, *Some Remarks on the Tragedy of Hamlet Prince of Denmark* was published. This piece has been attributed to Sir Thomas Hanmer.[30] It will be profitable for us to examine this essay in more detail than its intrinsic merit justifies. Besides being the first extended critical treatment of Hamlet that is extant, it is broadly illustrative of what may be called the eighteenth-century collective mind in reference to the play and its hero. Nearly everything Hanmer says is derivative. In the course of his "remarks," at some time or other he seems to take almost every possible point of view toward his subject—every attitude possible for a man of his period to take. Many of the things he says illustrate an English neo-classical mind of the more liberal tinge. Others are quite definitely empirical in tenor. Combined with this admirable scientific trait, he can take other positions that are distressingly unhistorical. Let me illustrate these various statements.

Hanmer's basic conception of Hamlet is orthodox. He says:

The Prince's Resolution to speak to the Phantom, let what will be the Consequence, is entirely suitable to his Heroical Disposition; . . ."[31]

We are now come to the sublimest Scene in this whole Piece, a Scene worthy of the greatest Attention; an Heroical Youth addressing the Shade of his departed Father, whom he tenderly loved.[32]

28. *Works,* VIII, 177.
29. *Shakespeare Restored* (London, 1726), pp. 86-7.
30. In my discussion of the *Remarks,* I treat Hanmer's questioned authorship as valid. However, it should be understood that such an attribution cannot be called other than doubtful. See C. D. Thorpe, "Thomas Hanmer and the Anonymous Essay on *Hamlet," MLN,* 49, 493-98.
31. *Op. Cit.,* (London, 1736), p. 22.
32. *Ibid.,* p. 27.

He accosts the Ghost with great Intrepidity; and his whole Speech is so full of the Marks of his Filial Piety, that we may easily observe, that his Tenderness for his Father gets the better of all Sentiments of Terror.[33]

In addition to possessing such qualities as these, Hamlet has others that make him a prince after Shaftesbury's heart, for Hanmer says of him:

and his Reflection upon his Father's Spirit appearing in Arms, is such as one would naturally expect from him; and the Moral Sentence he ends his short Speech with, suits his virtuous Temper, at the same Time that it has a good Effect upon the Audience, and answers the End of Tragedy.[34]

After saying these warmly appreciative things concerning Hamlet, it might seem surprising to find Hanmer taking sharp exception to the prince's "light and even ludicrous expressions" as his father's ghost is departing and cries from the cellarage. His madness, also; his unseemly conduct during the play; his obscenity with Ophelia; his levity after the killing of Polonius—all these offenses against decorum Hanmer deprecates. Since he includes an account of the story as found in Saxo Grammaticus, it is surprising that he does not make the historical connection— that a piece of work may be viewed partly in the light of its sources. Might it not be that Hamlet's character would be illuminated through such a comparison? Hanmer, however, is contented merely to describe the source so that he may show how far Shakespeare goes beyond it—not how he sometimes approaches it.[35]

Later in his essay, however, Hanmer brings up the subject of play versus source again, and this time he is surprisingly sound. He notes the puzzling fact that there is no real motivation for Hamlet's assumed madness. The madness merely makes his task of revenge more difficult, instead of easier.[36] What is more, the delay in killing the king is not adequately explained. Hanmer now does, however, what he did not do earlier: He calls upon Saxo to explain the delay:

To speak Truth, our Poet, by keeping too close to the Ground-work of his Plot, has fallen into an Absurdity; for there appears no Reason at all in Nature, why the young Prince did not put the Usurper to Death as soon as possible, especially as *Hamlet* is represented as a Youth so brave, and so careless of his own life.[37]

Then, with eminent good sense, this critic draws a conclusion not always kept in mind by later generations of critics:

33. *Ibid.*, p. 28.
34. *Ibid.*, p. 22.
35. *Ibid.*, pp. 5, ff.
36. *Ibid.*, p. 33.
37. *Ibid.*, p. 33.

The Case indeed is this: Had *Hamlet* gone naturally to work, as we could suppose such a Prince to do in parallel Circumstances, there would have been an End of our Play. The Poet therefore was obliged to delay his Hero's Revenge; but then he should have contrived some good Reason for it.[38]

Nor does this surprising critic stop here. A few pages later he makes this pentrating observation:

And the more I read him, the more I am convinced, that as he knew his own particular Talent well, he study'd more to work up great and moving Circumstances to place his chief Characters in, so as to affect our Passions strongly, he apply'd himself more to This than he did to the Means or Methods whereby he brought his Characters into those circumstances.[39]

From this remark, considered along with the other two just quoted, it is evident that as a critic of *Hamlet* Hanmer was well in advance of previous commentators. Indeed, his recognition of the gap that often exists between Shakespeare's characters in their "great and moving Circumstances" and the motivation used to bring about the situation, brings him very close to the position taken by modern historical scholars. If Hanmer had particularized here, he might have said that Shakespeare kept the awkward and archaic old plot of revenge, and placed in it a profoundly moving hero, far too rich in personality to move easily in such surroundings. Hanmer, of course does not say this. His words, however, show that he had some such thought in mind.[40]

At another point Hanmer is equally sound. He sees that the usurpation motif cannot be interpreted as having any large part in Hamlet's grief. The play simply does not give any marked evidence to substantiate such a position.[41] This is fine analysis of aesthetic data.[42]

One other comment of Hanmer's has significance, that setting forth his position on Hamlet's "cruelty," as displayed in the prayer scene:

Hamlet's Speech upon seeing the King at Prayers, has always given me great

38. *Ibid.*, p. 34.
39. *Ibid.*, p. 55.
40. Karl Young's essay, "Samuel Johnson on Shakespeare: One Aspect," (*U. of Wisc. Stud. in Lang. and Lit.*, *18*, 1923), contains an excellent discussion and appraisal of the critical tendencies of commentators through these years. For interpretative use here, I have taken several valuable hints from Mr. Young.
41. Dover Wilson, with a mistaken subtlety, builds up an elaborate case for the usurpation motif (*What Happens in Hamlet*, Cambridge, 1935, pp. 26, ff; 114, ff; 164, ff). Hanmer's position is much more sound.
42. Hanmer was also quite definitely on the right track in his analysis of the use of time in the play. He does not make a complete analysis that would bring out Shakespeare's "naive perspective" but he goes so far as to differ from Theobald. He maintains that the time supposed to elapse is fairly short. He ends his comment quaintly: "These Reasons and the whole Conduct of the Piece convince me, that this is one of *Shakespeare's* Plays, in which the least Time is employ'd; how much there is, I cannot pretend to say." (*Op. cit.*, p. 18)

Offense. There is something so very Bloody in it, so inhuman, so unworthy of a Hero, that I wish our Poet had omitted it. To desire to destroy a Man's Soul, to make him eternally miserable, by cutting him off from all hopes of Repentance; this surely, in a Christian Prince, is such a Piece of Revenge, as no Tenderness for any Parent can justify. To put the Usurper to Death, to deprive him of the Fruits of his vile Crime, and to rescue the Throne of *Denmark* from Pollution, was highly requisite: But there our young Prince's Desires should have stop'd, nor should he have wished to pursue the Criminal in the Other World, but rather have hoped for his Conversion, before his putting him to Death; for even with his Repentance, there was at least Purgatory for him to pass through, as we find even in a virtuous Prince, the Father of Hamlet. . . .[43]

These words, so often quoted, are the first example I have found of the "cruelty" motif. Later in the century when it became the vogue to criticize Hamlet's character adversely, the same charge appeared often. The definite significance that was given then to such a trait in Hamlet is important. At present, however, the main importance to us of Hanmer's remarks is their indication of an unhistorical blind spot which becomes increasingly manifest, as time passes, in certain other critics. Here we see to a marked degree one aspect of the sentimental influence that has already been noted as having so prominent a part in the theatrical interpretation of Hamlet's character. Certainly the Elizabethan audiences who were so avid for Kydian revenge plays did not object to a little "cruelty" on the part of their hero-avengers!

Such are the main outlines of Hanmer's interpretation. In his inclusive net he seems to catch almost every prevailing aspect of *Hamlet* criticism. I have omitted some of his judgments—those in which he repeats glibly the clichés of his time.[44] He shows on one issue a genuine historical perspective; on another a point of view that is hopelessly absolute. The very conclusiveness and synthetic quality of his picture of Hamlet are confusing. His interpretation exhibits all the swarming confusion of neo-classicism itself, when a number of its diverse elements are gathered together at one time. Of course his prince gives us none of the unity of impression that must have been provided by the contemporary stage, even in the portrayal of a Wilks or a Booth. His prince exhibits no

43. *Ibid.*, p. 41.

44. For example, of Shakespeare's characters in general, and thus, I suppose of Hamlet, he says: "His particular Excellency consists in the Variety and Singularity of his Characters, and in the constant Conformity of each Character to itself from its very first setting out in the Play, quite to the End." (*Ibid.*, p. 2.) Again he speaks of how "natural" Hamlet's reflections on his mother's hasty marriage are (*Ibid.*, p. 20). One variety of comment typical of the Eighteenth Century is that in which he points out some of Hamlet's words as "beauties." The prince's soliloquy after the ghost disappears is "exquisitely beautiful" (*Ibid.*, p. 31). In any number of other places, Hanmer follows the same critical method.

"conformity of a character to itself." However it is reasonable to believe that Hanmer's "real Hamlet" was most likely the "heroical youth" with filial piety, tenderness and resolution, who found himself entangled in "great and moving Circumstances." There may well be a difference between the picture provided by this critic's imagination and the aesthetic analysis made by his intellect. Such would seem to be the case.

After the 1736 *Remarks* there was nothing of importance in the way of formal criticism until William Guthrie's *An Essay upon English Tragedy* in 1747. John Upton's *Critical Observations on Shakespeare* of the previous year may be passed over, as it is almost exclusively of an emendatory nature. It gives nothing relevant to this study. Likewise, William Warburton's *Edition* of 1747 contains pedestrian comments that do not rise above his statement that Hamlet suffered from a "rooted melancholy sprung from thickness of blood."[45]

Guthrie, on the other hand, has value for us. His remarks illustrate well one tendency in eighteenth-century rationalistic aesthetics. For him, Hamlet is "Everyman." His portrait is not so much that of an individual as that of a species.[46] The critic is reacting here against what he considers an opposite trend in contemporary drama. He wishes to think of the prince as "ordinary," rather than as distinguished or unusual in quality. Let me quote:

This leads me to observe, though I have the prepossession of a whole age against me, that there is not the least necessity for the chief personage in a play to have either courage, wisdom, virtue, passion, or any other quality, above what is to be found in his real history, or in common life.

45. *The Poems and Plays of William Shakespeare* (London, 1821 Variorum), VII, 285.

46. Samuel Johnson gives the best expression of this aesthetic doctrine. In his *Preface to Shakespeare* (1765), he says:

> His persons act and speak by the influence of those general passions and principles by which all minds are agitated, and the whole system of life is continued in motion. In the writings of other poets a character is too often an individual; in those of *Shakespeare* it is commonly a species. (Walter Raleigh, *Johnson on Shakespeare, Essays and Notes*, Oxford, 5th Imp., 1925, p. 12.)

However, Johnson's classical expression of the doctrine is found in Chapter X of *Rasselas:*

> "The business of a poet," said Imlac, "is to examine, not the individual, but the species; to remark general properties and large appearances. He does not number the streaks of the tulip, or describe the different shades in the verdure of the forest; he is to exhibit in his portraits of nature such prominent and striking features, as recal the original to every mind; and must neglect the minuter discriminations, which one may have remarked, and another have neglected, for those characteristics which are alike obvious to vigilance and carelessness." (G. B. Hill, ed., Oxford, 1926, pp. 62-3.)

He [Shakespeare] has supported the character of Hamlet entirely by the force of sentiment, without giving him any of those strong markings, which commonly form the chief modern personage in a tragedy. He has not even made use of those advantages, with which the great historian from whom he took his subject might have furnished him. . . . Where is the poet but Shakespear, who could have worked so insipid a character [as that found in Saxo] into life by the justness of reflection, and the strength of nature, without applying those colours, which an inferior genius must have used to mark a principal figure. All we see in Hamlet is a well-meaning, sensible, young man, but full of doubts and perplexities even after his resolution is fixed. In this character there is nothing but what is common with the rest of mankind; he has no marking, no colouring, but its beautiful drawing, perhaps, cost Shakespear more than any one figure he ever attempted.[47]

Occasionally some curious critical document that as a whole has little value, may contain some note prophetic of future criticism. Such is the case with regard to *A Companion to the Theatre*. . . .[48] published in Dublin in 1751. The main object of the little book was to offer a paraphrase of, and commentary on, the drama about to be "enjoyed" by the theatre-goer. This author quite definitely shows that he does not think that a drama as enacted is necessarily self-explanatory. In view of the direction that *Hamlet* criticism at the end of the century takes, such a point of view in this Dublin critic is interesting. The one comment that is of especial value to us, however, involves the motivation given Hamlet's assumed madness. Hamlet himself seems quite the usual heroic prince. However, he "counterfeits a frenzy" to "conceal the true Cause of the Horror of his Mind." This is the earliest suggestion I have found that the older objective motivation of Hamlet's madness is being called in question. This critical bit is thus a straw in the wind.

The anonymous *Miscellaneous Observations on the Tragedy of Hamlet Prince of Denmark,* published in 1752, needs no more than a passing glance. The adjective "miscellaneous" was well chosen as part of its title. It is mainly a series of emendations interspersed with rather unilluminating observations. Hamlet appears usually as a virtuous person who can

---

47. *An Essay upon English Tragedy* (London, 1747), pp. 20-21.

In 1748, Peter Whalley published *An Enquiry into the Learning of Shakespeare* (London). In it he follows the best scholarship of his time, and assumes that Saxo's Latin history is the immediate source of *Hamlet.* For our purposes his comparison of the play with its "original" is not very illuminating. He shows little of Hanmer's ability to generalize fruitfully from the data before him. The best he can do is to deny that Shakespeare gained anything by his departure from his original, in the matter of an unhappy ending. He did not succeed in giving to *Hamlet* a "fine Distress, or any extraordinary Scene of Action." (*Op. cit.*, pp. v-vi.)

48. *A Companion to the Theatre: or a View of our most celebrated dramatic pieces . . . interspersed with remarks Historical, Critical, and Moral.*

make wise remarks at the proper moment. He displays "consummate judgment" in choosing Horatio as a friend.[49] In another place, however, the prince is pictured as a bit naïve in his surprise over the fact that the Danes have accepted Claudius as king.[50] This writer gives evidence of one undramatic habit of thought, induced by the study: he confuses Hamlet and Shakespeare, much as Theobald does. The play's satire against women is laid directly at the door of Shakespeare. "Concealed under the character of Hamlet, he lashes the pretty engaging Arts made use of by the Ladies of his Time, and even yet not out of fashion."[51] Thus in one way or another, this critic strips Hamlet of a good share of his autonomous life as a dramatic character.

From 1752 on, we need hardly stop before the time of the Johnson *Edition* of 1765.[52] Two pieces deserve passing attention: a curious poetic bit, and an essay by Goldsmith. In 1758 a "Dr. Ibbot" published "A Fit of the Spleen—In Imitation of Shakespeare," in Dodsley's *Collection* of that year. The only reason it deserves more attention than the thousand and one other echoes of *Hamlet* is its odd emphasis upon the procrastination motif. Possibly "Dr. Ibbot" finds Hamlet's words an opportunity to develop an authentic mood of his own. The only hint as to the time of composition is the statement that the last four lines are supposedly by Pope:

> Farewell, vain world! and thou its vainest part,
> O lovely woman! fram'd for man's destruction!
> Farewell, vain world! dwelling of ills and fears,
> Full of fond hopes, false joys, and sad repentance;

49. *Op. cit.*, (London), p. 31.
50. *Ibid.*, p. 20.
51. *Ibid.*, p. 34.
52. Mrs. Charlotte Lennox has a "source comment" in her *Shakespear Illustrated.* . . . (London, 1753). As with Hanmer, her point of departure for an examination of the play in relation to its source, is the assumed madness. She sees that as regards this point Saxo's account is properly motivated, but that *Hamlet* is not. The device of madness is "less essential to the Play than [to] the History." (*Op. cit.*, II, 272-3. Quoted from Karl Young, *op. cit.*, p. 190.) In her comment here, Mrs. Lennox seems aware of the "fossilized" nature of *Hamlet*. Like Hanmer, she makes a critical suggestion that shows genuine historical perspective.
The *London Chronicle* of Feb. 15-17, 1757 contains a review of a performance of the play. In substance, however, it is not a review so much as a discussion of the superiority of *Hamlet* to the account given by Saxo Grammaticus. In one way, the author says, the earlier account is superior. It contains an exemplification of poetic justice. There is also a brief discussion of Hamlet's eagerness to get the details of his father's appearance from Horatio and the guard. His manner of quick eager speech reveals "little touches" that are "agreeable to the Affections of the Mind, when we talk of a Person we love either absent or dead." (Quoted from James Agate, *The English Dramatic Critics*, London, 1932, pp. 19-21.)

For though sometimes warm Fancy lights a fire,
That mounting upwards darts its pointed head
Up, through the unopposing air, to heav'n,
Yet then comes Thought, and cold Consideration,
Lame Afterthought with endless scruples fraught,
Benumn'd with Fears, to damp the goodly blaze. . . .

So the struck deer, with some deep wound opprest,
Lies down to die the arrow in his breast;
There hid in shades, and wasting day by day,
Inly he bleeds, and pants his life away.[53]

This piece is at least prophetic of the early Nineteenth Century when critics will use the same words that Dr. Ibbot dwells upon, to discover in Hamlet a psychology and motives hardly dreamed of before.

Goldsmith's essay on *The Use of Metaphors*[54] contains a few remarks on Hamlet's "to be" soliloquy. What he says illustrates well what sometimes happens when a commentator picks a drama to pieces in his study. Losing sight completely of the dramatic relevance of the part being criticized, and forgetting that audiences for generations had found this soliloquy clear and meaningful, Goldsmith dissected it. His findings in part follow:

The soliloquy in Hamlet, which we have so often heard extolled in terms of admiration, is, in our opinion, a heap of absurdities, whether we consider the situation, the sentiment, the argumentation, or the poetry. Hamlet is informed by the Ghost, that his father was murdered, and therefore he is tempted to murder himself, even after he had promised to take vengeance on the usurper, and expressed the utmost eagerness to achieve this enterprise. It does not appear that he had the least reason to wish for death; but every motive which may be supposed to influence the mind of a young prince, concurred to render life desirable—revenge towards the usurper; love for the fair Ophelia; and the ambition of reigning.[55]

Goldsmith then proceeds to show how the soliloquy may be picked to pieces so that Hamlet's "whole chain of reasoning . . . seems inconsistent and incongruous."

This is indeed closet comment of a hopelessly "literary" nature. No critic could show himself further removed from any sense of dramatic

53. *Op. cit.,* V, 202-3.
54. Published in the *British Magazine* (1763?). Although given a place in practically every edition of Goldsmith's collected *Works,* one editor, Peter Cunningham, 1854, expresses doubt concerning its place in the Goldsmith canon. If one were to judge the quality of the essay by the remarks included on *Hamlet,* he would come to the conclusion that to eliminate the essay from the canon would not damage Goldsmith's reputation.
55. *Works* (ed. Cunningham, London, 1854), III, 316.

values, for Shakespeare makes neither Hamlet's love for Ophelia nor his "ambition of reigning" unmistakable dramatic motives. What is more, Goldsmith is unable to interpret even the plain meaning of the score in terms of its histrionic significance.

The notes of Dr. Johnson's 1765 edition of Shakespeare offer no radical departure in the eighteenth-century critical approach to Hamlet's character.[56] It is true, this edition contains the first vigorous interpretative notes on characters to be presented by an editor; that is, notes that, unlike Warburton's, are more than echoes of previous clichés or neo-classical truisms. Polonius, rather than Hamlet, is the character in *Hamlet* whom Johnson discusses at some length. As one would expect after reading his *Preface,* the generalizing doctrine there set forth, can be traced in the colors with which the old councillor is depicted. If Johnson had drawn Hamlet in similar detail, he probably would have given him an analogous "species" treatment.

What little Johnson says concerning Hamlet is illuminating, just the same. He can examine the aesthetic data of the drama, with a fair degree of objectivity. He sees that *Hamlet* is not a regulation play of action. Also, there is no adequate cause for the assumed madness. "Hamlet is, through the whole play, rather an instrument than an agent." He is a

56. Nichol Smith thinks that Johnson's notes on Polonius and Falstaff "herald the new subject—the study of Shakespeare's characters, and the study of Shakespeare through his characters." (*Shakespeare in the Eighteenth Century,* p. 80.) Smith points out that the development of critical method in treating Shakespeare's characters is evolutionary: "In matters of this kind we need not hope to find a definite beginning, nor need we look for the man with an undisputed claim to be called 'the first'." Besides mentioning the critics whose treatment of character is in a way pioneering work (*supra,* p. 50, notes 17, 18, and 19), he speaks of five papers contributed by Joseph Warton to the *Adventurer,* in 1753 and 1754. These are on *The Tempest* and *King Lear,* (Nos. 93, 97, 113, 116, and 122). Three other papers on King Lear, in *Gray's Inn Journal* (Nos. 65, 66, and 87), follow immediately after Warton's contributions. The new treatment of character, says Smith, grows out of the older method. Critics finally come to *practice* as well as to preach the doctrine that "Nature and Shakespeare are the same." Dramatic creations "come to be treated as historic beings. Simultaneously, criticism ceases to be pre-eminently judicial; it rather interprets." (*Op. cit.,* p. 83.)

In spite of what Smith says, it is difficult for me to see that Johnson's treatment of Shakespeare's characters is markedly new; or definitely "heralds the new subject." On the contrary, as brought out by Karl Young in his essay *(Op. cit.),* published five years before Smith's book, Johnson is in no sense a "modern sceptic." He lacks the particular flashes of critical intuition that make Hanmer and even Mrs. Lennox seem at moments so modern. He is indeed, free from the critical cant of the period. On the other hand, he sticks to the "species" dogma. Also he does not confuse art and life. On this score he is in no way prophetic of the critical heresies of the next decade— those of Richardson, Morgann, etc.

A commentary upon Smith's position is given by T. M. Raysor in "The Study of Shakespeare's Characters in the Eighteenth Century," *MLN,* 42, 495-500. Mr. Raysor adds details overlooked by Smith.

man "distracted with contrariety of desires, and overwhelmed with the magnitude of his own purposes."[57] There is no poetic justice.[58]

Johnson brings up also the matter of Hamlet's cruelty on occasion of overhearing the king at prayer.[59] A little later he takes up the same trait again. He says that the prince "plays the madman most, when he treats Ophelia with so much rudeness, which seems to us useless and wanton cruelty."[60] And of the apology to Laertes in Act V, he says: "I wish Hamlet had made some other defense; it is unsuitable to the character of a good or a brave man, to shelter himself in falsehood."[61] Yes, unsuitable, Hamlet's defenders might admit, but "good and brave men" do that very thing, and are forgiven for it.[62] The implication of Dr. Johnson's less favorable remarks is probably such an idea as this: words and actions do not always express the true character. If they did, who could pass guiltless before a bar of judgment! One can hardly doubt that for this critic, Hamlet was a good and brave man.

It is plain, I think, that much of what Johnson says concerning Hamlet was not new. Hanmer had already presented most of these critical ideas. True, of course, Johnson does not repeat Hanmer's more stupid remarks. He had a sturdy empirical instinct that kept him from acting as a mouthpiece for many of the staler clichés of rationalistic criticism. On the other hand, he never achieved such a moment of intuition and historical perspective as Hanmer did when he realized that Hamlet and the archaic plot in which he is placed are incongruous.[63] On the whole, as critic of *Hamlet*, Johnson looks back rather than forward.

57. Walter Raleigh, *Op. cit.*, p. 191. The phrase "distracted with contrariety of desires" suggests the interpretation that Richardson is to make the keynote of his 1774 essay. However, Johnson does not regard delay as a central dramatic motif in *Hamlet*. His phrase just quoted, together with the "overwhelmed with the magnitude of his own purposes" can be given an interpretation that keeps the prince a normal person. Hamlet has a great task on his hands; and like any other normal human being, must pause for a moment to collect his disturbed thoughts, before going ahead to his rendevous with destiny.

58. *Ibid.*, p. 196.

59. *Ibid.*, p. 193.

60. *Ibid.*, p. 196.

61. *Op. cit.*, p. 195.

62. After all, in his words to Laertes (Act V, ii, 237, ff) "Give me your pardon, sir," is he not merely trying to let others know how much he has suffered? Surely he is not trying to equivocate, or make others believe he was really mad. Words are but poor symbols with which to sketch the thought within. Even a normal man can have "that within which passeth show." Can Hamlet be censured for calling this "sore distraction" madness?

63. *Supra*, p. 55; and p. 61, note 56.

4

Formal Criticism, 1770-1800

I T IS a somewhat arbitrary device of exposition to set 1770 as the turning point in *Hamlet* criticism, for there have been hints of a change before this. I have noted these hints in my discussion. However, it is possible to see in this decade a very noticeable alteration in both the tone and content of what is said concerning Hamlet. Nearly every critic, in some respect, shows it. One, Richardson, offers a radical departure from former critical positions. As a whole, the change involves a more definite and more thoroughgoing negation of the direct perspective than has been seen before. I have sketched the undramatic tendencies always latent in eighteenth-century habits of thought—in fact, existing at the very heart of neo-classicism. Nevertheless, there is a difference between the undramatic attitudes of a Shaftesbury or Mrs. Montagu, and that of a Richardson. Shaftesbury and Mrs. Montagu did not turn so radically away from the traditional conception. They still had much in common with the seventeenth-century spectators who saw Burbage leap into Ophelia's grave, or with Addison's "trunkmaker in the gallery," and Tom Jones' friend, Partridge. In this decade, on the other hand, it is possible to catch signs of a vital and almost permanent change. The Hamlet of the theatre was a less active force. More and more the play was becoming something to be read and enjoyed in the study, less and less something to be seen on the stage. There can be detected also an accompanying tendency to use the criteria of real life as a yardstick of judgment.

The general results of the alteration I have sketched may be tabulated as follows:

1. a magnifying of certain character elements such as inconsistency and cruelty; a feeling on the part of critics that these elements made Hamlet a "complex character"; a growing tendency to "explain" him

2. a development of the procrastination motif

3. a development of the madness motif, which includes
    (a) a tendency to make more explicit the motivation of the assumed madness; such motivation followed subjective lines; the earlier objective motivation was largely subordinated

(b) a growing inclination to see Hamlet as really close to madness, or as actually mad

4. a development of the romantic tendency to read into Hamlet's character some prominent element in the psychology of the critic, the prince thus becoming a "man-of-feeling," a "young Werther," or the like

The decade of criticism now to be examined was opened by an essay written by Francis Gentleman, and published in 1770. Most of what he says need not detain us.[1] One paragraph, however, is interesting:

> In respect of characters, we are to lament that the hero, who is intended as amiable, should be such an apparent heap of inconsistency; impetuous, tho' philosophical; sensible of injury, yet timid of resentment; shrewd, yet void of policy; full of filial piety, yet tame under oppression; boastful in expression, undetermined in action; and yet, from being pregnant with great variety, from affording many opportunities to exert sound judgment and extensive powers, he is as agreeable and striking an object as any in the English drama.[2]

Gentleman is here using the method of intellectual dissection with which Goldsmith sought to destroy the artistic integrity of the "to be" soliloquy. In this case, though, it is not Hamlet's reasoning processes, but rather the whole fabric of his identity that is being attacked. The critic, however, cannot carry through, for he remembers that he has seen Hamlet in the theatre!

In spite of his perplexities concerning Hamlet's "inconsistencies," Gentleman admits that on the stage these jarring elements blend into a histrionic representation that is "agreeable and striking." Thus, he himself gives a perfect answer to the "charges" he has just made. Inconsistency, as far as it concerns Hamlet's character, exists only as a phenomenon of the study. On the stage, the odd, jarring diversities that somehow should not blend into a unity of impression, through a miracle of Shakespeare's art and genius, do so.[3]

Gentleman no doubt was perplexed by the gap between real life and

---

1. Much is a repetition of the ideas of former critics. His ideas on Hamlet's madness, the lack of proper motivation of the delay, and the failure to achieve poetic justice are of this nature. He seems to have nearly all of Hanmer's neo-classical prejudices. Some of the hero's remarks to his father's shade are "light"; he uses the word "hell"; some of his sentiments, especially those over the king at prayer are horrifying, "more suitable to an assassin of the basest kind, than to a virtuous and a feeling man." (*The Dramatic Censor*, London, 1770, p. 46.) On the other hand, he heartily approves of Hamlet's objection to suicide ("the dread of something after death") as "concise, persuasive, and highly consistent with the true principles of moral philosophy." (*Ibid.*, pp. 44-5.)

2. *Ibid.*, p. 55.

3. In fact, it is these various diversities that furnish the dramatic "bite" of the character. A telling contrast, and at times, an irony, is achieved by the combination into one character of such seemingly incongruous elements. Part of Shakespeare's suc-

art. Like others of his period, he did not see that the criteria of the first cannot be applied to a character creation whose only real life exists in the realm of art. True, Hamlet's "jarring" qualities cannot be fitted into a psychological unit. He must be apprehended with the aid of the more naïve perspective which the spectator, to get his full enjoyment, is willing to employ. As soon as this perspective is abandoned, as Gentleman here gives evidence of abandoning it, the artistic unity evaporates. It evaporates, that is, unless one does what critics were soon to do: remove Hamlet completely from his true sphere as a dramatic creation, and give him a new life off the stage as an entirely different type of character. Gentleman does not seem to wish to do that. Thus he remains perplexed.

Dr. James Beattie's estimate of Hamlet came next. In a letter to Mrs. Montagu dated as about 1772, he says in part:

> I have often seen Hamlet performed by the underlings of the theatre, but none of these seemed to understand what they were about. Hamlet's character, though perfectly natural, is so very uncommon, that few, even of our critics, can enter into it. Sorrow, indignation, revenge, and consciousness of his own irresolution, tear his heart; the peculiarity of his circumstances often obliges him to counterfeit madness, and the storm of passions within him often drives him to the verge of real madness. This produces a situation so interesting, and a conduct so complicated, as none but Shakespeare could have had the courage to describe, or even to invent, and none but Garrick will ever be able to exhibit.[4]

The description here of the prince as possessing a character "so uncommon, that few, even of our critics, can enter into it"; the conduct "so complicated"; the emphasis on irresolution; the suggestion of a state of mind on the "verge of real madness"—all of this is indicative of the "new Hamlet" that was replacing the more simple, more straightforward traditional figure.

The next year George Steevens published the first *Edition* of the Johnson and Steevens Shakespeare. In it, he adopted an attitude toward Hamlet that had in it a decided touch of hostility. At one point he says:

> Hamlet, at the command of his father's ghost, undertakes with seeming alacrity to revenge the murder; and declares he will banish all other thoughts from his mind. He makes, however, but one effort to keep his word . . . defers his purpose . . . he deliberately procures the execution of Rosencrantz and Guildenstern. . . . Their death . . . gives him no concern. . . . He is not less accountable for the distraction and death of Ophelia . . . he kills the king at last to revenge himself, and not his father.

---

cess is due to the fact that he made Hamlet, as he was later to make Othello and Macbeth, superior to his conduct. For a discussion of this, see E. E. Stoll, "Hamlet the Man," in *Shakespeare and Other Masters* (Cambridge, Mass., 1940), p. 127.

4. Sir William Forbes, *An Account of the Life and Writings of James Beattie, LL.D. . . . including many of his original letters* (Edinburgh, 1807), I, 283-4.

Hamlet cannot be said to have pursued his ends by very warrantable means; and if the poet, when he sacrificed him at last, meant to have enforced such a moral, it is not the worst that can be deduced from the play.

I have dwelt the longer on this subject, because Hamlet seems to have been hitherto regarded as a hero, not undeserving the pity of the audience, and because no writer on Shakespeare has taken the pains to point out the immoral tendency of his character.[5]

Here is a distinct suggestion of a tragic flaw—Hamlet defers his purpose, inexcusably. He was also cruel, emotionally unstable, and "immoral" in tendency. Steevens' later comments merely elaborate upon the foundation of this earlier position.

It is, however, the distinction of the Scotchman, William Richardson, a professor of humanity at Glasgow with little knowledge or appreciation of English dramatic tradition, to make the first unequivocal contribution to critical interpretation of the "new Hamlet."[6] In 1774, he included an essay on Hamlet's character in *A Philosophical Analysis of Some of Shakespeare's Remarkable Characters.* Now for the first time we get a critical approach that involves a definite "psychologizing" of Hamlet's character; an application of the criteria of real life. An attempt is made to show that Hamlet is not "inconsistent"; that all of his various words and actions fit into one harmonious picture, as part of one psychological whole. It is true that to achieve this goal, Richardson picks his items judiciously. For example, he ignores the prince's "cruel speech" over the king at prayer. Ten years later he is prepared to explain even this. What more could Hanmer, or even Steevens wish than that!

Richardson's general picture of Hamlet is of a thoroughly admirable character who is "moved by finer principles" than any mere self-interest. His actions and very thought are motivated by "an exquisite sense of virtue, of moral beauty and turpitude." His reactions are far more intense than those of the average person. This fact is seen in his state of mind at the moment he decides to put on an antic disposition. The description as given here is similar to that found in Dr. Beattie's letter to Mrs. Montagu. Hamlet is indeed in the grasp of emotions that almost tear him asunder. This is the characterization, which, ten years later, Richardson will deepen still further:

5. *The Plays of William Shakespeare* (London, 1773), X, 343-4.
6. Babcock (*The Genesis of Shakespeare Idolatry*, pp. 142, ff) says that Gentleman is the one who first broaches the "Hamlet problem." Nichol Smith gives the credit to Steevens for his remarks in 1773 (*Shakespeare in the Eighteenth Century*, p. 88). E. E. Stoll thinks that the dubious honor belongs to Richardson and Mackenzie (*Hamlet*, 1919, pp. 8-9). Each critic's point of view is understandable. It all depends upon how complete or explicit a break with tradition one asks for.

Conceiving designs of punishment, conscious of very violent perturbation, perceiving himself already suspected by the king, afraid lest his aspect, gesture, or demeanour should betray him, and knowing that his projects must be conducted with secrecy, he resolves to conceal himself under the disguise of madness.[7]

The effect of this account is plainly to throw the integrity of Hamlet's feigned madness under suspicion. The older objective interpretation of the assumption of madness is now almost discarded. Granted the fact that Hamlet's emotional reactions are intense, and that at moments he may almost feel the madness he feigns, just the same the older orthodox interpretation gave him exquisite finesse and self-control in his feigning.[8] But now, this was gone.

Richardson goes on to describe more fully the subsequent condition of the prince's mind, a condition which makes delay inevitable. He is gifted —or cursed—with a dual point of view. His violent conflict of emotions, the product of exquisite sensitivity, is traced in the following manner:

The tendency of indignation, and of furious and inflamed resentment, is to inflict punishment on the offender. But, if resentment is ingrafted on the moral faculty, and grows from it, its tenor and conduct will be different. In its first emotion it may breathe excessive and immediate vengeance: But sentiments of justice and propriety interposing, will arrest and suspend its violence. An ingenious mind, thus agitated by powerful and contending principles, exceedingly tortured and perplexed, will appear hesitating and undetermined. Thus, the vehemence of the vindictive passion will, by delay, suffer abatement; by its own ardour it will be exhausted; and our natural and habituated propensities will resume their influence.[9]

Of the unfortunate prince, thus paralyzed by conflicting emotions, Richardson goes on to say:

The mind of Hamlet, weary and exhausted by violent agitation, continues doubtful and undecided, till his sensibility, excited by a theatrical exhibition (the Hecuba speech), restores to their authority his indignation and desire of vengeance.[10]

Even then he does not act:

Still, however, his moral principles, the supreme and governing powers of his constitution, conducting those passions which they seem to justify and excite, determine him again to examine his evidence, or endeavour, by additional circumstances, to have it strengthened.[11]

7. *Op. cit.*, (Edinburgh and London), p. 126.
8. For example, recall Aaron Hill's description of Hamlet as he feigns madness, *supra*, p. 36.
9. *Op. cit.*, pp. 130-31.
10. *Ibid.*, pp. 131-2.
11. *Ibid.*, p. 132.

It is easy to see how the whole center of interpretation of Hamlet's character was shifted by Richardson to the most subtle psychological basis.[12] His treatment of the score represents a new reading, both absolutely and relatively. More especially, he is flagrantly unhistorical. *Hamlet* as a dramatic entity almost disappears. The prince whom he sketches might be the central figure in a novel of the modern introspective stripe. Where else he might find a place in art, I hardly know. The sturdy prince of tradition, even in the eighteenth-century guise of Garrick's delicately touched interpretation, the Hamlet who shows the "progress of impassioned sensation," has vanished. Garrick did not show a hero who put off his revenge because of emotional paralysis. He delayed because of a scruple that might have held up any avenger. The motif of delay had never before received the subtle treatment accorded it by Richardson. In fact, such a motif had not before been set forth as a dramatic item to arrest markedly the attention of the spectator.[13]

In this decade when critical opinion was crystallizing along new lines, there were several conservative notes. Mrs. Griffith's *The Morality of Shakespeare's Drama Illustrated*, 1775, shows older habits of thought.[14] Hamlet receives little attention at her hands, but what notice she gives

12. Another interesting aspect of Richardson's treatment of Hamlet here, is his description of the way his mind works. The critic is thinking in terms of associationist psychology, set forth definitely by David Hartley in his *Observations on Man*, 1747. For example, in discussing the manner in which Hamlet deliberately aggravates his own sense of his mother's guilt by shortening the period between his father's death and her remarriage, Richardson says:

> In the foregoing lines the reflections are general; but, in these that follow, they become particular; and the emotion waxing stronger, the imagination, by exhibiting suitable images, and by fitting to its purpose even the time between the death and the marriage, renders it excessive.
>> That it should come to this!
>> But two months dead! nay, not so much not two; . . .
> The emotion grows still more vehement, and overflows the mind with a tide of corresponding images.
>> Heaven and earth!
>> . . . Yet within a month!
>>> (*Op. cit.*, pp. 105-6.)

It is worthy of note that three years after Richardson's essay from which I have just quoted, Joseph Priestley discussed these same lines from *Hamlet*, and explained them explicitly in terms of associationist psychology (*A Course of Lectures on Oratory and Criticism*, London, 1777, pp. 92-4). It would seem likely that Priestley got his idea directly from Richardson. One should remember also the anticipation of both Richardson and Priestley in *Tatler* 106 (*supra*, pp. 50-51); and in the *Remarks* of 1736, pp. 20-1.

13. From now on it will at least arrest the attention of the critic! One of the best treatments of this aspect of *Hamlet* criticism is found in A. J. A. Waldock's *Hamlet, A Study in Critical Method* (Cambridge, 1931). See especially his remarks in Chapter VII, "The Nature of Delay."

14. *Supra*, p. 46, note 5.

him indicates that for her he had not the slightest trace of a tragic fault. She calls him the "gallant Hamlet." He is hardly procrastinating, cruel, inconsistent, or exquisitely sensitive.

Frederick Pilon, the actor, was conservative also. In fact, one would expect a man of the theatre to see Hamlet in traditional terms. A theatrical event of melancholy nature was at least partially responsible for his remarks. In this decade when the "new Hamlet" put in his appearance, David Garrick, the actor chiefly responsible for preservation of the traditional conception in the Eighteenth Century, passed forever from the English stage. He retired in 1776, and died in 1779. In 1777, a young actor named Henderson tried to carry on in Garrick's famous role. A careful reading of Pilon's critical tract[15] occasioned by Henderson's first performance, would indicate that this critic did not regard the young actor's success as phenomenal.

Pilon starts out by giving his own conception of the role:

He represents a Prince, in the bloom of life, plunged into a deep melancholy, at the death of a father, whom he tenderly loved. . . .
Hamlet's understanding is sound, and his sensibility exquisite. He is moreover adorned with every liberal accomplishment, which can distinguish the gentleman and the scholar; his reasonings are deep, and his passions ardent; and as both are excited by great and adequate motives, his character affords the most ample field for the display of theatrical abilities.[16]

It is interesting to see that this picture has some notes in common with Richardson, the sensibility that is "exquisite," for example. However, if one reads the entire tract he sees that Pilon interprets Hamlet as a prince who has control of himself! There is furthermore no question about the integrity of the assumed madness. It is definitely feigned, and is not a necessary device to cover up a conflict of emotions that border upon the very thing that is feigned.

In Pilon's pamphlet, the item of particular interest for this study is a remark concerning what its author considered an unfortunate omission in Henderson's version of the text. The actor left out Hamlet's reasons for sparing the king at prayer:

This principal link, being omitted in the representation, and no other cause, substituted, for Hamlet's continuing to procrastinate. he appeared weak and inconsistent, during the last two acts.[17]

Pilon thus put himself in the group with those who valued the tradi-

15. *An Essay on the character of Hamlet as performed by Mr. Henderson at the Theatre-Royal in the Hay-Market* (London, 1777).
16. *Ibid.*, pp. 3-4.
17. *Ibid.*, p. 19.

tional Hamlet. Henderson's omission of this link, the famous "cruel" lines that so many eighteenth-century critics objected to, was a sign of the times. Possibly the young actor felt that he was adding to Hamlet's character by doing away with such "immoral" lines. As Pilon points out, however, they are an absolutely necessary link in the action.

The next year, 1778, Steevens returned to the arena by adding a new emphasis to his earlier indictment of the prince. He says:

The late Dr. Akinside once observed to me, that the conduct of Hamlet was every way unnatural and indefensible, unless he were to be regarded as a young man whose intellects were in some degree impaired by his own misfortunes; by the death of his father, the loss of expected sovereignty, and a sense of shame resulting from the hasty and incestuous marriage of his mother.[18]

The "conduct" of Hamlet that Steevens speaks of is undoubtedly what he had described with such an acid pen in his *Edition* of 1773.[19] He is speaking of the Hamlet who is cruel, procrastinating, and emotionally unstable. The answer he suggests is devastating to the integrity of the traditional heroic prince. Like some of the remarks of Richardson, already noted, what is said here shows the growing tendency to magnify the cruel emotional stress that Shakespeare undoubtedly wished to set forth, and to minimize the calculation and intellectual artistry of the feigned madness. These critics indeed used an undramatic and unhistorical expedient to motivate the elements in Hamlet's character which they disliked. In fact the dislike itself may be explained as an unhistorical tendency on their part.

After a decade of such mixed tendencies, Henry Mackenzie swung the pendulum in the radical direction.[20] In two successive essays in the *Mirror*[21] he set forth his views on the Danish prince. As would be expected from Mackenzie, his Hamlet is a man-of-feeling:

The basis of Hamlet's character seems to be an extreme sensibility of mind, apt to be strongly impressed by its situation, and overpowered by the feelings which that situation excites. . . . Hamlet from the very opening of the piece, is delineated as one under the dominion of melancholy, whose spirits were overborne by his feelings. Grief for his father's death, and displeasure at his mother's marriage, prey on his mind; and he seems, with the weakness natural to such a disposition, to yield to their control. He does not attempt to resist or combat

18. *The Plays of William Shakespeare* (London, 1778), X, 412-13.
19. *Supra*, p. 65.
20. One other critic of these years can be classed with Pilon as upholding the traditional and conservative point of view,—Edward Capell in his *Notes and Various Readings to Shakespeare* (London, 1779-83). For a point of view that is at least implicitly antithetical to that of the "radical critics," see Capell's remarks on the omission of 25 lines in Act I (*Ibid.*, p. 125).
21. April 18 and 25, 1780.

these impressions, but is willing to fly from the contest, though it were to the grave.[22]

As would be natural for such a prince, he is an irresolute procrastinator:

With the strongest purposes of revenge, he is irresolute and inactive; . . . Naturally of the most virtuous and most amiable dispositions, the circumstances in which he was placed unhinged those principles of action, which, in another situation, would have delighted mankind, and made himself happy.[23]

What is more, he knows how to protect himself against his procrastination, for he is a most effective rationalizer. Of Hamlet's doubts concerning the authenticity of the ghost,[24] Mackenzie says: "This doubt of the grounds on which our purpose is founded, is as often the effect, as the cause, of irresolution, which first hesitates, and then seeks an excuse for its hesitation."[25]

In dealing with the matter of Hamlet's sanity, Mackenzie again resorts to a novel interpretation. He does not picture the prince as mad, but finding it necessary to fill in adequately his conception of Hamlet's unhinged condition, he extracts what he pleases from the feigned madness and makes it part of the real character. In this case, it is the melancholy which is real. When the prince describes his feelings to Rosencrantz and Guildenstern ("This goodly frame, the earth, etc."), he is speaking in earnest.[26] It is of course logical that Mackenzie should choose melancholy as the particular ingredient out of the feigned madness which he could profitably add to Hamlet's real character; for it fitted in well with the sentimental groundwork of the conception he had built up.

Sentimental indeed! Before, Hamlet had been "gentle," "delicate," "sensitive," and "melancholy," as Garrick's portrayal bears witness, but never before this, with the exception of what Richardson had said in 1774, had softness and sensibility been made the central core of his personality,—a weakening, debilitating dissolver of resolution and all power of action. From now on, for many critics the note of procrastination had

22. *British Essayists* (London, 1827), XXIV, 421-23.
23. *Ibid.*, pp. 420-1.
24. Hamlet, according to the accepted ideas of the time, had every right to question the authenticity of the ghost, unless it was confirmed for him. Mackenzie thus is most definitely unhistorical at this point, as well as at many others. He is not thinking of the play in terms of its time. On the ghost, see E. E. Stoll, *Hamlet* (1919), pp. 47, ff.
25. *Op. cit.*, p. 423.
26. *Ibid.*, p. 423. Mackenzie is not completely consistent in his discussion of the madness. In his second paper (April 25, 1780), he emphasizes the fact that the madness was definitely feigned throughout the play. Hamlet appears a considerably more rational person in this paper. It is the extreme interpretation as man-of-feeling, in the first paper, that seems to have been the influential angle of Mackenzie's treatment. Goethe, for example, pictures the same type of "soft" prince.

been irrevocably sounded. The next really original contribution did not come until Coleridge made his analysis.

Between Mackenzie and Richardson's second interpretation of 1784, there were no noteworthy additions to the critical picture.[27] Richardson's second essay deepened his earlier observations and added several new touches not found there.

One section of the preliminary remarks in this 1784 essay illustrates well how the scattered comments of an unfavorable nature current since 1770, have helped to motivate the "psychological" point of view. After mentioning the fact that Hamlet's character has been commented upon in this unfavorable manner, Richardson proceeds:

> In the conduct, however, which he displays, in the progress of the tragedy, he appears irresolute and indecisive; he accordingly engages in enterprizes in which he fails; he discovers reluctance to perform actions, which, we think, need no hesitation; he proceeds to violent outrage, where the occasion does not seem to justify violence; he appears jocular where his situation is most serious and alarming; he uses subterfuges not consistent with an ingenuous mind; and expresses sentiments not only immoral, but inhuman.
>
> This charge is heavy; yet every reader, and every audience, have hitherto taken part with Hamlet. . . . Let us enquire, therefore, whether those particulars which have given such offense, may not be considered as the infirmities of a mind constituted like that of Hamlet. . . .[28]

The critic then makes good his promise by adding to and subtracting from the list of Hamlet's infirmities. He adds the habit of amiable self-deceit. That disposed of the cruelty, an item that had caused so many commentators from Hanmer to Steevens, to wince. Richardson's justification follows:

> You ask me, why he did not kill the Usurper? And I answer, because he was at that instant irresolute. This irresolution arose from the inherent principles of his constitution, and is to be accounted natural: it arose from virtuous, or at least from amiable, sensibility, and therefore cannot be blamed. His sense of justice, or his feelings of tenderness, in a moment when his violent emotions were not excited, overcame his resentment. But you will urge the inconsistency of this account, with the inhuman sentiments he expresses:

27. In 1781, 1782, and 1784, the matter of Hamlet's cruelty was mentioned by various critics. In 1781 James Harris speaks of the killing of Polonius as being "unfeelingly cruel" (Babcock, *op. cit.*, p. 151); in 1782 Joseph Ritson in his *Remarks Critical and Illustrative*, defends Hamlet against the charges of Steevens; and in 1784 Davies in his *Dramatic Miscellanies* regards the speech over the king at prayer as "not only shocking but highly improbable" (III, 101). Davies' general attitude toward Hamlet contains no hint that he thought of him as a procrastinator or as otherwise than noble. I have indicated in my text the general significance of the "cruelty" motif.

28. *Essays on Shakespeare's Dramatic Characters . . . to which are added, An Essay on the Faults of Shakespeare; and Additional Observations on the Character of Hamlet* (London, 1784), pp. 149-50.

Up, sword, and know thou a more horrid pent [*sic*]:
When he is drunk, asleep, or in his rage, etc.
Then trip him up, etc.

In reply to this difficulty, and it is not inconsiderable, I will venture to affirm, that these are not his real sentiments. There is nothing in the whole character of Hamlet that justifies such savage enormity.[29]

To complete my account of Richardson's super-subtle prince,[30] I shall quote one more passage. Of the madness he now says:

Surely such disorder of mind, in characters like that of Hamlet, though not amounting to actual madness, yet exhibiting reason in extreme perplexity, and even trembling on the brink of madness, is not unusual. Meantime, Hamlet was fully sensible how strange those involuntary improprieties must appear to others: he was conscious he could not suppress them; he knew he was surrounded with spies; and was justly apprehensive, lest his suspicion or purposes should be discovered. But how are these consequences to be prevented? By counterfeiting an insanity which in part exists.[31]

Can this be the manly heroic figure who had pleased countless English audiences through generations? An impartial judge will admit, I believe, that Hamlet's "sanity" as set forth here has little in it more than its name to distinguish it from madness.

The "new Hamlet" of the Eighteenth Century is now before us. English criticism will add nothing else distinctive to his portrait. One other great interpretation, while not original, is done with such verve as almost to amount to originality. I am referring of course, to the account of the prince given in Goethe's *Wilhelm Meister.* This will be described in my account of foreign criticism.

To complete the English critical contribution for the century, it merely remains for me to add a number of miscellaneous items, and then to summarize the whole.

In 1785, J. M. Mason says:

29. *Op. cit.*, pp. 158-9.
30. If one cannot believe Hamlet's soliloquy in the passage I have just quoted, it is difficult to know what to believe in the play. Mr. Stoll discusses the technique of the soliloquy, in *Hamlet* (1919), p. 21.
One critic of Richardson characterizes his method in the *Hamlet* essays, as follows:
Richardson's whole account of Hamlet's character is that of a man with a thesis to prove. He picks out isolated speeches and strings them together; he neglects the obvious intent of the text, as above; he seeks out an interpretation which is so subtle as to be unobserved and unsuspected by any audience, forgetting that subtlety is not, can not be, a part of popular drama; moreover, he says that he simply does not believe the text when it contradicts his views. (E. L. McAdam, Jr., *The Shakespearian Criticism of Kames, Richardson, and Mackenzie*, Master's thesis, U. of Minn., 1929, p. 35.)
31. *Op. cit.*, p. 163.

I cannot read it [Johnson's characterization of Polonius] without heartily regretting that he did not exert his great abilities and discriminating powers, in delineating the strange, inconsistent, and indecisive character of Hamlet, to which I confess myself unequal.[32]

In 1786, William Craig in *Lounger* 91 developed critical views that manifestly drew their inspiration from Mackenzie. Craig, however, emphasizes Hamlet's melancholy almost exclusively. The whole piece is filled with eighteenth-century commonplaces on the subject.[33]

Thomas Robertson, another Scotchman, starts his 1790 essay[34] with a remark which shows that, like Richardson, he thought that Hamlet must have defenders. Oddly enough, he feels that even the stage may not do justice to the Danish prince:

The *Character* of HAMLET has been variously judged of by critics, and what might be expected, it has been still more variously represented by performers upon the stage. SHAKESPEARE himself seems to have apprehended that this would happen; and that injustice would be done a hero, who probably, in his estimation, ranked higher than any other that he has brought into the drama.[35]

It would be valuable indeed for our purposes here if this critic had gone into particulars as to just what special features of stage representation constituted an "injustice" to Hamlet. He does not. But since in this same criticism he shows himself as the proponent of a "paralyzed prince," we may almost conclude that at least one of his objections to performances he had seen is that *they* did not portray such a type. In support of such a position, is the fact that we have affirmative evidence that during these years Robertson could have seen the traditional stage figure; and no evidence whatsoever that he might have seen any other.

Be this as it may, the Scotch critic proceeds to develop his ideas on his puzzling hero, and thus do him the "justice" he deserves. His ideas are reminiscent of both Richardson and Mackenzie. In fact he shows that he is conscious of this very fact. His description of Hamlet's psychology, however, represented his own particular analysis. The prince's "radical and general character" was

a compound of many particular qualities; an exceeding high elevation of soul, an exquisite sensibility to virtue and vice, and an extreme gentleness of spirit and sweetness of disposition. With these were conjoined the most brilliant and cultivated talents, an imagination transcendently vivid and strong, together with what may be called rather an intuition, than an acquired knowledge of man-

32. *The Poems and Plays of William Shakespeare* (1821 Variorum), VII, 270.
33. *The British Essayists* (London, 1808), XXXVII, 254, ff.
34. Read in 1788 before the Royal Society of Edinburgh; published in 1790.
35. "An Essay on the Character of Hamlet, in Shakespeare's Tragedy of Hamlet," *Transactions of the Royal Society of Edinburgh* (1790), II, 251.

kind. And there may be added still, a singular gaiety of spirits, which hardly at any after period, the very gloomiest only excepted, seems to have failed him.[36]

Hamlet's character was thus compounded. His failure to act came as a result of a conflict of psychological forces that is similar to, yet different from, the conflict as seen by Richardson.[37] His nobility and "exquisite sensibility to virtue and vice" gave him indignation and desire for revenge, but then his gentleness and sweetness entered as further determining forces, with the result that he was left "like Samson, when his strength was gone from him."

In spite of his partial agreement with Richardson and Mackenzie, this critic felt that their views were too narrow. Hamlet is for him far more interesting than he could possibly be if sensibility alone were the chief ingredient of his character. He has a richness and a variety that make him most complex. His eloquence is "rich, tropical, daring, ardent, vehement." At moments, "an intrepidity breaks forth . . . beyond what is human." He is "the most splendid character of dramatic poetry"; his character comprehends "almost the whole of what is beautiful and grand." Again, he is "singularly and marvellously made up." In him, for the first time the world "saw a *man of genius* upon the stage."[38]

It is, I fear, impossible to gather together all of Robertson's analysis into a consistent critical formula. His predecessors, Richardson and Mackenzie, were simpler and more logical in their positions. However, it is evident that one of the keynotes of Hamlet's character for this critic was the baffling and brilliant diversity in his qualities. Robertson is not the first who thought of the prince in such terms during these years. Gentleman in 1770 had such a sense of the elements that make up his character. And in 1772, Dr. Beattie spoke of "a conduct so complicated"; Steevens too, saw him as made up of strange incompatible elements. Richardson recognized such a diversity in order that he might "explain" it. J. M. Mason spoke of it in 1785. It is possible, then, to find a certain unanimity

36. *Ibid.*, II, 254.

37. For Richardson, Hamlet's "moral faculty" is what gives him his "exquisite sense of virtue, of moral beauty and turpitude." This same moral faculty, however, gives him also his feelings of justice, etc. These second qualities are what cancel out and render impotent the first, and thus make him procrastinate. Robertson seems to see the sensibility as productive of the desire for revenge; the cancelling qualities, on the other hand, the gentleness and sweetness, do not owe their origin to sensibility. Mackenzie starts and ends with sensibility, a general debilitating quality that dissolves all power of action.

38. *Op. cit.*, pp. 254-65. It is evident that Robertson here is trying to have his critical cake and eat it, too. He wishes to make Hamlet over—to paralyze his active powers after the manner of Richardson and Mackenzie, and still keep the brilliant traditional, active hero. One may freely admit that this dual Hamlet would indeed be a man "singularly and marvellously made up."

as far as this point is concerned, in a number of these critics who have written on Hamlet since 1770.

In order to get a proper historical perspective, it will be profitable to place against such a Hamlet of "diversity," the far simpler figure as described by Guthrie in 1747. As will be remembered, Guthrie saw the prince in the light of a widely accepted neo-classical formula: he was a "species" hero, a "universal man." Like Johnson's tulip in Chapter X of *Rasselas,* he had no "marking or colouring" to make him different from other men. Not so with Robertson's Hamlet, whom we may take as the representative of the later group of critics. His is the highly individualized portrait of a man "singularly and marvellously made up." A dozen diverse character elements are held together in strange unity; or, if we go back to Steevens, the unity is non-existent—the diversity is all.

It may be said that this shift of emphasis which becomes increasingly evident over a period of forty years, is indicative of the breakup of the uniformitarian ideal so dear to the heart of eighteenth-century rationalism. The new ideal of diversity is the common element in a number of the tendencies, otherwise quite different, which have been labelled "romantic."[39] And, as I think I have shown, the net result of this discovery of "diversity" in Hamlet was the depiction of a strange new "psychologized" figure, whose existence in any realm of art must be apprehended

39. An acute present day critic says:
> In the aesthetics of literature the high neo-classical dogma demanded that the subject-matter and emotional content of a drama or epic should be limited to that which is universal in human experience and capable of appealing equally to all men in all times and lands. . . . In every domain, in short, the program of improvement or reform was one of simplification, standardization, the avoidance of the particular. . . .
>
> There has, in the entire history of thought, been hardly any change in standards of value more profound and more momentous than that which came when the contrary principle began widely to prevail—when it came to be believed that in many, if not all, phases of human activity, not only are there diverse excellences, but that diversity itself is of the essence of excellence; and that in art, in particular, the objective is neither the attainment of some ideal perfection of form in a small number of fixed *genres*, nor, on the other hand, the gratification of that least common denominator of aesthetic susceptibility which is shared by mankind in all ages, but rather the fullest possible expression of the abundance of differentness that there is, actually or potentially, in nature and human nature, and—for the function of the artist in relation to his public—the evocation of capacities for understanding, sympathy, and enjoyment, which are latent in most men, and perhaps never capable of universalization. (A. O. Lovejoy, "Optimism and Romanticism," *PMLA,* 42, 943.)

I need hardly point out the fact that one does not need to see the problem from the special point of view used by Lovejoy, in order to interpret the Hamlet of Richardson, Mackenzie and Robertson as "romantic." For example, Hamlet's "exquisite· sensibility to virtue and vice"; his "imagination transcendently vivid and strong"; his "intuition,

and enjoyed in the study, book in hand. He is an impossible figure for the stage. Between him and the traditional Hamlet there is little if any likeness.

Before putting a period to this section of my paper,[40] it will be well to speak of Edmund Malone, the great critic of Shakespeare who published his *Edition* in 1790. His remarks on Hamlet show that he regarded him as the traditional heroic figure. If he has read Richardson and Mackenzie he gives no sign of being infected by their romantic heresy. He takes the pains, however, to answer Steevens' charges of "cruelty," "outrage to decency," "brutal conduct to Ophelia," and the like. Rosencrantz and Guildenstern received the treatment they deserved; Hamlet did not mean to kill Polonius and thus drive Ophelia mad; and at her grave he did not intend to insult Laertes, but was incited by the "bravery" of the brother's grief "to vie with him in the expression of affection and sorrow."[41]

In one phase of their quarrel, Malone and Steevens fought a battle which indicates that the issues of historical criticism were emerging more clearly. After quoting from the Belleforest account of the trip to England, Malone says:

From the narrative it appears that the faithful ministers of Fengon were not unacquainted with the import of the letters they bore. Shakespeare, who has followed the story pretty closely, probably meant to describe their representatives, Rosencrantz and Guildenstern, as equally guilty; as confederating with the king to deprive Hamlet of his life. So that his procuring their execution,

---

rather than an acquired knowledge of mankind"—all these are suggestive of what most critics see in the Romantic Movement. Then, also, surely the Hamlet paralyzed by emotional conflict is romantic.

It is more than interesting to remember that for these later critics who went to the study and to psychology in search for a unity in the "diverse" Hamlet, there was a far simpler answer: They might have kept him on the stage and found the unity there, where it had always existed. (*Supra*, p. 64 and note 3.)

40. I will include also, the names of the following, who at some time or other in the late years of the Eighteenth Century dwell upon Hamlet's words or character. Usually their purpose is emendatory, and in no case do they offer anything new for inclusion in this study. Ritson and Mason have already been given cursory mention. The others are Thomas Warton, Sir William Blackstone, Richard Farmer, Isaac Reed, Henderson the actor, George Tollet, and Tyrwhitt. All of these commentators eventually were given a place in the *Variorum* Hamlet of 1821.

In 1796, James Plumptre published his *Observations on Hamlet* with the purpose of proving that the play should be interpreted in terms of Elizabethan politics. This might be labelled abortive historical criticism of a particularly sterile nature.

In 1799, Edward DuBois in *The Wreath* gave an example of what may be termed "parallel passage criticism." Hamlet's words are compared with passages from Homer, Lucian, Epictetus and Theocritus. No special effort is made to show that Shakespeare actually had these authors before him. The main purpose seems to be to sanctify Shakespeare's words by showing their similarity to those of the great classicists of antiquity. DuBois may be classed as a late century exponent of the "beauties school."

41. *The Plays and Poems of William Shakespeare* (London, 1790), IX, 424.

though certainly not absolutely necessary to his own safety, does not appear to have been a wanton and unprovoked cruelty, as Mr. Steevens has supposed in his very ingenious observations on the general character and conduct of the prince throughout this piece.[42]

Let me quote part of Steevens' answer:

I apprehend that a critick and a juryman are bound to form their opinions on what they see and hear in the cause before them, and not to be influenced by extraneous particulars unsupported by legal evidence in open court. I persist, in observing, that from Shakespeare's drama no proofs of the guilt of Rosencrantz and Guildenstern can be collected. They may be convicted by the black letter history; but if the tragedy forbears to criminate, it has no right to sentence them. This is sufficient for the commentator's purpose. It is not his office to interpret the plays of Shakespeare according to the novels on which they are founded, novels which the poet sometimes followed, but as often materially deserted.[43]

I do not have Malone's answer, if he ever made one. It is easy to see that both critics were partly right—although the issue between them was never completely clarified. Malone is the sounder of the two.[44] Hamlet's character needs explanation and interpretation in terms of the sources that Shakespeare used but never fully assimilated. Steevens was right also: one must take the aesthetic data offered and judge them. However, judgment must be relative as well as absolute. It happens that in this case a relative judgment is particularly necessary in order that one may interpret correctly the "fossilized" structure of the plot, a characteristic that conditions very markedly, at least for some readers, the impact and quality of the aesthetic data.

42. *Ibid.,* p. 400. In another comment Malone shows that he is equipped with an historical answer that might have been applied to Hamlet's treatment of Ophelia. In the Belleforest *Hystory of Hamblet,* the "faire and beautiful woman," who is the literary ancestress of Ophelia, is definitely used as a lure to trap the prince (*Op. cit.,* p. 255).

43. *Variorum* (1821), VII, 485.

44. One other item from the pen of Steevens suggests a type of dubious historical comment still seen. Of the queen's "He's fat, and scant of breath," he says:

It seems that John Lowin, who was the original Falstaff, was no less celebrated for his performance of Henry VIII and Hamlet. See the Historia Histrionica, etc. If he was adapted, by the corpulence of his figure, to appear with propriety in the two former of these characters, Shakespeare might have put this observation into the mouth of her majesty, to apologize for the want of such elegance of person as an audience might expect to meet with in the representative of the youthful prince of Denmark, whom Ophelia speaks of as "the glass of fashion and the mould of form." This, however, is mere conjecture, as Joseph Taylor likewise acted Hamlet during the lifetime of Shakespeare.

(*Poems and Plays* (1790), IX, p. 510.)

This critic did not realize that the *art* is the conditioning factor; and that thus the actor must make the accommodation. If possessed of adequate genius for acting the part, no Hamlet need worry about a little extra avoirdupois.

HISTRIONIC TRADITION AFTER GARRICK

As a background for the Shakespearian criticism of the later century with its dominant center of interest the study rather than the stage,[45] it will be well to glance once more at the histrionic tradition itself. Of this tradition, our *a priori* expectation would be to find some diminution in its vigor and popular appeal. This we do find, but in spite of such a fact *Hamlet* was still an active and potent force upon the stage. The best evidence in support of this conclusion is the fact that in the 1790's a procession of minor actors, and at least one actress, tried the role: Holman in 1792, Pope, and Seymour at Bury St. Edmunds in 1793; Cooke at Manchester in 1794; Cooper in 1795; Palmer and Mrs. Powell in 1796.[46] What is more, in 1798 an anonymous writer to the *Monthly Mirror* struck a chord that seems familiar when he says that in the schools, "at this season of the year, we have sucking Hamlets and Romeos by wholesale."[47] One can reasonably conclude that the acted play was still a living and vital tradition on the English stage.

Vital, yes, but with a difference. The old lusty days of Garrick were gone. For all of the Shakespearian repertoire there is recorded a decline in prestige and popularity as compared with earlier days. The evidence on this point seems conclusive.[48]

Beside the numerous minor actors who played Hamlet in the last years

45. It is of course accurate to use the term "Shakespearian criticism" here, rather than merely "*Hamlet* criticism." For example, the most important piece of romantic criticism in the last quarter of the century does not concern Hamlet at all. It is Morgann's *An Essay on the Dramatic Character of Sir John Falstaff*, 1777.

The ideas of minor critics sometimes offer an indication of how widespread has been the dissemination in any period of a particular critical position. A bit of evidence that the sentimental interpretation of *Hamlet* was widely accepted by 1794 can be seen in an essay "On the Character of Hamlet" by "Selim," *Thespian Magazine and Literary Repository*, 3, 82.

46. For comment on these minor actors, see in order: *Thespian Magazine and Literary Repository*, 1, 153, and 3, 29; *Ibid.*, 2, 357; *Ibid.*, 2, 364; *Monthly Mirror*, 2, 118; *Ibid.*, 2, 50.

47. 6, 353-5.

48. George C. D. Odell says: "A careful tabulation of performances recorded by Genest for the period of Kemble (1776-1817) shows no such result as was discovered in a similar study of the Garrick times. Hardly any play at either house was acted so regularly, year after year, as were the great tragedies in the time from 1742 to 1776. In fact, Hamlet, King Lear, and the rest sometimes disappear from the boards of either house for several seasons in succession. For instance, John Kemble made his first appearance with great success in Hamlet, yet he did not enact the character during the following season, and, having satisfied all theatre-goers in the part for four years thereafter, for some unaccountable reason he dropped it from his list for six successive seasons. Even at that, it failed to appear in the forty-one years we are considering for only thirteen seasons at Drury Lane, and but eight at the rival house." (*Shakespeare from Betterton to Irving*, II, 19.)

If my reasoning is correct, there is a fairly simple key to Odell's "unaccountable

of the century, one may place two others who were more famous. After the retirement of Garrick, for a few years the young actor, John Henderson, achieved considerable acclaim in the role. Then in 1783, J. P. Kemble made his début. He offered the only distinguished Hamlet in the closing years of this period. His interpretation was decidedly original. Under him Hamlet again became more explicitly an elocutionary prince. The portrayal which for Garrick had been a marvel of plasticity, a "working from within," grew hard, polished, and external. The intellectual vivacity and quickness of Garrick gave way, thus, for a less subtle and more obvious reading. The "progress of impassioned sensation" was no longer so superbly registered.[49] The play became more outward, more objective —more "action" in an orthodox sense.[50] A comment made by Davies, however, shows that for him at least, this new Hamlet of Kemble's was an outgrowth of the old. The interpretation was new, but the traditional continuity was not snapped:

Though, in drawing the outline of Hamlet it was scarcely possible Mr. Kemble should differ from preceding actors, yet his particular emphasis, pauses, and other novelties in acting, having surprised the public, and divided the critics; some of whom greatly censure, while others as warmly extol his peculiarities.[51]

This cursory examination may suffice as a treatment of the stage tradition of *Hamlet* in the last years of the Eighteenth Century. I have found no evidence that could lead me to believe that the frustrated, paralyzed Hamlet of the romantic critics had any counterpart on the stage during these years.[52]

---

reason": Those who were finding satisfaction in the new closet criticism of Richardson, Mackenzie, etc., were enjoying a pleasure that the stage could not compete with. The study, and a copy of the play were all such people would ask for.

49. "It is admitted that he was naturally slow and comtemplative, and his utterances tardy. It was said by some that his pauses were too long." (H. P. Phelps, *Hamlet from the Actor's Standpoint*, pp. 10-11.) Davies says, "Mr. Kemble's pauses are, I believe, very judicious, though to many they appeared long." (*Dramatic Miscellanies*, III, 150.)

50. Odell: Kemble made of the role "a polished gem of dramatic intensity; much of the fine poetry is gone; . . . but the whole thing moves with splendid vigour to its conclusion. Perhaps, after all, poetry is better in the ear of the student than in the mouths of ordinary actors." (*Op. cit.*, II, 54-5.)

Kemble's costume for the part was most original: "Mr. Kemble played the part in a modern court dress of rich dark velvet with a star on the breast, the garter and pendant ribbon of an order, mourning sword and buckles, with deep ruffles; the hair in powder, which in scenes of feigned distraction flowed disheveled in front and over his shoulders." (H. P. Phelps, *op. cit.*, pp. 10-11.)

51. *Dramatic Miscellanies*, III, 155.

52. Let me recall to the reader the quick objections that came from Frederick Pilon in 1777 (*supra*, p. 69), when Henderson's cutting of certain lines gave the impression of a procrastinating prince.

In his *Memoirs of the Life of J. P. Kemble* (Philadelphia, 1825), James Boaden does

The panorama of *Hamlet* criticism for a major segment of this study now lies before us. We have viewed it in both its narrower "theatrical" aspects, and in its larger more formal implications, as seen in the English tradition up to the year 1800.

The theatrical Hamlet is remarkable for its unity and for the continuity of tradition that it incarnates. This is true in spite of the fact that each period saw the prince freely through the lenses of its own special tastes and interests. This illustrates a simple histrionic truth: the stage is a jealous master; but, one must add, for a gifted genius like Garrick, who understands it, a faithful one. In the case of *Hamlet,* it forced a fairly consistent reading of Shakespeare's score. His dramatic purpose, his intention to portray an heroic, many-sided various prince was not mistaken by theatre or spectator through these two hundred years.

When we turn, however, to the full critical tradition, the unity is not so evident. Usually the heroic Hamlet is in the background of such criticism, but can be seen through one of a number of tendencies, including several that strip him of his dramatic individuality and life. The dissecting critical intellect, using a prerogative that might be termed particularly English in nature, sees the aesthetic data offered with varying degrees of completeness or of flagrant partiality. The result therefore is confusing and mixed. It is true, of course, that certain of the critics display at least moments of genuine historical perspective. For example, Hanmer, a commentator from earlier in the century, makes a general comment that shows rare intuition.[53] It was, however, a far different critical instinct that dominated at the end of the century; for then one particular brand of undramatic, unhistorical criticism gained the ascendancy, and produced the new Hamlet.

---

exactly what Murphy had done previously in regard to Garrick (*supra*, p. 59, note 2)— that is, he makes a retrospective interpretation that labels Kemble's performance as showing a Hamlet who had "melting softness," "weakness," etc., (*Op. cit.*, p. 55).

53. *Supra*, p. 55.

5

Hamlet in French Criticism

THE HISTORY of *Hamlet* in France,[1] up to 1800 is a simple story. Of the six or eight men whose views can be recorded, one of them, Voltaire, took most of the limelight. What is more, nearly everything said concerning the play can be described in terms of the artistic philosophy that ruled France for at least 'a century and a half, an aesthetic uniformitarianism that had its basis in the rationalism of the Enlightenment. As the Eighteenth Century progressed, the rigid and inelastic structure of this aesthetic formula was slowly liberalized. A more valid historical perspective made itself felt; and certain new social forces tended to give the thought and emotion of Frenchmen a different coloration. The dominant aesthetic formula, however, was not destroyed. What is more, it is not possible to catch more than a small echo of this liberalization of thought in *Hamlet* criticism. Nevertheless, its influence can be traced in a histrionic tradition, and in the reception which the French gave the Letourneur translation of 1776.

It was inevitable that the French, circumscribed as they were within the limits of an artistic temperament that allowed approval of one kind of tragedy, and one only, should have looked upon *Hamlet* as they did. Their standards were those of their own neo-classical tragedy as given a doctrinaire basis by seventeenth-century theorists, exemplified on the stage by Corneille and Racine, and interpreted for the Eighteenth Century by the plays of Voltaire himself.

Some of the cardinal points at which this classical tragedy[2] furnishes a contrast with the more naturalistic and romantic Shakespearian drama

1. The first mention of Shakespeare's name in France is dated between 1675 and 1684, and is found in a short note in a catalogue of books for the Paris National Library, compiled by Nicholas Clement, Royal Librarian. His appraisal of Shakespeare is prophetic of later French opinion: "Ce poète anglois a l'imagination assés belle, il pense naturellement, il s'exprime avec finesse; mais ces belles qualitez sont obscurcies par les ordures qu'il mêle dans ses Comedies." (J. J. Jusserand, *Shakespeare in France*, London, 1899, p. 173.) Few eighteenth-century Frenchmen, however, would agree with Clement concerning Shakespeare's "finesse."

2. For an incisive summary of the philosophical background and main characteristics of French classical art, see G. Lanson and P. Tuffrau, *Manuel D'Histoire de la Littérature Française* (4th edit., Paris, 1935), pp. 179-80; as well as the section on Corneille, pp. 185, ff.; and on Racine, pp. 272, ff. For sources of general neo-classical aesthetic background, see *supra*, p. 48, note 13.

are: its sense for verbal and mechanical perfection, its rigid separation of comedy and tragedy, its strict observance of the unities, its more restricted use of the supernatural, its more careful observance of poetic justice, its sense of decorum, and its "noble" heroes and heroines speaking, always loftily, in alexandrines. In this art, French aesthetics had its opportunity to register without impediment the full strength of its generalizing and idealizing tendencies.[3] Consequently, the tragedies lack the earthy tang which Shakespeare's great plays are never wholly without. They are less "realistic." The spectator, at least one used to the English drama, is continually reminded that he is witnessing art, not life. With Shakespeare he is prone to forget. It is doubtful whether the Frenchman wishes to forget. Part of his aesthetic pleasure seems bound up in the fact that he is continually conscious, at least in the inner regions of his artistic experience, that he is being properly edified by "Art." His vintage must be most decidedly a *vin travaillé*.

The first mention of the play that I have found, displays a point of view so typical of French critiques that one learns almost to take such an attitude for granted. De La Roche in 1717 looks upon Hamlet as a character created by a man of great genius but no taste. He must necessarily show himself to disadvantage because his creator makes him mouth buffooneries, either in soliloquy, or with the unspeakable grave-diggers. The grave-diggers were anathema to almost every French critic. Furthermore, what could be expected of a hero who appears in a play that observes no rules, or in which appalling cruelties take place on the stage?[4] This early critic is fully typical of the century.

The Abbé Prévost, in his youth at least, was more liberal than the average French critic. He had been in England, and while there no doubt saw a performance of *Hamlet*. Although he shares the prejudices of his countrymen concerning the crude nature of English art, he gets from it an aesthetic effect that he is honest enough to acknowledge. Of certain English tragedies, *Hamlet* among them, he says:

3. Besides the usual "species" doctrine (chapter 10, *Rasselas*), never absent long from any rationalistic aesthetic, there is in French artistic doctrine a pronounced strain of the related theory of *belle nature*, or idealized type-form. This dogma seems to me to have had a marked effect in shaping the spirit of French classical tragedy. The philosophical ancestry of the idea is complex, but it could come straight from the *Poetics* of Aristotle, where Sidney (*Apology for Poetry*) seems to have found it. Some of the French exponents of the idea are: Du Fresnoy, *De arte graphica*; Molière, *La gloire du Dôme du Val-de-Grace*; and Diderot, *A Mon Ami Monsieur Grimm* (Salon de 1767). The idea is occasionally given expression in English literature, as witness Sidney; Addison, *Spectator* 418; Hurd, *Notes on the Art of Painting*.

4. "Dissertation Sur la Poësie Angloise," *Journal Littéraire* (The Hague), 9, part 1, pp. 204-6.

Pour la beauté des sentiments, soit tendres, soit sublimes; pour cette force tragique qui remue le fond du coeur, et qui excite infailliblement les passions dans l'âme la plus endormie; pour l'énergie des expressions, et l'art de conduire les événements, ou de ménager les situations, je n'ai rien lu, ni en grec ni en françois, qui l'emporte sur le théâtre d'Angleterre.[5]

Like a true critic of the Eighteenth Century, the Abbé adds that in these tragedies, "l'on trouve mille beautés réunies."

As the Abbé grew older, his youthful enthusiasm for English plays must have dimmed, for in the article in which he describes *Hamlet,* his general appraisal strikes the tone used by most of his countrymen. He says of the play:

Cette étrange rapsodie, où l'on n'aperçoit ni ordre ni vraisemblance, et où le comique et le tragique sont confusément mêlés, passe pour le chef-d'œuvre de Shakespeare. On ne m'en croiroit pas, si je ne promettois d'expliquer dans quelque autre feuille les causes de cette admiration.[6]

Unluckily for us Prévost never fulfilled his promise made here. What he might have said if he had gone into more detail, whether he had really abandoned the more liberal views of his youth, we shall never know.

The earliest of Voltaire's incisive and brilliant critiques on *Hamlet* was almost contemporary with the comments of Prévost. His last words come over forty years later.[7] In essential details his verdict does not change, except for the animus and bitterness he displays against a writer who, he felt, was eclipsing Racine and Corneille. If some allowance is made for the inevitable exaggerations made possible by his brilliant style, and for the fact that the negative aspects of his opinion increase as he grew older, he may be called the most typical mouthpiece of French criticism on Shakespeare in the period.

It should be remembered that Voltaire thought so well of Shakespeare that he was willing to use dramatic situations and other hints from him to revivify the classical tragedy of his own country,— a tragedy that lacks action so decidedly that at times it almost degenerates into a series of conversations. Voltaire put a situation similar to that found in *Othello,* in *Zaïre,* and a ghost into *Sémiramis.*[8] He used hints from *Macbeth* for

5. *Œuvres Choisies de Prévost* (Paris, 1810-16), II, 281. (From *Mémoires et Aventures D'un Homme de Qualité,* 1728-31.)

6. Quoted from G. R. Havens, "The Abbé Prévost and Shakespeare," *MP,* 17, 195. (From *Pour et Contre,* 14, 72, dated 1737 or 1738.)

7. For critical comment on Voltaire in relation to Shakespeare, and in relation to French criticism as a whole, see: J. J. Jusserand, *Shakespeare in France;* T. R. Lounsbury, *Shakespeare and Voltaire;* F. Baldensperger, *Esquisse D'Histoire Littéraire,* deuxième série, Paris, 1910; and C. M. Haines, *Shakespeare in France.*

8. English critics and admirers of Shakespeare were quick to defend *Hamlet* against

Mahomet, and was influenced by Shakespeare's portrayal of Ophelia and Desdemona in the creation of some of his feminine characters.

In view of the facts I have just cited, Voltaire's early verdict upon Shakespeare is illuminating. What did he think of this dramatist whose material he was to use so freely? He tells us:

Il avait un génie plein de force et de fécondité, de naturel et de sublime, sans la moindre étincelle de bon goût, et sans la moindre connaissance des règles. Je vais vous dire une chose hasardée mais vraie, c'est que le mérite de cet auteur a perdu le théâtre anglais; il y a de si belles scènes, des morceaux si grands et si terribles répandus dans ses farces monstrueuses, qu'on appelle tragédies, que ces pièces ont toujours été jouées avec un grand succès. Le temps, qui fait seul la réputation des hommes rend à la fin leurs défauts respectables. La plupart des idées bizarres et gigantesques de cet auteur ont acquis au bout de deux cents ans le droit de passer pour sublimes. . . ."[9]

If Voltaire had not been the special pleader that he was, he might have suspected that the amazing success of these "farces monstrueuses" was due to an art not found in his own beloved French tragedies. He might have realized, too, that the winnowing hand of time is far too merciless to deal gently with a writer as crude as he professes to think Shakespeare. Voltaire was, however, well cloistered within the walls of his own tight system. His prejudices were far too rigid to allow him to advance very far in the direction of a valid historical criticism. He had before him a certain type of aesthetic data. He saw it in proportions that should have allowed him to draw an arresting conclusion. He could not, or would not, make this conclusion.

Voltaire did not leave his countrymen in doubt as to what they would find in *Hamlet* if they dipped into that amazing play. In the same article that contains the general estimate of Shakespeare just quoted, he brings up the inevitable subject of the grave-diggers. However, no one before him had castigated them with such a barbed whip of words:

Vous n'ignorez pas que, dans *Hamlet,* des fossoyeurs creusent une fosse en buvant, en chantant des vaudevilles, et en faisant sur les têtes des morts qu'ils rencontrent des plaisanteries convenables à gens de leur métier; mais, ce qui vous surprendra, c'est qu'on a imité ces sottises.[10]

Hamlet himself does not appear in this essay as the beer-drinking barbarian that he later becomes. Surprisingly enough, here he is an eight-

---

Voltaire's aspersions. For example, "Hermes," in a letter to the editor of the *London Magazine,* April, 1776 (p. 183), notes with satisfaction Voltaire's imitation of *Hamlet* in *Sémiramis.*

9. *Œuvres Complètes* (Garnier edit., Paris, 1877-85), XXII, 149, (from the 18th of the *Lettres Philosophiques*).

10. *Ibid.,* XXII, 149.

eenth-century rationalist of anti-clerical stripe. At least this is the meta-morphosis he undergoes in Voltaire's version of the "to-be" soliloquy. Later on, the old warrior may have felt a twinge of conscience, for he put a literal translation by the side of his first version. In 1734, however, Hamlet exclaims:

> Eh! qui pourrait sans toi supporter cette vie,
> De nos prêtres menteurs bénir l'hypocrisie. . . .
>   Arrêtez.
>
> Il défend à nos mains cet heureux homicide,
> Et d'un héros guerrier fait un chrétien timide.[11]

In regard to what was to be found in *Hamlet* and the necessary judg-ment to be passed upon it, as well as upon the hero, Voltaire later was to go into still more detail. In the meantime other critics gave their verdict. In 1738, Louis Riccoboni of the Italian theatre in Paris, used *Hamlet* as a typical example to illustrate his statement that "The English Dramatic Poets have, beyond Imagination, stained their Stage with Blood. . . ."[12] He notes with amazement the fact that English audiences "listen with Admiration, and applaud with Transport" when Hamlet makes a moral dissertation upon the skull of a jester. It is quite evident that this critic has no conception of, or sympathy for, the "memento-mori" tradition. And he cannot appreciate the lusty tragic appetite of a more masculine period. He can merely look on in shocked amazement.

As a whole, the French comments upon *Hamlet* in this century have a negative cast. Such a fact must be plain already. La Place in 1746, how-ever, could give his words a more constructive tone. To begin with, he considered some of Shakespeare's plays worth translating into French. A prose version of *Hamlet,* largely in paraphrase, forms part of *Le Théâtre Anglois* published in 1746. In this clipped and uninspired work it is difficult to find much of Shakespeare. The poetry has all evaporated. For example, Ophelia's lovely death is given as follows: "La Reine vient an-noncer, en pleurant, qu'Ophelia s'est noyée, dans un accès de folie."[13] The important thing to remember, however, is not the blindness of La Place to the real beauty of *Hamlet,* but the fact that he considered it worth "translating" at all.

La Place like Voltaire, had a rationalistic aesthetic. In one place he

11. *Ibid.,* p. 151. C. Serrurier has made a detailed analysis of Voltaire's "transla-tion" in comparison with the original. If one did not realize it before, what this critic says will make him see vividly the faithlessness of Voltaire's version. ("Voltaire et Shakespeare—a propos du Monologue D'Hamlet," *Neophilologus,* 5, 205-9.)

12. *Réflexions Historiques et Critiques sur les Différents Théâtres de l'Europe* (quoted from the English version, London, 1741, p. 170).

13. *Op. cit.,* (London, 1746), II, 378.

gives a verdict on the shortcomings of *Hamlet* if viewed in terms of aesthetic uniformitarianism. He says:

Ce sont là des tableaux, des discours, et des écarts, qui ne peuvent être justifiés dans aucun tems, ni dans aucun pays, parce qu'ils sont contraires à la vérité, à la raison, et aux bienséances générales, qui sont les mêmes partout.[14]

But, he says in effect, these are merely the "blemishes" of an author whose "beauties" far outnumber his faults.

Although La Place says nothing of a more specific nature concerning the play, and never discusses Hamlet as a character, it is legitimate to draw at least an implied verdict from his apology for Shakespeare in general. He says about what one would expect from Pope. In fact, he used Pope as one of his main sources of information and critical opinion. La Place's knowledge of English literature was hardly notable; but his words are generous. He shows, within the limits of his aesthetics, an appreciation for the English dramatist. Shakespeare is the first and greatest poet of England. His characters are always true, always sustained, always natural, always individualized. He is less able to reflect than to portray the warmth of human emotions.[15] As a critic of Shakespeare, La Place is about as inspired as the man he borrowed from. His verdict on Hamlet, if he had expressed it, would most probably have been the conventional one that an orthodox rationalistic critic of this century would give. If he had been an Englishman, he could have written the *Miscellaneous Observations* of 1752. They are keyed at his aesthetic level.

That even as early as 1746 there were Frenchmen who caught a broader glimpse of critical matters than either Voltaire or La Place, can be seen in the words of J. F. Marmontel. What he says was suggested by the translation of La Place. He admits that Shakespeare's plays have an appeal possessed by no French tragedies. Shakespeare uses resources for moving the spectator not permitted on the French stage,—for example, Hamlet's interview with the ghost, and the fencing match. In admitting the superior power, in this direction, of Shakespearian drama, Marmontel asks with regret, "Pourquoi nos poètes s'interdiraient-ils ces grands ressorts de la pitié et de la terreur?"[16] Thus we see that this neo-classical critic tempers his dogmatism. He has seen new things. The historical perspective of French criticism is widening.

Voltaire did not change. The great liberal in other realms of thought was a conservative in art. And even there what liberalism he had allowed himself in his youth was fading. What is more, when he thought of

14. *Ibid.*, I, lxxviii (from "Discours sur le Théâtre Anglois").
15. *Ibid.*, I, xxviii-xxxi.
16. *Œuvres de Marmontel* (Paris, Belin, 1819-20), VII, 276.

Shakespeare, his thoughts almost inevitably turned to *Hamlet*. It will be remembered that in 1734 his verdict on the play was still fairly generous. Hamlet was at least capable of words that could be given a twist most congenial to this arch deist of the Enlightenment. Unfortunately the prince was not consistent. He could not soliloquize in terms congenial to Voltaire all the time. He also must act: he had an assumed madness to carry out, and a tragic mission to perform. His mistake was that, although he was partly an Elizabethan malcontent he must, to please this exacting critic, act with the decorum prescribed for French classical tragedy. Needless to say, Voltaire's verdict was adverse. In 1752, he says of the play and its hero:

C'est une pièce grossière et barbare, qui ne serait pas supportée par la plus vile populace de la France et de l'Italie. Hamlet y devient fou au second acte, et sa maîtresse devient folle au troisième; le prince tue le père de sa maîtresse, feignant de tuer un rat, et l'héroïne se jette dans la rivière. Hamlet, sa mère, et son beau-père, boivent ensemble sur le théâtre: on chante à table, on s'y querelle, on se bat, on se tue. On croirait que cet ouvrage est le fruit de l'imagination d'un sauvage ivre. Mais parme ces irrégularités grossières, qui rendent encore aujourd'hui le théâtre anglais si absurde et si barbare, on trouve dans *Hamlet,* par une bizarrerie encore plus grande, des traits sublimes, dignes des plus grands génies.[17]

These words show that Voltaire still conceded, though unwillingly, the fact that Shakespeare's plays possessed an appeal for him. By 1761, however, the French critic's words took on the animus that they were to show for the rest of his life. He now realized that Shakespeare was gaining favor among the French. The English dramatist had been mentioned frequently in the *Encyclopédie* of Diderot and d'Alembert, the first volumes of which came out in 1751. In 1756, *Le Nouveau Dictionnaire historique* had six pages allotted to him. A clearer and better knowledge of the Elizabethan period and its great dramatist was crystallizing in the minds of Frenchmen. Their tastes were becoming more catholic.

This growing demand for information concerning Shakespeare, a demand that led inevitably to a wider dissemination of his works, was being reinforced by deep flowing currents of thought and emotion. These were to temper the lives of Frenchmen in fields far outside aesthetics. The taste for the sentimental, with its appetite for tears and its desire for a stronger emotional stimulation than was offered by the aridity of an extreme rationalism, found one outlet in the treatment of melancholy and

17. *Op. cit.,* IV, 502 (from "Dissertation sur la Tragédie," published with *Sémiramis*).

The next year, an English critic wrote a warm defense of Hamlet against Voltaire's aspersions. See *Grays-Inn Journal*, No. 41, July 28, 1753.

sepulchral subjects. After 1760 the taste for the "somber" appeared. This is the counterpart in French literature of the emotional appetite that in England was satisfied by the graveyard poets, and by Ossian—even by *Clarissa Harlowe.*

Another related aspect of these same tendencies was the taste for wildness and irregularity. The French people went to Shakespeare and *Hamlet* and found these qualities also. In his article on "génie" for the *Encyclopédie,* Diderot says that "Le sublime et le *génie* brillent dans Shakespeare comme des éclairs dans une longue nuit." The work of génie must have "l'air irrégulier, escarpé, sauvage."[18] It was not new to say that Shakespeare had these qualities. Voltaire had already said much the same thing. It was novel, however, to imply a genuine admiration for Shakespeare because of them.

To return to Voltaire and 1761. It is against the background I have just sketched that one must understand the growing willingness of the French to find Shakespeare more pleasing; and Voltaire's deepening animus against him. What seems finally to have aroused him to a sense for the dangerous state of things, was an anonymous article in the *Journal Encyclopédique,* in 1760. Here again was the now familiar statement that Shakespeare was "un grand génie poétique." He had far too much inner fire to submit to rules. Corneille, on the other hand could do so. He was only "un excellent poète dramatique."[19] Although this judgment was not extreme, nor very "insulting" to Corneille, Voltaire felt that matters were going too far. He would not concede now that *Hamlet* had any admirable features. In 1752 he had admitted that Shakespeare possessed genius; now, however, such a quality had little significance in view of the fact that the English dramatist lacked the ability to shape his material according to the conventions of neo-classical tragedy. In 1761, Voltaire set forth this point of view in his famous *Appel à toutes les Nations:*

Il n'y a peut-être pas un plus grand exemple de la diversite des goûts des nations. Qu'on vienne après cela nous parler des règles d'Aristote, et des trois unités, et des bienséances, et de la nécessité de ne laisser jamais la scène vide, et de ne faire ni sortir, ni entrer aucun personnage sans une raison sensible; de lier une intrigue avec art, de la dénouer naturellement, de s'exprimer en termes nobles et simples, de faire parler les princes avec la décence qu'ils ont toujours, ou qu'ils voudraient avoir; de ne jamais s'écarter des règles de la langue! Il est clair qu'on peut enchanter toute une nation sans se donner tant de peines.[20]

Voltaire now seems to have forgotten that he himself took the trouble

18. *Œuvres Complètes* (Paris, 1875), XV, 37.
19. Baldensperger, *op. cit.,* p. 171.
20. *Op. cit.,* XXIV, 203.

once to translate some of the words of this poet who could not speak in terms "noble and simple." Would he now say that he himself had given Shakespeare's words this quality through his translation? Probably he did not stop to figure the matter out. By 1764 all he knew was that Hamlet's manner of expressing himself was quite reprehensible. Commenting upon the soliloquy that starts, "O, that this too too solid flesh would melt," recently praised by Lord Kames, Voltaire says: "et quelques Français pourront dire que Gilles, dans une foire de province, s'exprimerait avec plus de décence et de noblesse que le Prince Hamlet. . . ."[21]

The final words I shall quote from Voltaire are found in the same article of 1764. They put more briefly and exactly his later estimate of *Hamlet:* "Le fond du discours d'Hamlet est dans la nature: cela suffit aux Anglais. Le style n'est pas celui de Sophocle et D'Euripide; mais la décence, la noblesse, la justesse des idées, la beauté des vers, l'harmonie, sont peu de chose."[22]

No later words of Voltaire's, even including his celebrated letter to the Academy, of August 25, 1776, need be considered here. This last great effort was called forth by Letourneur's translation, with the indisputable evidence of the popularity of Shakespeare that its reception offered. At some time or other, Voltaire seems to have said nearly everything concerning Hamlet that other French critics of the period said. However, when he came to realize the full implication of his estimate, he fulminated in critical rage. He had not expected that the French people would ever grow to like this author who was little more than a gifted and irrational savage; nor his hero, Hamlet. He finally saw that it had been indiscreet of him to show that he had found anything admirable in a character who at best could merely display moments of rationality or surprising sublimity; but whose words and actions, the rest of the time, were hardly to be spoken of in polite society. He was the raw material of a hero, hardly more. From the French point of view, the literary form in which he appeared was not dramatic, for "Art" was a necessary ingredient of the dramatic.

In his "Second Discours Préliminaire," 1765, to *Le Comte de Comminge,* Baculard d'Arnaud gave evidence that he had caught to a considerable degree the power of *Hamlet* when experienced in its Shakespearian dimensions. He was moved by the terrible power of the ghost scene, where "geste si expressif" and "silence ténébreux" add to the great effect.[23] Possibly d'Arnaud is merely analysing one source of the "sub-

21. *Ibid.*, XXV, 161 (from an article in *La Gazette Littéraire,* April 4, 1764).
22. *Ibid.*, XXV, 161.
23. Third edition (The Hague, 1765), p. lii.

limity" that Voltaire had spoken of in connection with the play. The implication of his words is important for this study. Did he see Hamlet in the terms that would be appropriate for the rest of his interpretation, —as an heroic and agonizing son who must avenge the murder of his father? It seems most probable that he did.

With the exception of several isolated critical bits that I shall speak of in connection with the histrionic tradition of the play, there is little more to record. In view of the growing popularity of Shakespeare, this is amazing. Possibly, however, it is evidence that Voltaire had given expression quite well to critical instincts in the French people too deep rooted to be modified greatly by the forces working in the other direction.

After Voltaire's great defense of French tragedy in August, 1776, Baretti was moved to reply in favor of Shakespeare. He finds Voltaire's version of the "to-be" soliloquy, written so many years before, "une tirade . . . bruyante, légérement saupoudrée de quelques pensées impies."[24] But of Hamlet himself Baretti had nothing illuminating or new to say. The best he could offer was a Johnsonian comment regarding Shakespeare's characters in general. They represent "point des individus, mais des espèces." Baretti's slender comment is the last I have found that in the slightest degree can be interpreted as referring to the problem of Hamlet's character.

Before concluding, I should like to set back the chronology of this discussion far enough to take note of the attenuated histrionic tradition that formed the stage history of *Hamlet* in eighteenth-century France.[25] In 1751 and again in 1765, Garrick gave an interpretation of the role in dumb show. In 1769 the play made its appearance on the Parisian stage in the adaptation of Ducis.

This adaptation quite definitely capitalized on the growing interest in Shakespeare, and on the current taste for the sentimental and "somber." For his source, Ducis, who knew no English, had to depend upon La Place's paraphrase, and for inspiration, upon two engravings sent him by Garrick,—one was of Shakespeare himself, and the other of Garrick in the role.[26] The result was unique. There is possibly some of Shakespeare remaining in La Place. By no stretch of the imagination can any be

24. *Discours sur Shakespeare et sur Monsieur De Voltaire* (1777; reprint Lanciano, 1911), p. 24.

25. There are records of visits of English players to France in the late Sixteenth and early Seventeenth Centuries. The English plays performed must have been in the mangled form of dumb show, or otherwise vulgarized. Whether *Hamlet* ever had even such a performance is unknown (Jusserand, *op. cit.*, pp. 50, ff).

26. Jusserand, *op. cit.*, pp. 416, ff.

found in Ducis! The love interest almost obligatory in French tragedies
was furnished by making the relations of Hamlet and Ophelia much
more explicitly that of lovers. Ophelia is made the daughter of Claudius.
Hamlet gets his knowledge of the shameful death of his father through a
ghost who meets him in the coulisse. Hamlet, vowing vengeance but
also weeping easily, parades through the palace carrying an urn containing the ashes of his venerated parent. Ophelia, in a fashion like that of
the heroines of Corneille, is torn between conflicting emotions—love for
Hamlet, and duty to her father. Possibly the hero was meant by Ducis to
have a touch of the "sauvage," for Ophelia calls him "tigre impitoyable."
At the end, Claudius besieges the palace and is killed by Hamlet. Ger-
trude, broken-hearted at her own degradation, kills herself. The lovers
live happily ever after. At the end, as he surveys his own triumph after
accumulated agonies, Hamlet says:

> Que tes remords sur toi fassent du haut des cieux
> Descendre et les regards et le pardon des dieux!
> Privé de tous les miens dans ce palais funeste,
> Mes malheurs sont comblés; mais ma vertu me reste;
> Mais je suis homme et roi: réservé pour souffrir,
> Je saurai vivre encor; je fais plus que mourir.[27]

What shall one say concerning this strange artistic mélange which
proved successful on the French stage?[28] If we judge the feeling of the
French for Shakespeare by it, would it not be necessary to conclude that
they could not appreciate him at all? Such a conclusion would be most
rash. Frenchmen might read Hamlet appreciatively, but they could not
bring thmselves to see it on the stage where, of necessity a collective aesthetic response was called for. They did not wish "unadulterated nature"
in their heroes; or a situation that would rouse within them too great a
sense of horror.[29] As far as the stage was concerned, they remained conservative. They must take this crude English hero whose Elizabethan
ancestry was most hazy to them, and refine away his malcontent "crud-

---

27. Œuvres de J. F. Ducis (Paris, 1826), I, 149.

28. One amusing indication of French audience reaction to the Ducis Hamlet is
furnished by the Lettre d'un Jeune Homme, à l'auteur de La Tragédie d'Hamlet
(Paris, 1769). Even in Ducis, this writer found violations of decorum. For him the faint
traces of malcontentism as registered by Ducis, were unpleasant. He wishes the queen
to be more remorseful, and Ophelia's plight to be made more pathetic.

The one completely unfavorable reaction I have found is that of Diderot. He
finishes his trenchant review of the play by saying, "Je finis en vous disant que je
m'accommoderai encore mieux du monstre de Shakespeare, que de l'épouvantail de M.
Ducis." (Op. cit., VIII, 476.)

29. On the other hand, aesthetic conservatism made the English demand for their
stage the very "crudities" that kept the play, in its Shakespearian form, off the French
stage (supra, p. 32).

ities." They must make him classic. They must keep the horror in the coulisse!

Paradoxically, however, the people who could give their approval to Ducis in 1769, could also read avidly Letourneur's edition of 1776, dedicated to the king, and published with a large subscription list.

It is possible, then, to say that within the limits of their characteristic aesthetic dualism, the French "understood" *Hamlet*. They seem to have enjoyed even the grave-diggers. Such an implication may be gathered from the spirited words of Cubières in 1777, in which he describes the French mania for the somber. He is speaking, he says, of those farces in which,

des Fossoyeurs de Cimetière font de froides plaisanteries sur les crânes de leurs aïeux; où l'on voit des Spectres, des Revenans [sic], encore couverts du drap mortuaire, venir faire des discours pathétiques aux assistans, où l'on prodigue les échaffauts, les cercueils, les potences, les coupes empoisonnées et mille autres ressorts puériles de terreur, qui ne parlent qu'aux yeux et ne disent rien à l'âme.[30]

But it is well to remember that the "fossoyeurs de cimetière" spoken of so contemptuously by this critic never escaped from the pages of *Hamlet* to exhibit their drolleries on the French stage. There they and the "sauvage" prince with whom they bandy words, remained. In so far as Frenchmen of these years discovered Hamlet, it was in the study from the pages of Letourneur.

Our final conclusion must be that when all allowances are made, Voltaire still remains the most typical critical mouthpiece of the century.[31]

30. Quoted from a letter to a "femme sensible," *La Manie des Drames Sombres* (Paris, 1777), p. 3.

31. I have discussed in some connection or other, most of the French critics of importance who said anything about either Shakespeare or *Hamlet* in the period. The ones that I have neglected do not seem to me to have a vital connection with this study. To make the record more complete, however, one may add the following critics as possessing at least some importance in Shakespearian criticism: the Abbé LeBlanc, *Lettre d'un François*, 1745; C. J. F. Henault, *Nouveau Théâtre François*, 1747; S. Mercier, *Du Théâtre: ou Nouvel Essai sur l'art dramatique*, 1773; Martin Sherlock, *A Fragment on Shakespeare*, 1786; and J. F. La Harpe, *De Shakespeare*, 1799.

6

Hamlet in German Criticism[1]

GERMAN CULTURE in this century is the story of a period when the creative forces of a people, long almost dormant, awakened, and after manifesting themselves in a series of rapid changes, blossomed into a splendid literature. The progress of this evolution includes a time when rationalism and imitation of the French shaped the reigning aesthetic ideal, with Gottsched as its leading spirit. After revolt from Gottsched, led by the two Swiss professors, Bodmer and Breitinger, Germany "assimilated the best ideas of English and French individualism."[2] Chronologically it was at the time when the Germans were throwing off the fetters of rationalism that by some striking intuition they discovered Shakespeare and *Hamlet,* and found there a most congenial and potent spiritual food.

Hamlet criticism began in the decade between 1750 and 1760. The play has, however, a histrionic tradition in Germany that dates back a century and a quarter before this decade. The first unequivocal record of this tradition is found in an almanac for the year 1626: "Den 24 Junius Ist eine Trag-

1. In this section I shall deal incidentally with some of the *Hamlet* criticism in neighboring countries influenced by German tradition. The general subject of the play on the continent outside of Germany is too large a subject for discussion here. Briefly put, a few important facts are these: English comedians in the Seventeenth Century played as far north as Copenhagen and Stockholm; as far east as Danzig, Königsberg and Warsaw; and as far south as Vienna and Innsbruck. Whether *Hamlet* was on their repertoire for these places, we do not know. There is little to record concerning either Shakespeare or *Hamlet* in Denmark, Norway, Sweden, Holland, Italy, Spain, Poland or Russia before the Nineteenth Century. Denmark had a prose translation of the plays by 1780; Sweden had none until considerably later. In Holland the play was being staged in 1793 with a happy ending, the latter probably due to such influence as that of Heufeld in Germany. In Italy, Antonio Conti adapted *Julius Caesar* into Italian as *Il Cesare,* 1726. With this exception, what little Italy knew about either Shakespeare or *Hamlet* before the Nineteenth Century, it gathered from Voltaire and Ducis. A Spanish version of the Ducis *Hamlet,* by Cruz, is dated 1772. Russia and Poland do not enter into the picture until the Nineteenth Century.

Two sources that supply at least a rapid discussion of this subject are J. G. Robertson, "Shakespeare on the Continent," *CHEL,* V, chapter 12; and C. H. Herford, "A Sketch of the History of Shakespeare's Influence on the Continent," in *The Post-War Mind of Germany, and Other European Studies,* 1927. There are a number of such specialized accounts as M. B. Ruud's *An Essay towards a History of Shakespeare in Denmark,* 1920. Lack of space will not permit their inclusion here. For the reference to Holland, above, see *Thespian Magazine and Literary Repository,* 2, 366.

2. J. G. Robertson, *A History of German Literature* (rev. edit., Edinburgh), p. 239.

oedia von Hamlet einem printzen in Dennemarck gespielt worden." This performance took place in Dresden, and was given by a company of English comedians.[3] As the same group of actors gave performances that year or the next in Köln, Frankfort and Torgau, it is probable that *Hamlet* was acted in these places also.[4] Whether this first recorded performance was a full-fledged adaptation or some mangled form of dumb show, we do not know. It is possible, however, that a form of the drama more acceptable to German audiences was soon available, for companies of native German actors, generally students, sprang up. It seems probable that a German adaptation of *Hamlet* was part of the repertoires of these companies. This supposition derives weight from the fact that such an adaptation, the *Bestrafte Brudermord,* exists in an early eighteenth-century manuscript, the prototype of which must have had its origin at a considerably earlier date.[5]

An examination of the *Bestrafte Brudermord* will answer this question: How much of the substance of *Hamlet* could a German audience of 1710, or earlier, assimilate? The answer is that they could take the essential dramatic situation in a cruder, more elemental form than it is found in Shakespeare's play. In origin the German play would seem to be definitely linked with Quarto 1.[6] In spirit it is primitive and naïve, even more so than is Quarto 1, which in several important aspects is itself more "Kydian" than Quarto 2. When we get beneath the basic situation, that of a man who carries out a command of revenge enjoined upon him by his father's ghost, we find that the *Bestrafte Brudermord* differs greatly from both of the Shakespearian quartos. There are no splendid soliloquies, little real melancholy, no poetic death of Ophelia, no graveyard scene,—one might almost add, no Shakespeare.[7] There is a distinctly primitive comic element of vulgar buffoonery. For example, the ghost boxes the ears of a sentry. In another place, where Hamlet is to be executed by bandits, he falls to the ground just as they fire, thus causing them to kill each other. Of Hamlet himself it is interesting to note that

3. W. Widman, *Hamlets Bühnenlaufbahn,* p. 15.

4. *Ibid.,* p. 17.

5. *Ibid.,* pp. 17-18.

6. The latest scholarship on this subject, the relationship between Quarto 2, Quarto 1, and the *Bestrafte Brudermord* is found in two articles by E. E. Stoll: "*Hamlet* and *The Spanish Tragedy*, Quartos 1 and 2: A Protest," MP, 35, 31-46; and "*Hamlet* and the *Spanish Tragedy* again," MP, 37, 173-186. The standard treatment of the matter up to this time has been that of Sir Edmund Chambers, in *William Shakespeare,* 1930. Pioneering work on the relationship of the German play to the quartos was done by Wilhelm Creizenach. He sums up his scholarship on the subject in " 'Der Bestrafte Brudermord' and its Relation to Shakespeare's 'Hamlet.' " MP, 2, 249-60.

7. For an excellent comment, see Friedrich Gundolf, *Shakespeare und der Deutsche Geist* (Berlin, 1911), pp. 36-8.

he loses most of his introspective qualities. There is less possibility here to interpret him as a procrastinator than in either of the quartos, for the difficulties he must undergo in carrying out his revenge are more external. For example, in one place Hamlet says to Horatio:

My worthy friend, Horatio, through this assumed madness I hope to get the opportunity of revenging my father's death. You know, however, that my father is always surrounded by many guards; wherefore it may miscarry. . . .[8]

It is of course impossible to retrace the steps through which this play came into being, or to know what materials its authors or adapters had before them as they wrote. But one can feel with some conviction that the material concerning the guards, just quoted, as well as other primitive items, could well have been in the old *Hamlet*. But origin aside, it is quite evident that this adaptation was prepared for an audience capable of only a "lowbrow" aesthetic reaction; they are given horseplay instead of humor, and horror instead of terror. It is legitimate, I believe, to pass a critical judgment that goes beyond the "audience," and say that this adaptation was the only type of production that the German spirit, —expressing itself of necessity in the contemporary idiom popular on the stage—was capable of shaping out of Shakespeare.

The name of the great English dramatist was not connected with the *Bestrafte Brudermord*. However, the process through which a valid knowledge of both Shakespeare and *Hamlet* was to be gained had already started. In the years between 1682, when Shakespeare's name was first mentioned in Germany, and 1741, when the first more valid translation of one of the dramas, Borck's *Der Tod des Julius Cäsar* in alexandrines, was published, there had been a slow infiltration of at least some of the external facts concerning Shakespeare into the German mind.[9] Borck's translation is French in tone, showing the influence of Voltaire and classical tragedy. That the phrase "external facts" is not a misnomer when used in this connection, is borne out by no less a critic than Lessing, who can say in 1749: "Shakespear, Dryden, Wycherley, Vanbrugh,

8. Act II, v (Furness Variorum *Hamlet,* II, 128).

9. A detailed account of this process of acquisition may be found in J. G. Robertson, "The Knowledge of Shakespeare on the Continent at the beginning of the Eighteenth Century," *MLR,* 1, 312, ff. See also Widmann, *op. cit.,* pp. 35-6. There are probably not more than half a dozen such early references to Shakespeare. These include one in Morhof's *Unterricht von der teutschen Sprache,* 1682. Morhof admits that he knows little concerning Shakespeare, beyond his name. Other casual references are dated 1694 and 1703. In 1709 Shakespeare received mention in the *Allgemeines historisches Lexicon* of Buddeus. Buddeus took what he says from Fuller's *Worthies* of 1682. In 1725 the Swiss poet Bodmer refers to "Shakespear der Engelländische Sophocles"; in 1740, evidently under the influence of the Italian, Antonio Conti, he changed his orthography to "Sasper."

Cibber, Congreve sind Dichter, die man fast bei uns nur dem Namen nach kennet, und gleichwohl verdienen sie unsere Hochachtung sowohl als die gepriesenen französischen Dichter."[10]

In 1749 Lessing could say this. In 1773 the first German adaptation of *Hamlet* for the stage opened in Vienna. The years in between these two dates comprise a period in which a genuinely critical basis for the acceptance of Shakespeare was laid; a period in which the first criticism of *Hamlet* appears.

In the decade between 1750 and 1760, a gifted German Jew, Moses Mendelssohn, gives us the first bit of *Hamlet* criticism that I have found. Both Mendelssohn and his friend Nicolai, who also was reading Shakespeare appreciatively, are interesting for another reason. Their mutual friendship for Lessing probably had a marked effect upon the latter's critical tendencies.[11] To the men already mentioned may be added one other, who was influenced by Mendelssohn, the poet Ewald Kleist.

By 1757 Mendelssohn had read *Hamlet* and had made a translation of the "to-be" soliloquy into blank verse. Later he revised his version several times. His first draft is far from a perfect translation, for in addition to its metrical roughness, it does not catch the shadings of Hamlet's thought. Also, it suffers from a touch of morbidity, a graveyard flavor not in the original. The images of death are given with words that involve a note of physical corruption quite foreign to the exact thought.[12] In another place an extreme image is chosen to represent Hamlet's more poetic and less violent:

The slings and arrows of outrageous fortune

10. *Sämtliche Schriften* (Stuttgart, 1881-1919), IV, 52 (*Beiträge zur Historie und Aufnahme des Theatres*).

11. This friendship may quite possibly have had more influence upon Lessing than later critics have usually allowed. Lessing has nearly always been given the credit for being the pioneer in German Shakespearian criticism, with little or no importance assigned to his friends Nicolai and Mendelssohn. An article by F. W. Meisnest, "Lessing and Shakespeare," *PMLA*, 19, 234, ff., says that before 1758, all Lessing knew about Shakespeare had been gathered second hand through Voltaire, La Place's translations, and a few articles that had appeared in German periodicals (*Ibid.*, p. 247). As early as 1754 Nicolai gives evidence of a first-hand knowledge of Shakespeare; and Mendelssohn may have been less dependent intellectually upon Lessing than some critics suppose. (See also, Daniel Jacoby, "Der Hamlet-Monolog III, i und Lessing's Freunde Mendelssohn und Kleist," *Jahrbuch*, 25, 115-16.)

12. *Gesammelte Schriften* (Berlin, 1929-32), I, 202. Jacoby, *op. cit.*, pp. 118-19., prints a part of Mendelssohn's later version of the soliloquy; and also a translation of part of the one starting "O, what a rogue and peasant slave am I!"

Mendelssohn's more concrete imagery may be seen in the use of the word "verwesen" in place of the less concrete "sterben," in Hamlet's second "To die; to sleep," and a few lines later, in his translation of the prince's "When we have shuffl'd off this mortal coil" as "wenn einst dieses Fleisch vermodert."

Mendelssohn makes this phrase,

des strengen Schicksals
Blutdürstige Pfeile.

In his later revisions, he comes much closer to Shakespeare's tone and thought.

In a treatise on aesthetics published in 1758,[13] where he included part of his first draft of the soliloquy, Mendelssohn says that these famous lines are the finest example he can offer of one type of the sublime. Although he couches his description in general terms so that it includes all heroes in such a situation, and names several tragedies whose heroes in soliloquy illustrate his point, Hamlet is the character to whom he refers most directly. What is more, it is Hamlet's words in this connection that he uses for illustration.

Mendelssohn says that in soliloquy, an heroic soul incorruptible in its thought, speaks. When its resolution is fixed, its speech is quick and incisive. But when in doubt as to a course of action, the soul "reich und unerschöpflich an Gedanken," bends over and contemplates its own mental and emotional life. At this moment of temporary irresolution, the thoughts take on a coloring of eloquence, power and passion. They become sublime. Here Mendelssohn uses a vivid figure of speech to describe the power and magnificence of this mental phenomenon: "Die unentschlossene Seele schwankt wie von Wellen getrieben von einer Seite zur andern, und reisset die Zuhörer allenthalben mit sich fort. . . ." The splendid conflict ends when the soul hears the voice of virtue telling it what choice to make. It then fixes its resolution, and afterwards does not waver again.[14]

This fine interpretation of Hamlet's inner life at a great moment seems appropriate indeed from the pen of the first German critic. Like many who will come after him, he saw the hero's introspection in terms of a rich significance. If Mendelssohn were referring exclusively to Hamlet here, his term "unerschöpflich" would make him prophetic of Coleridge. It would be uncritical, however, to consider him as definitely "romantic" in his approach. This is true in spite of his exclusive interest in Hamlet's inner life, and the morbid touch in his translation.[15] He dis-

---

13. *Betrachtungen über das Erhabene und das Naïve in den schönen Wissenschaften.*
14. *Gesammelte Schriften,* I, 201.
15. Ewald Kleist seems to have been influenced through Mendelssohn's translation of the "to-be" soliloquy to write two poems, 1757 and 1758. They illustrate well how Hamlet's words through an intermediary source, could strike a chord of sympathy in a sensitive spirit, and help him to give expression to a romantic mood. In emotional

plays a genuine sense of historical perspective and a sanity that will not always be found in later German critics of *Hamlet*. Probably his translation was motivated by the fact that he could make it vicarious expression. Nevertheless his interpretation as described above, does not warp the words out of their dramatic context. What he says concerning Hamlet makes us wish he had written more. Later German criticism might with profit have imitated his objectivity of approach.

Before there could exist any very widespread knowledge of *Hamlet*, it was necessary that someone give the general public a full translation of the play. This task fell to a man of more pedestrian genius than that of Mendelssohn. In 1759 Lessing recommended a translation of Shakespeare "mit einigen bescheidenen Veränderungen." His wish was fulfilled within the next decade by Wieland, who issued between 1762 and 1766 the translation of twenty-two of Shakespeare's dramas, *Hamlet* among them. Wieland was in no sense a great translator. His *Hamlet* is best described by saying that it represents a prose version of Warburton's text, limited by the translator's scanty knowledge of Elizabethan English. He adds and subtracts, at times is too cursory, and at others too verbose. The grave-diggers scene, for example, is represented with a short paraphrase. He makes no attempt, however, to recast the play,[16] a form of procedure that was to be the typical method of a number of future German critics, from Heufeld and Schröder to Gerhart Hauptmann. Wieland makes the statement that it is his desire to give a faithful and complete transcript of Shakespeare. For his task he used the German language and the German capacity of understanding as it existed in 1762-66. Obviously, this was his necessary procedure. Mendelssohn in a flash of

---

origin the poetry seems similar to the English graveyard poetry. It is also touched with the mood of "revolt." His "Grablied" follows:

> Allein, du wirst auch nicht mehr sehn,
> Dass sich der Tugendhafte quält,
> Sich seiner Blösse schämt und darbt,
> Und seine Lebenszeit verweint,
> Indessen dass in Seid' und Gold
> Der Bösewicht stolzirt und lacht.
> Du wirst nicht sehn, dass ein Tyrann
> Die Ferse frei gebornem Volk
> In den gebognen Nacken setzt. . . .
> Kein Narr, kein Höfling wird dich mehr
> Mit dummer Falschheit peinigen,
> Und keine Rachsucht sicht auf dich
> Mit scheelen Blichken eines Wolfe.
> (Jacoby, *op. cit.*, pp. 121-3).

16. For a detailed description and analysis of Wieland's translation of *Hamlet*, see F. W. Meisnest, "F. W. Wieland's Translation of Shakespeare," *MLR*, 9, 12-40.

intuition could light up the "to-be" soliloquy; Wieland on a less creative level could set forth the whole play. What is more, it is probable that he did the task as well as it could have been done at that time.[17] Even on the stage, Wieland's *Hamlet* was, compared to the *Bestrafte Brudermord,* an immeasurable advance. Its greatest importance, however, lies in the fact that it helped to make possible a stage version in the next decade.

Lessing's various references to *Hamlet* in the *Hamburgische Drama-turgie,* starting in 1767, offer little clue to his actual feeling about the hero. Earlier he had praised Mendelssohn's version of the "to-be" solil-oquy,[18] and had made a general reference to the play in his *17th Litter-aturbrief* of 1759. Here he does little more than refer casually to *Hamlet.* In number 5 he translates part of Hamlet's instructions to the players, and recommends them as a golden rule for actors. In numbers 11 and 12 he compares the ridiculous ghost in *Sémiramis* with the ghost of Ham-let's father—to the advantage of Shakespeare. Such criticism, important as it was in helping to destroy the last vestiges of the idea that French clas-sical aesthetics was the sum total of all wisdom, and Shakespeare a bar-barian,[19] helps us little.

Herder's chapter on "Shakespeare" in *Von deutscher Art und Kunst,* 1773, opening with its virtual apotheosis of the dramatist, "hoch auf einem Felsengipfel sitzend!" contains a cryptic and puzzling description of Hamlet. In an earlier redaction of his chapter, Herder had taken ex-ception to those "beauty-hunting" critics who saw Hamlet merely as "trübsinniger Raisonneur," rather than also as "der würdige Königs-sohn, und der so Menschlich rührende *good fellow,*" who against his will

17. Gundolf is of such an opinion. In his chapter on Wieland in *Shakespeare und der Deutsche Geist,* pp. 161, ff., he is critical indeed in his judgment of Wieland's trans-lations. However, he goes on to say, "Die Erklärung dafur liegt nicht in Wieland's gutem oder trägem Willen, sondern in dem Zustand der Sprache deren er sich zu bedienen hatte, in der persönlichen Sphäre seines Spracherlebens." (p. 172).

18. *Sämtliche Schriften,* XVII, 128.

19. That there were critics possessed of the inclination to make sharp remonstrance against the growing popularity of Shakespeare is seen by the following words from the pen of Josef v. Sonnenfels, the "dictator of Vienna's taste":

> Niemand läuft vielleicht so sehr nach der Art des unschicklichen Witzes, als eben Shakespear, dieses abenteuerliche Genie, welches sehr oft in einem und demsel-ben Stücke die zwie äussersten Empfindungen ohne Mittelband vereinigt und den Leser mit Thränen in den Augen zu lautem Gelächter nötigt. . . . Shakespeares Stücke sind also immer Ungeheuer, wo der Held, der nur itzt in Gold und Purpur erschien, mit pöpelhaften Reden der Schänke zuwandert, worin wider Wahrscheinlichkeit, Sitten und Anstand verstossen wird, und die bei allen den Flammen tragischen Genies mehr bewundert als nachgeahmt zu werden verdienen. (from *Briefe über wienerische Schaubuhne,* 1768, as quoted by Widmann, *op. cit.,* p. 57.)

must be "Bote der Rache" and "Werkzeug des Schicksals."[20] In the completed chapter as published, "Hamlet vorbeiirrt in seiner Mutter Kammer vor dem Bilde seines Vaters!" Herder then shows him at the grave of Ophelia, "der rührende *good Fellow* in allen den Verbindungen mit Horaz, Ophelia, Laertes, Fortinbras!" It is because he possesses such a nature that Herder can speak of "das Jugendspiel der Handlung, was durchs Stück fortläuft und fast bis zu Ende keine Handlung wird."[21]

Herder would not deny that Hamlet at times could be "trübsinnig." In 1801 he gave an interpretation that made the prince both sentimental and speculative.[22] Here, however, he pictured him as having qualities less subjective, qualities that showed him as dramatically a more estimable character, but nevertheless as at the same time, a "pathetic good fellow" who spent his time in "Jugendspiel," and only at the last moment could become serious, and act. Is there not here a distinct hint of a hero who is hardly equal to the serious task imposed upon him? It would be a mistake I feel, to force too precise a meaning upon Herder's words, or to give them too much importance. This much is certain: his picture of Hamlet is not a satisfyingly heroic one. It seems to make too insignificant Hamlet's deeper qualities, those that so appealed to Mendelssohn.

So far it has been possible to find only fragmentary bits of genuine *Hamlet* criticism. The same year in which Herder published his comment, however, marks the beginning of a tradition of theatrical criticism called into being by one of the most amazing phenomena in the history of the stage. On January 16, 1773, the first recorded performance of *Hamlet* under Shakespeare's name, took place in Vienna. Later in the same year another adaptation was performed in Biberach. In 1774 performances followed in Pressburg; in 1775 in Prague and Salzburg; and in 1776, in Innsbruck and Pest. In 1776 also, the first adaptation of the play by Schröder appeared in Hamburg, and in 1777, in Berlin. In 1778 Schröder acted the role for the first time. From then on the floodgates were open. There passed over Germany and the territory surrounding her, what one critic has well called a "Hamlet-fever." The next few years saw performances in practically every town of any size in Germany.[23] With player and public alike the drama had amazing popularity. Reichard in his *Theaterkalender* for 1780 remarks, "Nach keiner Rolle haben

20. *Sämmtliche Werke* (ed. Suphan, Berlin, 1877-1913), V, 234.
21. *Ibid.*, V, 224.
22. See the quotation as given by Furness in the Variorum *Hamlet*, II, 276-8.
23. A detailed account of these performances, including dates, actors and representative criticism is given by Widmann, *op. cit.*, pp. 120-177.

Schauspieler mehr gegeizt als nach Hamlet."[24] Schink says, "Nie ist wohl irgend ein englisches Trauerspiel mit dem allgemeinen Beyfall in Deutschland aufgenommen, nie irgend eines mit einem solchen Heisshunger von Zuschauer und Publikum verschlungen worden als dieser Hamlet."[25]

Both of the leading adaptations of the play were based on Wieland's text. Both were just as thoroughly adaptations as that of Ducis, in France. Neither Heufeld nor Schröder mangled the play, however, past all recognition, as Ducis did.

Heufeld came first. He shortened the action considerably. Rosencrantz and Guildenstern are made into one person. Ophelia does not go mad. There are no trip to England, no grave-diggers, no appearance at the end, of Fortinbras. Laertes and the duel are omitted. The king is stabbed by Hamlet. The queen drinks poison and admits her guilt before she dies. Hamlet, on the other hand, does not die, but is victorious over his enemies. The object seems to have been to make the play a "family tragedy."[26] In Schröder's adaptation of 1776 many of Heufeld's changes were kept. As in Heufeld, there were no churchyard scene, no duel and the prince was victorious and alive as the play closed. However, in many small ways Schröder made his version more like Wieland's.[27] And more important, when he came to act the part himself, he succeeded best of any German actor in giving the role a Shakespearian flavor.

The total result of these changes may be easily seen. The main situation remained—a son visited supernaturally by his father's ghost; a command of revenge finally carried out. However, much of Shakespeare's complex Elizabethan richness was deleted. Many tragic tones were lost. Some of Hamlet's best chances to show himself an active prince were taken from him—for example, his trip to England and the duel. He must talk more and do less; and even in speech he suffered, for some of his finest lines were taken from him, his splendid soliloquy as the soldiers of Fortinbras pass by, and the ironic tang of his words in the graveyard. Hamlet's whole situation was made less desperate, less heart-wringing. And at the end there could be no great tragic katharsis.

Nevertheless, even after the worst is said, this "Verwässerung" as Widmann calls it, still contains much of Shakespeare. There was enough left so that audiences in Germany and the surrounding territory seem to have been willing to applaud almost any actor who could speak Hamlet's lines with a fair degree of elocutionary ability.

From the copious theatrical criticism of the time, one may reconstruct

24. *Ibid.*, p. 120.
25. *Ibid.*, p. 121.
26. *Ibid.*, pp. 48-9.
27. *Ibid.*, pp. 60-1.

his own picture of these performances of *Hamlet*. Widmann records a good sampling for our use. For example, Joseph Lange, who first took the role in the Heufeld adaptation, was pictorial and "plastic" in method. He was declamatory and cold. Notwithstanding these deficiencies, enough of the magic of Shakespeare's lines seems to have survived to make an impression on the Viennese audience.[28]

In Hamburg Johann Brockmann first took the role, preceding Schröder there by two years. The individual quality of each actor is seen best in contrast with the other. Brockmann did not go beyond the narrowed limits of the tragic situation in the "Verwässerung." He acted the part of a man for whom the experiences he must pass through were, to quote one critic, "nur ein vorübergehendes schreckliches Ereignis." He made the madness laughable, not tragic. He played the whole piece on the level of wit and scorn. He did not touch the heart deeply. Schröder, on the contrary, seems to have felt the inner meaning of the role. He understood the profound tragedy of the situation. Thus he could make up somewhat for the deficiencies of his script by an interpretation which he was inspired to give through his own study of the unaltered play.[29]

Many other actors took the role. In fact, their name is legion. Reinecke for example, played it with a heavy emphasis on Hamlet's sadness. "Er kömmt mit niedergesenktem Leib und langsamem Schritt daher, bleibt ganz in Nachdenken verzunken. . . ." All of the intellectual vivacity and spring-like quality in the prince of Shakespeare's lines was missing. This Hamlet was heavy and German; we see almost exclusively his broken heart.[30] Another actor, Czechtitzky seems to have succeeded through his splendid "external" qualities,—his looks, "jeder Zoll ein Prinz!" his voice, his nobility of bearing. I shall not describe the many others.

It seems evident that on the whole the performances were what one would expect. In spite of changes in the script, the role was kept an active and heroic one. There was no romantic Hamlet.[31] The "to-be" solil-

28. *Ibid.*, pp. 47, ff.

29. *Ibid.*, p. 74.

30. *Ibid.*, pp. 108-10.

31. It seems the incurable habit of critics who appear later, to look back and give a retrospective interpretation in terms of a new zeitgeist. Like Murphy and Boaden in England, Robert Prutz, near the middle of the Nineteenth Century, did it for Germany. Of the "Hamlet-fever," he says:

> Vielmehr dieser Beifall war eine unmittelbare, bewusstlose Folge jener tiefen, innerlichen Verwandtschaft, welche zwischen dem Helden des Stücks, dem sentimentalen, grübelnden, in Skepsis verschmachtenden Prinzen von Dänemark und der sentimentalen, grübelnden, weltschmerzlichen Stimmung der damaligen deutschen Welt bestand. Man schaute in Hamlet sich selber an; ein solcher Grübler über der Reflexion die That versäumend, war auch das deutsche Volk; so, an der

oquy that so fascinated Mendelssohn, was never slighted. On the other hand, I find no appearance of Herder's "pathetic good fellow."

Although the general tone of this theatrical criticism is one of acceptance and approbation, there are a few notes of dissent. Some, of course, are unfavorable analyses of the interpretations of certain actors. Others question the suitability of showing the play at all. Let me give one of each type. One critic praises Karl Wahr, a minor actor in the role, saying:

Viele Akteurs verkennen den Hamlet ganz; sie halten ihn fur einen feurigen, mutvollen Jungling, wovon er doch im Grunde das Gegentheil ist. Hamlet muss als ein bedächtiger, gesetzter und nachdenklicher Jungling vorgestellet werden, und so hat ihn Hr. Wahr gespielt.[32]

Ideas know no boundary line of country or nationality. Ayrenhoff, a tragic dramatist himself and imitator of Racine, pens words very similar in import to what was being said in these very years by an English critic, George Steevens. Ayrenhoff was so aroused over the Heufeld production that he could write:

Shakespeares Dramen sind noch tiefer unter der Kritik als die allerschlechtesten gothischen Gebaüde. . . . Vom sophokleischen Oedip bis zum Götz von Berlichingen gibt es keinen so schlecht durchgefuhrten, albernen, unmoralischen Charakter als—Hamlet![33]

The "Hamlet-fever," spectacular though it was, may best be regarded as another milestone in Germany's acquisition of Shakespeare. A Hamlet who realized fully the potentialities with which the dramatist endowed him so richly, could not emerge from such versions as those of Heufeld and Schröder. Nor can we pass very definite censure upon the producers, for no translator had given them an authentic script. What is more, even Schröder's modest attempts to bring the play closer to Shakespeare met with an unenthusiastic public. In 1777 he attempted to add Laertes and the grave-diggers to his performance, keeping however, the happy ending. The spectators forced him to return to his original version.

Finally, in 1799 *Hamlet* was performed in a version based on the Schlegel translation. Its blank verse and the quality of its lines made it essentially "real Shakespeare." Beschort took the leading role. The public was not warm in its approbation. Ten years passed, and a number of minor changes were made in the script before Schlegel won his triumph over Schröder.

To complete an account of German criticism, I shall now turn from

Sophistik des eigenen Gefühle, thatlos, ruhlos, zehrte auch die deutsche Jugend sich ab. (quoted in *Widmann*, p. 122.)

32. *Ibid.*, p. 57.

33. *Ibid.*, pp. 56-7.

theatrical matters to comment upon the work of three critics who published views on *Hamlet* in the last decade of the century. I am speaking
of Goethe, Christopher Garve and Friedrich Schlegel.

Goethe's literary indebtedness to Shakespeare forms a subject in itself.
I cannot attempt a treatment of it here. His important critical comment
on *Hamlet* is found, of course, in *Wilhelm Meisters Lehrjahre,* 1795-6. I
cannot find that what he says there was ever superseded by later critical
dicta. It is possible, however, to illuminate his treatment of the prince,
as given in *Wilhelm Meister,* through the citation of things said later. I
shall do this as I proceed.

Although the criticism in *Wilhelm Meister* is not presented as Goethe's
own opinion, I shall interpret it as such. Justly or unjustly, and in spite
of the remonstrances of certain modern scholars,[34] this criticism has generally passed for its author's own estimate.[35] He did not disclaim it later,
nor give a new view that was out of harmony with his (or Wilhelm's)
earlier one. Indeed, in one place where Goethe is quoting a comment
which takes it for granted that he is giving his own views, he makes no
effort to deny such an implication. We all know that at times his works
are heavily autobiographical in nature. It is also true that Goethe's critical intelligence was often inextricably tangled with his creative impulses.[36]
It is well to keep these facts in mind as we look at the famous dictum on
Hamlet.

It will be best to let Wilhelm Meister speak for himself. I shall quote
at some length, merely connecting the citations with any necessary explanatory remarks. In this way it will be possible to preserve some of the
verve and tang of Goethe's style, an important consideration if one wishes
to catch the full value of this great document.

Wilhelm has been studying with a view to acting the leading role
himself. His method of beginning study was, he says:

Die stärksten Stellen, die Selbstgespräche und jene Auftritte zu memoriren, in
denen Kraft der Seele, Erhebung des Geistes und Lebhaftigkeit freien Spielraum
haben, wo das bewegte Gemüth sich in einem gefühlvollen Ausdrucke zeigen
kann.[37]

34. See Gundolf, *op. cit.,* p. 318; and Wm. Diamond, "Wilhelm Meister's Interpretation of Hamlet," *MP.,* 23, 89-101.

35. A. W. Schlegel says, "But let us say nothing further regarding Hamlet's character after what Wilhelm Meister has said. Let us write no *Iliad* after Homer!"
(*Sämtliche Werke,* 1844, VII, 32; quoted by Diamond, *op. cit.,* p. 101.)

36. In this respect, F. Schlegel's estimate of Goethe is interesting:
    "Goethe schwelgt viel zu sehr im Genusse seines vollendet schönen Selbsts,
    als dass er mit treuer Enthaltsamkeit eines bescheidenen Forschers die
    Werke eines anderen Dichters erklären könnte." (quoted by Diamond, *op.
    cit.,* p. 101.)

37. *Werke* (Weimar, 1887-1912), I, Abteilung, XXII, 26.

He finds his study both vicarious experience and a journey into strange places:

Auch glaubte ich recht in den Geist der Rolle einzudringen, wenn ich die Last der tiefen Schwermuth gleichsam selbst auf mich nähme, und unter diesem Druck meinem Vorbilde durch das seltsame Labyrinth so mancher **Launen und** Sonderbarkeiten zu folgen suchte.[38]

Wilhelm now finds himself lost in these strange mental regions. He cannot come to an adequate understanding of this "inconsistent" character. The further he wanders through these "Irrgänge," the more discouraged he gets. Finally he hit upon a solution. It was, however, a dangerous step for Wilhelm, so far as his future as a critic of *Hamlet* was concerned. He went back of the play to examine the previous life of its hero:

Ich suchte jede Spur auf, die sich von dem Charakter Hamlets in früher Zeit vor dem Tode seines Vaters zeigte; ich bemerkte, was unabhängig von dieser traurigen Begebenheit, unabhängig von den nachfolgenden schrecklichen Ereignissen, dieser interessante Jüngling gewesen war, und was er ohne sie vielleicht geworden wäre.[39]

Now comes Wilhelm's central interpretation of the character of the hero. Most justly, however, this "critic" does not call him a hero. Here is the prince, whose "previous life" never dreamed of by Shakespeare, is now uncovered, I cannot say for the first time, for English critics had already caught similar glimpses of him:

Zart und edel entsprossen wuchs die königliche Blume, unter den unmittèlbaren Einflüssen der Majestät, hervor; der Begriff des Rechts und der fürstlichen Würde, das Gefühl des Guten und Anstandigen mit dem Bewusstsein der Höhe seiner Geburt, entwickelten sich zugleich in ihm. Er war ein Fürst, ein geborner Fürst, und wünschte zu regieren, nur damit der Gute ungehindert gut sein möchte. Angenehm von Gestalt, gesittet von Natur, gefällig von Herzen aus, sollte er das Muster der Jugend sein und die Freude der Welt werden.[40]

To the characterization found in the striking paragraph just quoted, Wilhelm now goes on to add further details. Hamlet's love for Ophelia is not strongly passionate, but rather, "ein stilles Vorgefühl süsser Berdürfnisse." In every way his nature seems compounded of mellow sweetness and all other good qualities. He likes neither idleness nor violent employment. He is gentle, courteous, sweet, able to forget and forgive an injury, and forever inimical to the mean and unworthy. Hatred could hardly enter into his gentle soul, unless it were used in order that he might despise heartily enough the hypocrisies of the royal court.

38. *Ibid.,* p. 26.
39. *Ibid.,* p. 27.
40. *Ibid.,* p. 27.

To this exquisitely delicate soul must now come a frightful experience. It will clarify Goethe's picture, I believe, if I add here the central idea in his conception of modern tragedy as expressed some years later in *Shakespeare und kein Ende.* In this critical piece he makes a distinction between ancient and modern tragedy. In modern tragedy the fatal outcome is achieved when an insufficient human will is raised through circumstances from without, to the level of irremissible necessity.[41] In *Hamlet* this external agency is the ghost and its revelations.[42] Keeping in mind Goethe's words in this later essay, let us return to *Wilhelm Meister.*

Our last glimpse of Hamlet left him still untouched by serious misfortune. As will be remembered he is still "outside the play,"—what he would have been if the events in the play had never taken place. But they do take place. His father's death and the accession of his uncle to the throne which he had thought would be his, were a blow indeed:

Er fühlt sich nun so arm an Gnade, an Gütern, und fremd in dem, was er von Jugend auf als sein Eigenthum betrachten konnte. Hier nimmt sein Gemüth die erste traurige Richtung. Er fühlt, dass er nicht mehr, ja nicht so viel ist als jeder Edelmann; er gibt sich für einen Diener eines jeden, er ist nicht höflich, nicht herablassend, nein, herabgesunken und bedürftig.[43]

Then came the marriage of his mother, as if to set the seal to his misfortunes. He now felt not only completely bowed down, but also orphaned as well. Sadness and reflectiveness now seem the very nature of one who did not originally have such tendencies. Soon, however, there falls the last and final blow, the supernatural revelation:

Denken Sie sich . . . diesen Jüngling, diesen Fürstensohn recht lebhaft, vergegenwärtigen Sie sich seine Lage und dann beobachten Sie ihn, wenn er erfährt, die Gestalt seines Vaters erscheine; stehen Sie ihm bei in der schrecklichen Nacht, wenn der ehrwürdige Geist selbst vor ihm auftritt. Ein ungeheures Entsetzen ergreift ihn; er redet die Wundergestalt an, sieht sie winken, folgt und hört.—Die schreckliche Anklage wider seinen Oheim ertönt in seinen Ohren, Aufforderung zur Rache und die dringende wiederholte Bitte: Erinnere dich meiner![44]

The sequel to this gripping scene is strange indeed, and yet not surprising—that is, if one remembers the soft and gentle prince upon whom the command of revenge has just been laid:

Und da der Geist verschwunden ist, wen sehen wir vor uns stehen? Einen jungen Helden, der nach Rache schnaubt? Einen gebornen Fürsten, der sich glücklich

41. "Nun aber kommt ein äusserer hinzu, und der erhitzt sich öfters dadurch, dass ein unzulängliches Wollen durch Veranlassungen zum unerlässlichen Sollen erhöht wird."

42. *Werke,* I, Abteilung, XLI, 62.

43. *Op. cit.,* pp. 73-4.

44. *Ibid.,* p. 75.

fühlt, gegen den Usurpator seiner Krone aufgefordert zu werden? Nein! Staunen und Trübsinn überfällt den Einsamen; er wird bitter gegen die lächelnden Bösewichter, schwört, den Abgeschiedenen nicht zu vergessen, und schliesst mit dem bedeutenden Seufzer: Die Zeit ist aus dem Gelenke; wehe mir, dass ich geboren ward sie wieder einzurichten.[45]

Hamlet now presents the strangest of all paradoxes. He is driven onward to an action by a power from without that has planted within him a "will" which he cannot resist; he cannot act, however, until this driving external compulsion coalesces with his own native will. To use a figure, he must furnish the fuel upon which this devouring flame planted within, is to feed. Or better still, let us take Goethe's own figure of speech:

Und mir ist deutlich, dass Shakespear habe schildern wollen: eine grosse That auf eine Seele gelegt, die der That nicht gewachsen ist. . . . Hier wird ein Eichbaum in ein köstliches Gefäss gepflanzt, das nur liebliche Blumen in seinen Schoss hätte aufnehmen sollen; die Wurzeln dehnen aus, das Gefäss wird zernichtet.[46]

In one last striking paragraph, Goethe gives us a picture of Hamlet as he writhes under the mighty purpose that has been planted within him. From now on, it must be his inseparable companion, a terrible visitor whom he cannot accept and dare not cast out—the very shadow of his fate:

Ein schönes, reines, edles, höchst moralisches Wesen, ohne die sinnliche Stärke, die den Helden macht, geht unter einer Last zu Grunde, die es weder tragen noch abwerfen kann; jede Pflicht ist ihm heilig, diese zu schwer. Das Unmögliche wird von ihm gefordert, nicht das Unmögliche an sich, sondern das, was ihm unmöglicht ist. Wie er sich windet, dreht, ängstigt, vor—und zurücktritt, immer erinnert wird: sich immer erinnert und zuletzt fast seinen Zweck aus dem Sinne verliert, ohne doch jemals wieder froh zu werden.[47]

There is one other critical item that has at least an oblique interest for us. A little later in the narrative, Goethe has Wilhelm propose a scheme of revision and concentration through which *Hamlet* may be made into a true "family tragedy," analogous, I suppose, to some of the Greek dramas. He makes the reservation, however, that his changes shall not affect the outlines of Hamlet's character. In his desire to make the play over, Wilhelm is here, of course, reflecting the obsession for the classical which forms so strong an ingredient in Goethe's artistic philosophy. He is also following a method which, as we have seen, Heufeld and Schröder had already carried out in presenting their stage versions of the play. In

45. *Ibid.*, p. 75.
46. *Ibid.*, p. 76.
47. *Ibid.*, p. 76.

spite of many differences in detail, all three attempted to make *Hamlet* over into more of a "family tragedy."

It can hardly be an accident that in the very pages that contain this discussion of the play, Serlo, one of the characters makes a statement that applies directly to the Wilhelm-Goethe treatment of Hamlet:

Wenig Deutsche, und vielleicht nur wenige Menschen aller neuern Nationen, haben Gefühl für ein ästhetisches Ganzes; sie loben und tadeln nur stellenweise; sie entzücken sich nur stellenweise: . . .[48]

The superb poetry of isolated passages in *Hamlet* has so fascinated Goethe that critically he remains lost in "Irrgänge." Although he flatters himself that he achieves a view of the character as a whole, he has not done so. He has lost its dramatic reality completely—and that, in.spite of the fact that he was closely connected with the German theatre himself, and in 1809 was to produce the play. He is a Mendelssohn with a difference; for Mendelssohn did not attempt a general remoulding of Hamlet's character in terms of the one mood he enjoyed so much.

The result is that Goethe produced a Hamlet of his own creation, vividly and masterfully set forth. His prince could never walk the stage of any theatre, and present himself adequately to an audience. In fact, an audience even in Germany would be expecting something else,—not this sentimental and "psychologized" figure that represents a confusion of art and life. Where is the malcontent prince with his masculine, vigorous and even bawdy speech and action—with his amazing richness of incongruous character elements? Had not Goethe ever seen a German "Verwässerung" that gave in at least a partial degree illustration of the strange artistic alchemy through which this incongruity becomes histrionic unity? Goethe was acute enough to catch the truth of such an aesthetic miracle; but I do not believe he ever did.

Finally, then, it must be said of Goethe that like Richardson and Mackenzie in England, he did not understand the Elizabethan background from which Hamlet sprang. There is more excuse for Goethe, for they were English, and he was a foreigner. On the other hand, he was a genius; they were not. Yet it is probably just because he was a genius that he is not a great critic. In spite of his great gifts, he made an absolute and unhistorical interpretation. His criticism bears, therefore, most definitely the limitations that must follow in the wake of all such flagrant impressionism.[49]

48. *Ibid.*, p. 157.

49. That *Hamlet* the play, and Hamlet the character still possess much the same fascination for at least one contemporary German that they had for Goethe, and with partially similar results, is seen in Gerhart Hauptmann's two pieces, *Hamlet in Wit-*

After Goethe, two other late century critics deserve mention. One of them, Christopher Garve in 1796 has an interpretation that is even less convincing than Goethe's. Hamlet has a "thirst for revenge" that amounts to a monstrous passion. His whole psychology is imaginative and fantastic. In view of the fact that Garve accepts the madness as feigned, his subsequent discussion is puzzling.[50] He says that at times Hamlet really behaved like a man of shattered wits. One might ask Garve why he should not have behaved thus. Was he not taking such a part? The critic then goes on to say that there was no cause for real madness; and that, anyway, Hamlet played the part too well for that. Garve had all of the material here for an answer to his difficulties, but he lacked the subtlety to see his way clear. One wonders, again, whether this critic had ever seen an actual performance where he might have caught a sense of the genuine plausibility of Hamlet's character, madness and all.

It is possible that Friedrich Schlegel had read Goethe[51] before giving his estimate of Hamlet in *Die Griechen und die Römer,* of 1797. The central conception of each has points in common. Schlegel, however, succeeded in taking his own rather individual approach. He places Hamlet against a background of the universe. As far as man is concerned, there

tenberg, and his novel *Im Wirbel der Berufung,* 1936. The play takes up Hamlet's school career before the events chronicled in *Hamlet* start. The novel is more definitely autobiographical than *Wilhelm Meister.* It contains Hauptmann's own adaptation of Hamlet; the play is performed in the course of the story, and around it much of the action centers. As in Goethe, there is also a critical discussion of the play and hero. In the adaptation it is Hamlet, not Laertes, who bursts in upon the king and says, "Give me my father!" The usurpation motif is made an explicit part of the dramatic situation. Hauptmann believes that such an adjustment would restore the play to something closer to Shakespearian dimensions. His Hamlet is more masculine and active than Goethe's. It is hardly more Shakespearian. Like Goethe, he uses Shakespeare as a point of departure, and creates his own art in the process. And, one might add, like Goethe he thinks he is being a critic.

I am indebted to Professor F. L. Pfeiffer of the German Department in the University of Minnesota for calling to my attention this interesting contemporary material.

50. "Ueber die Rollen der Wahnwitzigen in Shakespears Schauspielen, und über den Charakter Hamlets ins besondre," in *Versuchte über verschiedene Gegenstände* . . . (Breslau, 1796), II, 468, ff.

51. In 1798 Schlegel discussed Goethe's novel in *Charakteristik der Meisterischen Lehrjahre von Goethe.* He seems to recognize the main trend of Goethe's critical method when he says, "Die . . . zerstreute Ansicht des Hamlet ist nicht sowohl Kritik als hohe Poesie." However, after saying this, and leading us to believe that he sees Goethe's criticism in a historical light, he gives no further indication that he does have any such conception of the matter. His attention in this critique is fixed upon Wilhelm's plans for remodelling *Hamlet,* rather than on his interpretation of the character of the prince. (Sämmtliche *Werke,* Vienna, 1822-25, X, 143-4.)

One must not forget, of course, the apt and telling verdict that Schlegel, in another connection, passed upon Goethe's critical capacities (*supra,* p. 105, note 36). But, in view of what Schlegel himself says concerning Hamlet in 1797, it seems quite doubtful whether he ever had a clear sense of the weakness of the Goethean interpretation.

is an eternal dissonance between him and the world he lives in. Tragedy is the picture of how this dissonance destroys him. As far as Hamlet is concerned, no gods need destroy him because he contained within himself the seeds of ruin. What was necessary in order that he may sink to defeat was that he be placed in a situation that would bring into play these internal forces. An unusual set of circumstances concentrated all the forces of his noble nature in his mind, and destroyed his active powers. The boundless disproportion between his thinking and active self, this paralysis from which Hamlet suffered, was the eternal dissonance made active and potent. His spirit breaks and is overwhelmed in "Ueberfluss von müssigem Verstand."

In the play, Schlegel says, every part radiates from and reacts back upon a central point. This point is Hamlet's character. The drama is the most typical of all Shakespeare's plays. What is here and there scattered in the others, appears in *Hamlet* as a whole. Its central impression is one of complete despair.[52] In another piece Schlegel speaks of the drama as "dieses fürchterliche Trauerspiel, welches zwischen Verbrechen und Wahnsinn schwankend, die sichtbare Erde wie einen verwilderten Garten der lüsternen Sünde, und ihr hohles Innres, als den Wohnsitz der Strafe und der Pein darstellt. . . ."[53]

As can be seen, both Goethe and Schlegel make the paralysis of Hamlet of central importance in the play. Thus Aristotle's dictum that in a tragedy action comes first as the conditioning factor, and character second, is reversed. Of the two, however, it is Schlegel who makes this un-Aristotelian position explicit.

If Schlegel's Hamlet were pictured as possessing a mind less "vacuous" and more contemplative, he might be considered prophetic of the philosophical prince developed by early nineteenth-century criticism as strikingly exemplified in Coleridge. As it is, however, in spite of the fact that he does not phrase his criticism directly in terms that make Hamlet a "soft prince," Schlegel's relationship seems with the past—with such critics as Goethe, Mackenzie and Richardson, rather than with the future.

Let me summarize the critical tendencies I have been describing. If we except the *Bestrafte Brudermord,* which may be termed an early abortive attempt to assimilate *Hamlet,* the views I have tabulated cover a span of little more than forty years. They represent the partial working out of three forces which must interact and blend if the Germans were to

52. *Friedrich Schlegel . . . seine Prosaischen Jugenschriften* (J. Minor, ed., Vienna, 1882), I, 106-7.
53. *Sämmtliche Werke,* X, 143.

assimilate the play in any form like its Shakespearian proportions. There must be an adequate knowledge of classical backgrounds. To this must be added some grasp of the Elizabethan period of English literature, especially of its dramatic aspects. And third, *Hamlet* itself must be perceived as part of a vigorous contemporary histrionic tradition.

It is not difficult to pass judgment upon the criticism of these forty years in the light of such a standard. The Germans did gain an impressive classical background. This allowed them to see the dogmas of French neo-classicism in their proper light; and gave them the opportunity to approach Hamlet without the crippling intellectual and emotional presuppositions of a Voltaire or a Gottsched. One less fortunate result of this interest in the classic was the numerous attempts to make *Hamlet* over into a "family tragedy."

Second—the difference between the translations of Wieland and those of A. W. Schlegel is one measure of what progress the Germans made in an assimilation of Elizabethan literature. But as one views the almost uncanny instinct with which the German critic, starting with Mendelssohn, gave his appreciation to an introspective Hamlet, he comes to the conclusion that forces were at work that made it impossible for a German to keep from exaggerating this alluring side of Hamlet's character. *Hamlet* as poetry and as isolated passage drew attention first, from inevitable emotional preference. The corrective knowledge that could be gained only by study of the play as a complete artistic entity came only after the earlier impressions were more or less fixed.

Third—there existed no histrionic tradition to do its part in correcting and making sane, interpretations that first took shape in the study. That tradition must grow. The early critics were compelled to read the script without assistance from the stage. And when a dramatic tradition, as embodied in the stage of Heufeld and Schröder, came into being, it offered no Danish prince of Shakespearian dimensions. What is more, from their pages one cannot tell that Garve or Friedrich Schlegel, or Goethe called upon even this tradition to help them. They did not see Hamlet in his dramatic proportions.

My survey of German criticism of the Eighteenth Century leads me to conclude that its contradictions and paradoxes were inevitable. They were the result of a complex of forces—aesthetic, social and racial—coming to focus upon the attempt of a people to understand a foreign poetic masterpiece; a masterpiece, I might add, that for several reasons offered a fruitful opportunity for critical misinterpretation.

PART THREE

The Nineteenth-Century Hamlet

7

English Histrionic Tradition:
Evolution and Decline, 1800-1821

INTRODUCTION

THE chronological divisions of this study are in one sense hardly more than a mere convenience for purposes of exposition. Such divisions, moreover, may become positively detrimental if they obscure the fact that *Hamlet* criticism presents a historical development —a continuity of ideas related organically to the general fabric of ideas of which it constitutes a part. Such an ordered development should be expected here. It happens, indeed, that in this case English tradition can be described with little more than passing reference to foreign ideas. *Hamlet* as a *cause célèbre* had just begun to penetrate the consciousness of English critics. Occasionally they were aware of a Voltaire or a Goethe,[1] but as a whole, their ideas, at least in so far as they assume relevance for us, seem admirably adapted for examination in isolation. Where I discover definite and traceable relationships, however, I shall record them.

This critical tradition, through 1821, may be treated under the two conventional headings—histrionic tradition and formal criticism. The material follows pretty well the lines of development that might be postulated of it in advance by anyone who has watched the growth of *Hamlet* criticism so far, and who also has some general knowledge of early nineteenth-century ideas, and the philosophical climate in which they grew.

It is a fact of common knowledge that the first three-quarters of the Nineteenth Century in England were such that its finest creative energies did not manifest themselves in the drama, or encourage the growth or even the continuity of a healthy dramatic tradition. When its choicest spirits were interested in the drama, they produced a *Manfred,* a magnificent but unstageable *Cenci,* or a *Strafford.* Or defying the theatre completely, they manifested themselves in a *Prometheus Unbound,* the

---

1. In the later Eighteenth Century, several English critics took notice, with considerable annoyance, of Voltaire's acid remarks on Shakespeare. In 1799, an English translation of the section on *Hamlet* in *Wilhelm Meister* appeared in the *Monthly Mirror,* 7, 235, ff.

only possible stage for which is the reader's imagination. It is a common-place to say that the reigning romanticism was of such a type as to foster histrionic futility in the creation of new plays. What is more, on the *Hamlet* stage tradition it cast a strange alchemizing influence, an influence that is part of our story here.

In my last chapter I spoke of a noticeable decline in the prestige and popularity of the acted Shakespearian plays, a phenomenon that Odell traces from 1776 on through the early years of the next century. *Hamlet* in particular, had its part in this process of histrionic decline and change.

But even in such a period of "decline" the *Hamlet* stage tradition gave unmistakable evidence of a continued vitality. That this is true may be seen in the succession of minor actors who took the role in the first years of the century. Theatrical records mention Brunton in 1800; Young, Siddons and Lacy in 1801; Cooke again, and also an unidentified "young gentleman" in 1802; Charles Kemble in 1803; Master Betty in 1805; Alexander Rae at Bath in 1806; and Henry Johnston in 1807.[2] Of these portrayals, at least those of Charles Kemble and Master Betty had momentary success. In fact Master Betty created such a popular furore as to curtail seriously the gate receipts of the famous J. P. Kemble himself. The fame of this young actor reached the rural ears of Wordsworth, who wrote to Sir Charles Beaumont for information concerning him. It is recorded that the younger Pitt adjourned the House of Commons so that its members might see the boy prodigy perform the role.[3]

With reference to these minor actors, it is generally their existence itself as Hamlets that is important as evidence, testifying as it does to a continued popular demand for the play. To such evidence must be added, of course, a record of the successes, both aesthetic and material, of the great actors—J. P. Kemble, Edmund Kean and Macready.

Of Kemble in Hamlet, Dutton could say in 1800: "Such, indeed, are the unrivalled beauties of Mr. Kemble's personification of the character, that, frivolous and debauched as is the public taste, the Play never fails to attract a crowded audience."[4] In 1814, Kean's first appearance on the London stage in the role brought him £660.[5] Of Macready, the third great actor, we have a different type of testimony. From his own words it

2. See Harold Child, "The Stage-History of *Hamlet*," in *Hamlet* (ed. J. D. Wilson, Cambridge, 1934), p. lxxxvii; T. Dutton, *The Dramatic Censor* (London, 1801), III, 158; Leigh Hunt, *Critical Essays* (London, 1807), pp. 40-1; *Monthly Mirror*, 10, 245, ff; 11, 412 and 419-20; 12, 261-4; 15, 345; *Theatrical Inquisitor and Monthly Mirror*, 5, 276-7.

3. E. de Selincourt, ed., *The Early Letters of William and Dorothy Wordsworth, 1787, 1805* (Oxford, 1935), p. 425.

4. *Op. cit.*, III, 135.

5. Phelps, *op. cit.*, pp. 12-13.

can be gathered that his success in 1835 was only the culmination of a long provincial "rehearsal" that started in Newcastle in 1811.[6]

To this background of facts demonstrating a continued vitality in the acted play, it is now necessary to add the data that tell another story, one of lessened prestige and decline. Between 1776 and 1817, *Hamlet* did not appear at all during 13 seasons at Drury Lane, and during 8 seasons at Covent Garden.[7] The remark of an unknown writer in a theatrical journal is indication of a change in aesthetic valuations and theatre-going habits. He says, "Such plays as *Hamlet* and *Macbeth* are but little calculated for the multitude."[8] The last few years of the period 1800-1821 were the beginning of what Odell calls "the leaderless age."[9] With the retirement of J. P. Kemble, Kean was the only actor to achieve distinguished success in the part. It is probably of significance also, that for these later years there seems to be no such abundance of minor Hamlets as make so interesting the first decade of the century.[10] All in all, there is a decided lack of positive evidence that might aid us in viewing the period as other than one of histrionic decline for either the Shakespearian drama in general, or *Hamlet* in particular.

Fortunately there is a certain type of direct evidence that assists us in sketching more fully this less favorable side of *Hamlet* stage history for the years 1800-1821. Surely there were no more potent moulders of aesthetic opinion during these years than were Wordsworth, Lamb, Coleridge and Hazlitt. Any expression of ideas on the subject from these men is of high importance. Such a record, including a substantiating utterance from the pen of Leigh Hunt, exists. These critics in most unequivocal terms display either an ignorance of, or a downright antipathy for stage performance of *Hamlet*.

The ideas of these five men fall into two divisions. Wordsworth and Hunt take the position that the portrayal of Hamlet is "above" contemporary acting genius. Wordsworth in 1805 writes to Sir George Beaumont, concerning Master Betty:

I wish much to have your further opinion of the young Roscius, above all of his "Hamlet." It is certainly impossible that he should understand the character,

6. *Ibid.*, p. 18.
7. Odell, *op. cit.*, II, 19.
8. *Theatrical Inquisitor and Monthly Mirror* (1814?), 5, 403.
9. Odell, *op. cit.*, II, 117, ff.
10. The management of Covent Garden could furnish no better a Hamlet than Young's when they reopened their newly decorated house in 1817. (See Hazlitt, "Young's Hamlet," *Times*, Sept. 9, 1817, *Works*, ed. Waller and Glover, London 1903, XI, 394-5.) For Hazlitt's amusing account of another minor performer, see *Ibid.*, VIII, 480. One other now forgotten actor is "Mr. Montgomery from Dublin" who played Hamlet at Dover, in 1816. (See *Theatrical Inquisitor and Monthly Mirror*, 8, 320.)

that is the composition of the character. . . . I never saw *Hamlet* acted myself, nor do I know what kind of a play they make of it. . . . They are both [Hamlet and Richard III] characters far, far above the abilities of any actor I have ever seen. Henderson was before my time, and, of course, Garrick.[11]

And Leigh Hunt in 1807, after describing his unfavorable reaction to Elliston's performance, says:

The character of Hamlet however seems beyond the genius of the present stage, and I do not see that its personification will be easily attained by future stages; for its actor must unite the most contrary as well as the most assimilating powers of comedy and tragedy, and to unite these powers in their highest degree belongs to the highest genius only.[12]

It is clear that neither Wordsworth nor Hunt had any high opinion of the "present stage," nor of the histrionic ability of any existing Hamlet. Their opinion concerning the contemporary stage is of course in agreement with the facts as we know them. Surely, however, there are deeper motivations beneath the words of each. As concerns Wordsworth, what these motivations were, we can only guess. He at no time set forth what he regarded as the "composition" of Hamlet's character. We can know, however, that any Hamlet he enjoyed can have had very little relevance to the actual stage, for he obviously felt no interest in it, and displays total ignorance of what a histrionic Hamlet might be like.

On the other hand, Hunt's opinion we may respect, for he sets forth his bill of particulars covering the stage Hamlet that would satisfy him:

It must be the praise of a man, who shall possess a genius capable of more than the art of acting, to personate Hamlet, the gallant, the philosophical, the melancholy Hamlet, that amiable inconsistent, who talked when he should have acted and acted when he should not even have talked, who with a bosom wrung with sensibility was unfeeling, and in his very passion for justice unjust, who in his misery had leisure for ridicule and in his revenge for benevolence, who in the most melancholy abstraction never lost the graces of mind or the elegancies of manner, natural in the midst of error. But let me not attempt to describe the indescribable.[13]

With due allowance for Hunt's romantic hyperbole here, and for the obvious influence upon him of those critics who from Francis Gentleman on down had been setting forth Hamlet as "inconsistent," it is to this critic's credit that he persisted in reading the *Hamlet* score in dramatic terms. In pronouncing unfavorable judgment on the contemporary stage, it is possible of course that its ineptitude was incidental to his opinion— in other words, that no performance of *Hamlet* could have satisfied him.

11. de Selincourt, *op. cit.*, pp. 489-90.
12. *Critical Essays*, pp. 182-3.
13. *Ibid.*, pp. 40-1.

However, his attitude toward the problem of a contemporary Hamlet is clear.

Lamb, Coleridge and Hazlitt form the second group of critics whose point of view is most relevant here. It will be wise to deal here merely with the downright *fact*—their undisgused antipathy to a stage *Hamlet* of any kind, and their corresponding preference for a play to be enjoyed in the calm privacy of the study. To go further than this at the moment would involve a discussion of the whole critical attitude of each writer.

Concerning Lamb, let me say only this. He saw all of the acted plays of Shakespeare as a pastime to be énjoyed only in the thoughtless days of youth. For him now in his maturity, a stage *Hamlet* meant little more than a gesticulating, declamatory prince, mouthing a "to be" soliloquy. It is evident that the acted play had less than no savor for him. His attention had been turned toward the study, where he had found the Hamlet really to his liking.[14] In my next chapter, I shall set forth at some length the nature of Lamb's full criticism.

For Coleridge, one illuminating excerpt from a newspaper report of his lectures delivered at Bristol in 1813-14, will serve:

He never saw any of Shakespeare's plays performed, but with a degree of pain, disgust, and indignation. He had seen Mrs. Siddons as Lady, and Kemble as Macbeth:—these might be the Macbeths of the Kembles, but they were not the Macbeths of Shakespeare. He was therefore not grieved at the enormous size and monopoly of the theatres, which naturally produced many bad and but few good actors; and which drove Shakespeare from the stage, to find his proper place in the heart and in the closet, where he sits with Milton, enthroned on a double-headed Parnassus; and with whom everything that was admirable, everything praiseworthy, was to be found.[15]

Hazlitt, the last of the three, makes specific reference to the stage play, in the following terms: "We do not like to see our author's plays acted, and least of all HAMLET. There is no play that suffers so much in being transferred to the stage."[16]

In such uncompromising terms as these, Lamb, Coleridge and Hazlitt put themselves on record. What I would stress as of immediate importance here is the fact that it is in such a climate of ideas as this that we must set the stage history of *Hamlet* for the years 1800-1821. Such antipathy may well threaten the histrionic integrity of the play, in both

14. Lamb's ideas are set forth in his famous essay of 1811: *On the Tragedies of Shakespeare, Considered with Reference to their fitness for Stage Representation.*
15. T. M. Raysor, *Coleridge's Shakespearean Criticism*, (Cambridge, Mass., 1930), II, 278-9.
16. From "Hamlet" in *Characters of Shakespear's Plays* (*Works*, I, 237).

the years with which we are dealing and in the later century. This conflict between adherents of stage and closet had reverberations that extend far beyond the year 1821.

The ground has now been cleared for a presentation of the last and most interesting question with which this chapter has to deal. What kind of a Danish Prince appeared on the English stage during these years? Was he a simple continuation of histrionic interpretations in harmony with the eighteenth-century tradition, albeit in a new period when the importance and prestige of the Shakespearian stage were declining; and when romantic closet interpretations were creating even more than in the late Eighteenth Century, a type of prince impossible of realization on any stage? Or were there other changes motivated by this new criticism?

The answer to these questions may be found in records that set forth the stage tradition as developed by three actors—Charles Kemble, J. P. Kemble, and Edmund Kean. Of the numerous other Hamlets who took the stage during these years, I shall make no mention here.

Charles Kemble, brother of the more famous John Philip, and father of Fanny, is deserving of mention for one reason. He maintained that Hamlet was really mad, and acted the prince accordingly. We have no evidence, however, that his prince elicited more than passing approval from the public. His daughter says of him:

I have acted Ophelia three times with my father, and each time in that beautiful scene where his madness and his love gush forth together like a torrent swollen with storms, that bears a thousand blossoms on its stormy waters, I have experienced such deep emotion as hardly to be able to speak. The exquisite tenderness of his voice, the wild compassion and forlorn pity of his looks, bestowing that on others which of all others he most needed; the melancholy restlessness, the bitter self-scorning; every shadow of expression and intonation was so full of the mingled anguish that the human heart is capable of enduring, that my eyes scarce fixed on his ere they filled with tears, and long before the scene was over, the letters and jewel-cases I was tendering to him were wet with them.[17]

In spite of such eloquent testimony, one feels that this Hamlet was too far off the beaten track to achieve any marked success.

I have already described the early career of J. P. Kemble. It is now important that his further record, this time as a nineteenth-century actor, be examined. Did Kemble, because of either the intrinsic nature of his histrionic genius, or because of the demands of a changing taste or critical temper, alter his portrayal of the role? If so, how far did the change go?

After the lapse of more than a hundred years, the answer to these

17. Phelps, *op. cit.*, pp. 11-12.

questions is not easy. Nevertheless, records do point to some evolution in the character of Kemble's Hamlet. For one thing, this careful actor himself would never have been satisfied with a static interpretation of the role. The very nature of his genius demanded a continued study of the part, a refinement upon refinement, a dynamic virtuosity.

One substantial item of concrete evidence is Kemble's acting version of the play as published in the collected edition of 1815. The cuts seem to have been made with the purpose of speeding up the action of the play. Odell says of it:

Kemble made of it a polished gem of dramatic intensity; much of the fine poetry is gone; also, as usual, all the Norweyan business, Polonius's advice to Laertes, etc.; but the whole thing moves with splendid vigour to its conclusion.[18]

Another effect of Kemble's changes was in the direction of a greater classical decorum throughout. He eliminated many of Hamlet's wild and whirling words to Horatio, both from the ghost scene in the first act, and from the dialogue after the play-scene.[19] It can be seen that such changes are the very ones that Charles Kemble could not afford to make, for the effect would be to make the hero too sane and balanced a prince.

Kemble's changes in the script and in interpretation seem ultimately to have been motivated by the intrinsic nature of his peculiar unification of the role. I have already commented upon the fact that this Hamlet did not have the vivacity and aliveness of Garrick's. That great actor achieved an inner unity that preserved Hamlet's many-sidedness, his infinite variety; Kemble's unity was more external, more a matter of mannerism and appearance. Most decidedly he threw a "manner" over the part. This was noticed by Hazlitt, who says of him:

There is a perpetual undulation of feeling in the character of Hamlet; but in Mr. Kemble's acting, "there was neither variableness nor shadow of turning." He played it like a man in armour, with a determined inveteracy of purpose, in one undeviating straight line . . . remote from the natural grace and indolent susceptibility of the character.[20]

This comment of Hazlitt's, along with others from several sources permits one to say that the temper of the times had its effect upon Kemble's portrayal. Contemporary critics noticed the fact that he knew how to set forth characters that were dominated by one passion or feeling. He seems to have given this role a meditative, ruminatory, sepulchral cast,—a col-

18. *Op. cit.*, II, 54-5.
19. Child, *op. cit.*, p. lxxxv-lxxxvi.
20. "Mr. Kemble's Retirement," the *Times*, June 25, 1817 (*Works*, VIII, 377). The estimate of another critic, Richard Cumberland is in substantial agreement with that of Hazlitt here. See comment in *Theatrical Inquisitor* (1813), 2, 100.

oring which may well be termed romantic. An illuminating bit of evidence along this line is the Lawrence portrait of Kemble. Its keynote is one of sepulchral melancholy.[21] Boaden says of him: "His person seemed to be finely formed, and his manners princely; but on his brow hung the weight of some 'intollerable wo.' "[22] A paragraph or two further on, the same biographer shows definitely that he is thinking of Kemble's acting in terms of a prince who had lost some of his heroic characteristics. Describing the manner in which Hamlet should utter the panegyric on his father, beginning "He was a man," Boaden speaks of Kemble's "flood of tenderness," his tears—and continues: "I know the almost stoical firmness with which others declaim this passage; . . . but I must be excused, if I prefer the melting softness of Kemble, as more germane to "the weakness and melancholy of Hamlet."[23]

In glancing over the evidence I have been reviewing, one might be impelled to question its objectivity. One might wonder whether Kemble wished to portray a romantic or unheroic prince. What is the genuinely histrionic *Ding an sich* at issue here?[24] How can Odell's reading of the evidence as pointing to the acted play as a "polished gem of dramatic intensity" be reconciled with the words just quoted from Boaden, or, for that matter, with a surprising passage in somewhat similar vein from the pen of Hazlitt the year after Kemble's death?[25] Of Boaden it may be said that, writing after Kemble's death, he makes no distinction between the actor's early and later renditions of the part. Of Hazlitt, that it would be critically unwise to see a significance in his words that does not take into account the obviously casual and impressionistic nature of his various pronouncements. Together, the latter's verdicts do not form any firm unity.

21. Percy Fitzgerald, *The Kembles* (London, 1871), II, 369-70; and Child, *op. cit.*, lxxxiv.
22. *Memoirs of the Life of John Philip Kemble, Esq.*, p. 53.
23. *Ibid.*, p. 55.
24. For our purposes there is of course no such aesthetic entity apart from the mind and imagination of the spectator who receives it. Valuable as evidence from Boaden and Hazlitt is, one wishes for the verdict of the average theater-goer of the times. From a theatrical point of view, his word would bear definite weight. For Garrick we have such a verdict; but for the later Hamlet of Kemble, unfortunately we do not.
25. That year, Hazlitt wrote:
> There he was, the sweet, the graceful, the gentlemanly Hamlet. The scholar's eye shone in him with learned beauty; the soldier's spirit decorated his person. . . . The beauty of his performance was its retrospective air: its intensity and abstraction. His youth seemed delivered over to sorrow. . . . Later actors have played the part with more energy, walked more in the sun—dashed more at effects, piqued themselves more on the girth of a foil; but Kemble's *sensible, lonely Hamlet* has not been surpassed.   (quoted by Fitzgerald, *The Kembles*, II, 370-1).

The matter may be summed up thus: Kemble undoubtedly did make some concessions to the tastes of his audiences. However, when one speaks of his later Hamlet as "sepulchral," "romantic," etc., one must take heavily into account the intellectual and emotional bias of the critic who offers the evidence.[26] Surely for anyone who regards Kemble's career as a whole, with some feeling for the nature of the *Hamlet* theatrical tradition, it would appear unnecessary that this nineteenth-century prince be seen as "weak," nor even so "melancholy" as to obliterate all other character features. The evidence does not make such an interpretation necessary.

Edmund Kean, who first appeared on the London stage as Hamlet in 1814, offered a marked contrast to Kemble. His acting of the part might be termed a "return to nature." He was not declamatory, nor "noble," nor classical. He did, however, put again on the stage a prince of impassioned sensation, whose inner life was a kaleidoscope of impressions. James Hackett reports him in these terms:

He seemed to me . . . more ably to illustrate the soul of Hamlet than any actor whom I have seen in the part; its intellectuality and sensitiveness were wrought into transparent prominency; every particle of its satire was given with extraordinary pungency; its sentiment was on each occasion very impressively uttered, and the melancholy was plaintively toned and sympathy-winning; the action was full and natural and never ungraceful, the passion heart-stirring, and the poetry was read with correct emphasis and a nice ear to rhythmical measure.[27]

He was an expert and graceful fencer, a devout son to his father, and a tender lover to Ophelia. He did not follow Kemble in toning down the wildness of the prince's whirling words.

In fact, it was the contrast which his interpretation offered to Kemble's that gave Kean the cue for his success. As Molloy says:

The force and fervour, earnestness and passion of the Drury Lane tragedian brought his [Kemble's] cold and pompous, stiff and ponderous manner into sharp contrast.[28]

Another critic and biographer, with Kemble in mind, says:

He did not, in his appearance indeed, precisely answer our previous notions of

26. At least one critic, Gilliland, describes moments in Kemble's performance when he gave the role a touch of frenzy, with an implication of weakness. The actor's convulsed features are described in much the same manner as Macready's were to be, later (See *A Dramatic Synopsis*, London, 1804, pp. 121-2). However, Gilliland himself is so little worthy of critical notice, that his evidence cannot be given any marked weight.

27. Phelps, *op. cit.*, p. 14.

28. J. F. Molloy, *The Life and Adventures of Edmund Kean, Tragedian* (London, 1888), I, 178-9.

Hamlet; because, by a strange error, we had been accustomed to associate with the character, a grave, noble, attenuated figure,—the ideal personification of grief; whereas our son "is fat, and scant of breath." However this might have been, Kean represented ably the better part of the princely Dane,—the intellectual part. We beheld, or rather felt, the real sadness of his soul, the nobility of his nature, his filial affection, his spirit lost in starry contemplation,—in abstraction 'from the things that be.' We saw "the rapt soul sitting in the eyes."[29]

Indeed, one cannot go through the old records without coming to the conviction that Kean had offered a new and markedly different reading of the Shakespearian script; that he had put upon the stage a more valid and authentic prince than theatre-goers had seen since Garrick; that, in fact the spirit of that great actor had been incarnated anew in a vital, albeit quite individual portrayal. Still another critic, in words of unreserved approval says of his portrayal:

In short, it did not on the first glance seize immediately on the outward eye, but it drew out upon it more and more fixedly the inward observation of the mind, which it awed into a solemn attention. Disdaining to employ any adventitious aids in his interpretation of the character, he played it to the understanding, not to the eye; he never for a moment lost sight of the fact that he was clothed in the sable garb of a man so deeply immersed in the soundless depths of a divine philosophy as to become indifferent to the agitations of the surface, and whose emotions, welling up spontaneously from the heart, could not be faithfully expressed by the dry pedantry and indissoluble hardness which characterized Kemble's performance of the part. In Hamlet, which he was ever inclined to regard as his best character, Kean threw open the flood-gates of his riches, learning, and discrimination; and while his performance displayed the richest hues of imagination and the finest impulses of the human mind, it was interwoven with flowers scattered so profusely about as to become permanently enshrined among the memories of every mind which is dedicated to the reception of the product of undeniable genius, depth, and originality.[30]

It is pertinent now to ask this question: In what way can the literary historian connect this attractive Hamlet, so different from Kemble's, with the times? He was surely not a weak procrastinating prince. Nor was he a fit subject for a Lawrence portrait. And, one must admit the force of the evidence that in spite of the fact that Mrs. Garrick found some of his utterances "too tame," he was appreciably more like the great actor than was Kemble. The key to this question may be found, I think, in Hazlitt's criticism of him. That critic found Kean's performance full of "sharp angles and abrupt starts; too splenetic and rash." He said of him that "He threw a severity, approaching to virulence, into the common observations and answers."[31]

29. Bryan W. Procter, *The Life of Edmund Kean* (London, 1835), II, 62-3.
30. F. W. Hawkins, *The Life of Edmund Kean* (London, 1869), I, 178-9.
31. "Hamlet" in *Characters of Shakespear's Plays* (*Works*, I, 237).

It is evident that what Hazlitt was objecting to was the fact that Kean had found again one element in the varied potency of Hamlet's words, an element that could be very displeasing to some nineteenth-century men. That quality was malcontent bite and "virulence."[32] In abandoning any such outwardness of interpretation as Kemble's, in refusing to cast over the part any manner, Kean was under the necessity of achieving an inner unity that would bind together all of the varied phases of a complex character creation. With all due credit to this great actor, he could not quite succeed in the task,—or at least he could not succeed for such a spectator as Hazlitt. Hazlitt, schooled in almost fifty years of closet criticism, could not furnish his share of the actor-spectator rapport necessary to allow an actor to create successfully a complex character like Shakespeare's Hamlet. It seems sound to say that others in Kean's audiences must have been in the same predicament. Besides the ravages of closet criticism, two hundred years and over had passed since *Hamlet* had first been staged. One can hardly imagine an early audience being too critical of a prince who was "splenetic and rash"! Considerations such as these would lead one to believe that the modern critic who calls Kean a "romantic genius type of actor," who played the part as a "sequence of impressive moments," is right.[33] The times were not propitious for the appearance of a Hamlet who could make a critic like Hazlitt accept all of his varied and kaleidescopic "moments" as part of the possible experience of one mortal man. Thus, one must admit that Shakespeare's greatest play could not be realized in its histrionic fullness and entirety on the stage of the early Nineteenth Century. However, if Kean had had Kemble's chance of being a close successor to Garrick, he might have been more potent that was that actor in protecting the acted tradition from the insidious erosions of romantic criticism.

Such is the histrionic picture that one must keep in mind if he wishes to see the *Hamlet* criticism of this period in correct perspective. All three of the performances just described in detail bear most definitely the marks of the social milieu of which they were a part. None can be properly understood unless it be remembered that the role was interpreted in a period of histrionic decline. The vitality and popular appeal of the play, even in this period, show the force of a two-hundred-year tradition. Change, however, was in the air. The Kemble and Kean Hamlets each, bear impressive witness to this fact.

32. A recent biographer and critic brings out the fact that Kean "was drawn by natural sympathy to sharp, acid, double-dealing knaves, or to heroes who are possessed by tempest-like passions." (H. N. Hillebrand, *Edmund Kean* (New York, 1933), p. 133.

33. Child, *op. cit.*, lxxxviii.

8

English Tradition: Formal Criticism, 1800-1821

OF the English critical landscape during these years, it may be said at once that there was one major tendency, and one only. That tendency was in its most important intention and result anti-histrionic and definitely romantic. It was a historical continuation of a movement that started with Richardson and extended far beyond the year 1821. Besides the major critics there were a number of minor figures who do not fall into any one category. I shall speak of these in passing. Their inclusion is necessary to complete the critical roster.

These years give evidence of no genuine advance in historical perspective. Along such lines what truth is achieved was the result of an occasional lucky impressionism. There was no advance built upon surer foundations than those constructed by Steevens and Malone. For *Hamlet*, one lucky discovery was added to historical data during the last years covered by this study. In 1821 the First Quarto of the play was brought to light. It took many years, however, before this valuable document was put to profitable use by Shakespearian scholarship.

In my succeeding discussion of English criticism, I shall treat: first, the minor figures of the early century; second, the romantic critics whose ideas form the fundamental contribution for these years; and third, the miscellaneous lesser critics who appeared in the years 1817-1821, offering an interpretation of synthesis and anti-climax.

THE MINOR CRITICS: 1800-1807

The critics of these years who wrote before Coleridge, Lamb and Hazlitt had become, for our purposes articulate, are an unexciting lot.[1] Their ideas are heavily derivative and synthetic. Clichés were the order of the day. The one critical method that was congenial to such writers was an intellectual hospitality in which truism, quotation and painful inconsistency fit together into one pattern.

Dibdin in 1800, devoted over ten pages of his voluminous *Complete History of the Stage* to a rambling discussion of *Hamlet*.[2] He likes the

---

1. For the whole period 1800-1821, six of these critics, Dibdin, Gilliland, Leigh Hunt, Oxberry, Campbell and Boswell, are not mentioned by Ralli at all.
2. III, 54, ff.

play but feels he must admit the fact that it possesses many blemishes. In true eighteenth-century style he catalogues these blemishes, but then proceeds with gusto to set forth its "beauties." It is evident that he considered Hamlet himself heroic. Because of the fact that this critic confused Hamlet and Shakespeare so thoroughly, it is impossible to make much from his direct remarks on the prince.

Thomas Gilliland's remarks on Kemble's *Hamlet,* dated 1804, are phrased as a tissue of reminiscences dating back to Cibber. In spite of the fact that Kemble's portrayal of the role, as Gilliland describes it, was not that of an active prince in the full Shakespearian tradition,[3] the implication of this critic's approach is that he interprets him as the traditional hero.

The year after Gilliland, E. H. Seymour set forth his views. He was just as decidedly unoriginal, but in another direction. In justice to him, however, let me add that he had an active desire to wrestle with the problem of *Hamlet* in its historical relations. But he could not achieve results. He gets little further than a condemnation of Steevens' worst crudities, and the statement that if Shakespeare had had the proper chance to revise his play, many of the items that bother the puzzled reader would have been eliminated. It is clear that Seymour was a reader rather than a spectator, for he says of the prince:

Shakespeare never meant to display in Hamlet a pattern of purity or insipid perfection, in which no one would be found to feel an interest; but rather, on the contrary, a striking example of human frailty; a young man with noble propensities and estimable habits, contemplative, learned, and wise, but at the same time passionate, irresolute, and capricious.[4]

Henry Pye's work completed the critical production of these minor figures for the decade. In 1807 he published his *Comments on the Commentators of Shakespear.* Suffice it to say of him that his remarks hardly rise above a condemnation of Steevens and a partial approval of Malone.[5] Like Seymour he struggled with problems of historical interpretation but could not make genuine critical advance over his predecessors. He, like Dibdin and Gilliland, implies that he considers Hamlet heroic and energetic.

Intrinsically insignificant as the work of these four men is, one may find in it a measure of value. For one thing, these men probably represent the point of view toward *Hamlet* of the average critical intellect in

3. *A Dramatic Synopsis,* pp. 121-4; see also *supra,* p. 123, note 26.
4. *Remarks, Critical Conjectural, and Explanatory,* II, 204-5.
5. Of the various minutiae that claim Pye's attention, the most interesting is the problem of the king and the dumb-show. Here he anticipates Dover Wilson by over a century.

this decade before the great romantic critics finally turned the tide for many years to come toward that of a reader's psychology formulated almost exclusively in the study. Hopelessly confused and derivative as their ideas are, three out of four of them seem to have looked upon Hamlet as the traditional heroic prince.[6]

It will be illuminating to compare the critical tone of these men with that of several others who appeared in the closing years of the twenty-one I am here covering. These latter put forth their ideas after the romantic critics had made their main pronouncements on the play.

THE MAJOR MOVEMENT: 1807-1821

Lamb, Coleridge and Hazlitt brought to virtual completeness the English romantic position on *Hamlet*. Of the others who might have written illuminating remarks, only two need mention—Wordsworth and Keats; and their remarks are very slight indeed. Because the ideas that shaped this body of criticism are closely related to the mental and emotional patterns that gave the period its dominant coloring, the romantic Hamlet I am about to describe has a deep significance for any student of nineteenth-century literary history.

It is disappointing to find that apart from the most casual of references Wordsworth had nothing to say on the play or its hero. Nor is it possible to infer his attitude from any general remarks. One may surmise that he shared with his fellow romantics their habitual attitude of idolatrous eulogy. In one of his prefaces, he speaks of Shakespeare's "almost omnipotent genius."[7] We feel instinctively that he might have developed a critical philosophy concerning *Hamlet* similar to that expressed by his fellow romantics. We have already seen that he considered Shakespeare and *Hamlet* beyond the capacities of the contemporary stage;[8] and that indeed, he cared so little for the Shakespearian stage that he had never seen *Hamlet* performed. His only other remark of interest is one recorded by the Bishop of Lincoln, in which he says: "There is more mind in 'Hamlet' than in any other play, more knowledge of human nature. The first act is incomparable."[9] Wordsworth's remark here concerning the first act involves the subject of high dramatic tension; and may easily be an echo of Coleridge's brilliant and suggestive words on the same subject. All in all, one cannot find in Wordsworth much evidence of careful thought on the general subject of *Hamlet*.

6. One other who saw Hamlet in traditional terms was Thomas Holcroft. See his "The Art of Acting," in the *Theatrical Recorder* (1806), 2, 44-6.

7. In the "Essay, Supplementary to the Preface," 1815.

8. *Supra,* pp. 117-18.

9. A. B. Grosart, ed., *Prose Works* (London, 1876), III, 460.

Keats says just enough to tantalize us. He had proved *Hamlet* "upon the pulses." It was Hamlet's grief and melancholy that came home upon him, for in a letter written at the time of the desperate illness of his brother Tom, he says: "You will know exactly my meaning when I say, that now I shall relish Hamlet more than I ever have done."[10] In another letter Keats says:

The middle age of Shakespeare was all clouded over; his days were not more happy than Hamlet's who is perhaps more like Shakespeare himself in his common every day Life than any other of his Characters.[11]

The third reference is the most appealing of all, for it occurs in Keats' last letter to Fanny Brawne, dated August 1820. Here he equates his own mental stress and agony with Hamlet's:

Shakespeare always sums up matters in the most sovereign manner. Hamlet's heart was full of such Misery as mine is when he said to Ophelia "Go to a Nunnery, go, go!" Indeed I should like to give up the matter at once—I should like to die. I am sickened at the brute world which you are smiling with. I hate men, and women more.[12]

It is of course impossible to build up from such slight references any detailed picture of Hamlet as Keats saw him. He chose one aspect and one only for comment or allusion,— and this aspect was the one that, by analogy with his own situation, came home to his heart. This prince like himself he conceived as having tasted the worst realities of suffering and defeat. For if the Hamlet of the nunnery scene is like the Keats of the August letter to Fanny Brawne, he was indeed an anguished and helpless victim against whom life had done its worst. The "paralysis" that seems here suggested is what we have learned to see as typical of the romantic Hamlet.

LAMB

Each of the three great romantic critics displays, of course, a family likeness to the others. There is in each also an individuality of critical temperament that stamps his position as different from that of the other two. I desire as best I can, to capture these critical individualities for my pages.

Lamb's position on Hamlet is set forth in two documents: his *Tales of Shakespeare* of 1807; and his arresting essay of 1811, already mentioned.[13]

The account of 1807, written in collaboration with his sister as part of a book for children, must represent Lamb's early and derivative conception

10. M. B. Forman, ed., *The Letters of John Keats* (New York, 1935), pp. 141-2.
11. *Ibid.*, pp. 346-7.
12. *Ibid.*, p. 503.
13. *Supra*, p. 119, note 14.

of the prince. Its dominant coloring is sentimental. In harmony with the method used by earlier romantic critics, Lamb and his sister made Hamlet a psychological study. His "inconsistency" vanishes. The motivations that Shakespeare left obscure are straightened out. For example, strong guards again surround the king as in the older accounts. Sad to say, however, this addition of the more primitive external difficulty does not make the story these writers tell crystal clear. They still feel vividly the problem of Hamlet's procrastination; and proceed to motivate it at the expense of his heroic character by giving him sentimental scruples:

The presence of the queen, Hamlet's mother, who was generally with the king, was a restraint upon his purpose, which he could not break through.

Besides, the very circumstance that the usurper was his mother's husband filled him with some remorse, and still blunted the edge of his purpose.

The mere act of putting a fellow-creature to death was in itself odious and terrible to a disposition naturally so gentle as Hamlet's was.

His very melancholy, and . . . dejection of spirits . . . produced an irresoluteness and wavering of purpose, . . .

he could not help having some scruples upon his mind, whether the spirit which he had seen was indeed his father, or whether it might not be the devil, who . . . might have assumed his father's shape only to take advantage of his weakness and his melancholy, to drive him to the doing of so desperate an act as murder.[14]

The weak and unimpressive Hamlet who emerges from the quotations just given represents Lamb's early view. Another and quite different prince appears in the essay of 1811. Besides representing Lamb's mature Hamlet, it phrases once for all what may be called almost the official romantic point of view toward the problem of a proper critical approach to both Shakespeare and *Hamlet*.

In an earlier chapter I have spoken of the fact that each of the great romantic critics displays an antipathy toward the Shakespearian stage. It is now time to examine more precisely the motivation for such an attitude. In his essay of 1811, Lamb says:

It may seem a paradox, but I cannot help being of opinion that the plays of Shakespeare are less calculated for performance on a stage, than those of almost any other dramatist whatever. Their distinguished excellence is a reason that they should be so. There is so much in them, which comes not under the province of acting, with which eye, and tone, and gesture, have nothing to do.[15]

In these words Lamb set forth his credo. It is other than histrionic excellences that Lamb found the distinguishing feature of Shakespeare. In-

14. Everyman Edit., p. 280.
15. *Works* (ed. Lucas, London, 1903), I, 98, ff.

deed he went so far as to say that the acted plays have no other aesthetic function than to provide enjoyment for the thoughtless days of youth. Moreover,

dearly do we pay all our life after for this juvenile pleasure, this sense of distinctness. When the novelty is past, we find to our cost that instead of realizing an idea, we have only materialized and brought down a fine vision to the standard of flesh and blood. We have let go a dream, in quest of an unattainable substance.

How cruelly this operates upon the mind, to have its free conceptions thus crampt and pressed down to the measure of a strait-lacing actuality, may be judged from that delightful sensation of freshness, with which we turn to those plays of Shakespeare which have escaped being performed, and to those passages in the acting plays of the same writer which have happily been left out in performance.[16]

Here indeed an unadulterated romantic attitude speaks forth. This critic has abandoned the stage. As he says further along in the same passage, he dislikes especially the ranting and elocution which "withers and blows upon a fine passage," but one can easily see that his objection to the acted plays was more fundamental than that. Even a Garrick would chill the artistic sensibilities of this critic. He wished no "strait-lacing actuality" ever again to trouble or limit his "free conceptions!"

It was from such credo as this that Lamb's mature conception of Hamlet grew. The irresolute, gentle wavering prince of the *Tales* now took on other shades of emphasis:

But Hamlet himself—what does he suffer meantime by being dragged forth as a public schoolmaster, to give lectures to the crowd! Why, nine parts in ten of what Hamlet does, are transactions between himself and his moral sense, they are the effusions of his solitary musings, which he retires to holes and corners and the most sequestered parts of the palace to pour forth; or rather, they are the silent meditations with which his bosom is bursting, reduced to *words* for the sake of the reader, who must else remain ignorant of what is passing there. These profound sorrows, these light-and-noise abhorring ruminations, which the tongue scarce dares to utter to deaf walls and chambers, how can they be represented by a gesticulating actor, who comes and mouths them out before an audience, making four hundred people his confidants at once . . . he must accompany them with his eye, he must insinuate them into his auditory by some trick of eye, tone, or gesture, or he fails. . . . And this is the way to represent the shy, negligent, retiring Hamlet. . . .

I am not arguing that Hamlet should not be acted, but how much Hamlet is made another thing by being acted.[17]

What shall one say of this Prince of Denmark? He is indeed "nine parts" a Hamlet of soliloquy, and even the soliloquy is so interpreted as

16. *Ibid.*, I, 98, ff.
17. *Ibid.*, I, 100-101.

to rob it of any histrionic reality,—any "trick of eye, tone, or gesture." This is a prince whose utterances no longer have an "active" quality, no longer possess the vibration and passion which histrionic tradition has always given them. His words sink to "noise-abhorring ruminations"; he becomes in truth the "shy, negligent, retiring Hamlet."

But one may well ask in bewilderment: Is the "one part" that Lamb left for all else in Hamlet's character, *enough* to cover his active qualities, those exhibited in his varied adventures with the ghost, with the players, in the play scene, or during the trip to England? Or at Ophelia's grave, and in the fencing match? Again, does the script of the play allow one to interpret the soliloquies as coming from "holes and corners and the most sequestered parts of the palace"? Lamb's answer might be that we are too obsessed with the exigencies of stage presentation, an embarrassment that he had cast off forever.

This "shy, negligent, retiring Hamlet" might be termed a thoughtful version of the older sentimental prince. It is obvious that such a character could not be cruel or sharp in nature. What then did Lamb do with such awkward features when Hamlet's words seemed to suggest them? He was not willing to blame the feigned madness for sharp words to Polonius or Ophelia. With regard to the latter, he says that there may be "a profound artifice of love, to alienate Ophelia by affected discourtesies, so to prepare her mind for the breaking off of that loving intercourse, which can no longer find a place amidst business so serious as that which he has to do." If not such an artifice, such words and actions were, like Hamlet's puzzling manner toward Polonius, the "tokens of an unhinged mind."[18]

It is clear from a careful examination of this celebrated essay that Lamb obtained the type of Hamlet he wished,—the negligent, shy figure by soft pedalling or explaining away the annoying sections that he disliked. Obviously, stage presentation did not allow him to do this. It was only in the study that such a feat of alchemizing could be accomplished. And Lamb says, reminiscent of Maurice Morgann, that to absolve Hamlet of all censure, one must see the "whole of his character."[19]

As may be seen, Lamb's Hamlet has some family likeness to other romantic interpretations; but it is at the same time most individual also. This prince has his own literary (not dramatic!) personality. If one omits the embarrassing suggestion of madness with which Lamb tainted his shy prince, the other character elements merge into a recognizable unity. No other Hamlet is quite like this ruminating figure. He represents a flagrantly absolute but arresting interpretation of the Shakespearian script.

18. *Ibid.,* I, 103.
19. *Ibid.,* I, 103.

COLERIDGE

As an equipment for his task Coleridge, the most influential critic of *Hamlet* that has ever lived, combined a keenly analytical and penetrating mind with romantic tendencies. It was because of his powers of analysis, his ability to take the actual aesthetic data before him and examine them without destroying their essential dramatic integrity, that he achieved results most potent of all romantic critics before and after him. Although it is true that the final result is almost if not quite impossible of realization on any actual stage, the Coleridgean Hamlet represents a reading of the script so illuminating and even dramatically so convincing that one may say this great critic all but succeeded in rewriting the play.

Before going into detail concerning this Hamlet, it will be helpful to record several facts that cast light upon the mental and emotional prepossessions which Coleridge brought to his task.

First of all, it must be admitted that this critic was decidedly weak in any sound historical knowledge of Elizabethan literature and life. Here he shared a limitation with his times. What is more, he had little editorial acuteness, no knowledge of sources beyond that provided for him by such students as Steevens and Malone. Even such knowledge he did not always accept. His general knowledge of Elizabethan literature was fragmentary and inadequate.[20] It can be seen, therefore, that Coleridge did not possess the saving knowledge that his keenly logical and assimilative mind might have used to high profit in a judgment on *Hamlet*.

To this lack of historical knowledge Coleridge added the general attitude of idolatry—a critical approach that he shared with most of the romantics. In one place he says:

Shakespeare knew the human mind; and its most minute and intimate workings, and he never introduces a word, or a thought, in vain or out of place: if we do not understand him, it is our own fault or the fault of copyists and typographers; but study, and the possession of some small stock of the knowledge by which he worked, will enable us often to detect and explain his meaning. He never wrote at random, or hit upon points of character and conduct by chance; and the smallest fragment of his mind not unfrequently gives a clue to a most perfect, regular, and consistent whole.[21]

Such an attitude toward Shakespeare as this would inevitably tend to heighten the unhistorical bias that Coleridge already possessed. It was in itself an unhistorical tendency.

Of his own method of critical study, Coleridge says:

20. Raysor, *op. cit.*, I, xliv-v. In several respects, Coleridge's Shakespearian criticism shows genuine historical acuteness. For full discussion, see Raysor's complete introduction, *Ibid.*, I.

21. Raysor, *op. cit.*, II, 145.

Each scene of each play I read as if it were the whole of Shakespeare's works—the sole thing extant. I ask myself what are the characteristics, the diction, the cadences, and metre, the character, the passion, the moral or metaphysical inherencies and fitness for theatric effect, and in what sort of theatres. All these I write down with great care and precision of thought and language . . . and thus shall not only know what the characteristics of Shakespeare's plays are, but likewise what proportion they bear to each other.[22]

This passage gives evidence both of the critical soundness and also of the romantic weakness of Coleridge's approach to *Hamlet* criticism. In connection with the latter, one can see prefigured the usual romantic over-emphasis on passages in the play (usually the soliloquies) especially congenial to the critic's taste. One can see the danger of šuch a piecemeal analysis that loses sight of the play as a dramatic unit. But aside from such a prefigured weakness, the passage furnishes also an illuminating commentary on a critical method that formed the very heart of Coleridge's individuality as interpreter of *Hamlet*.

The plays to be examined were, he says, produced by a dramatist who "knew the human mind; and its most minute and intimate workings." They are filled with subtleties that can be detected only by the most careful examination of "diction, metre, character, passion, moral or metaphysical inherencies." It is significant that then Coleridge adds as final data for examination "fitness for theatric effect, and in what sort of theatres."

It is clear that if Coleridge meant what he says here, he was not abandoning the Shakespearian theatre in the same sense that Lamb abandoned it when he found as the most important item in the plays "that which comes not under the province of acting, with which eye, and tone, and gesture, have nothing to do."[23] This critic was concerned with the aesthetic minutiae as described above, to see how far they were registered in "action,"—that is, in eye, tone and gesture. In his mind he seems to be preserving a distinction between the dramatic genre and the exclusively literary form, a distinction of which he was thinking when he says that in *Venus and Adonis,* through the use of images Shakespeare was trying to "provide a substitute for that visual language, that constant intervention and running comment by tone, look and gesture, which in his dramatic works he was entitled to expect from the players."[24]

We are now ready to examine Coleridge's ideas on Hamlet. In Shake-

22. Wm. Knight, ed., *Memorials of Coleorton* (Edinburgh, 1887), I, 47.

23. Actually, Coleridge was willing to abandon the Shakespearian stage, as we may gather from the passage I have quoted, *supra,* p. 119. However, his motives for this attitude were not intrinsically undramatic. I shall have more to say on this point later in the present chapter.

24. From critique of *Venus and Adonis* in *Biographia Literaria.*

speare's portraiture of him, does our critic see the dramatist at work picturing the human mind in "its most minute and intimate workings"? The answer to this question emerges with startling distinctness from a mass of marginalia, lecture reports and isolated critical essays.[25]

Coleridge's central conception may be stated in a few words. He sees the prince as a man of great and splendid intellectual power, but with little ability to translate his impulses into action. He is above all else the prince whose

> native hue of resolution
> Is sicklied o'er with the pale cast of thought

In presenting such a Hamlet Coleridge gives both an interpretation of the essential outlines of his character, and a most arresting system of psychology:

In Hamlet I conceive him to have wished to exemplify the moral necessity of a due balance between our attention to outward objects and our meditation on inward thoughts—a due balance between the real and the imaginary world. In Hamlet this balance does not exist—his thoughts, images, and fancy [being] far more vivid than his perceptions, and his very perceptions instantly passing thro' the medium of his contemplations, and acquiring as they pass a form and color not naturally their own. Hence great, enormous, intellectual activity, and a consequent proportionate aversion to real action, with all its symptoms and accompanying qualities.[26]

All romantic Hamlets are for some reason or other "paralyzed." So, indeed, is the Coleridgean prince. However, his paralysis, shot through as it is with an intellectual quality, is dynamic and yeasty. Besides the active quality of the mind itself, there is another activity that is almost pathological. The mental energies that should be released in action cannot find their natural outlet:

If there be an overbalance in the contemplative faculty, man becomes the creature of meditation, and loses the power of action. Shakespeare seems to have conceived a mind in the highest degree of excitement, with this overpowering activity of intellect, and to have placed him in circumstances where he was obliged to act on the spur of the moment. Hamlet, though brave and careless of death, had contracted a morbid sensibility from this overbalance in the mind, producing the lingering and vacillating delays of procrastination, and wasting in the energy of resolving the energy of acting. Thus the play of *Hamlet* offers a direct contrast to that of *Macbeth*. . . . [27]

25. I shall quote the evidence from Coleridge's criticism without regarding as a relevant issue the date of each notation. For practical purposes it makes little difference; for it is difficult to see that there was in any way a "development" in Coleridge's ideas on Hamlet.

26. Raysor, *op. cit.*, I, 37.

27. *Ibid.*, II, 272-3.

There is more than one suggestion in Coleridge of a Hamlet who writhes in such hopeless throes, trying to resolve energies that cannot take their normal course. Indeed one might be tempted to interpret Hamlet's overpowering intellectual activity as partly a sublimation of such energies; but this would be reading into Coleridge a later conception. In several places, however, Hamlet's helpless impotence is stressed. He displays "vacillation and purely convulsive energies. He acts by fits and snatches." Even at the time when the duel is almost upon him, he has not changed:

He is all dispatch and resolution, as far as words and present intentions are concerned, but all hesitation and irresolution, when called upon to carry his words and intentions into effect; so that, resolving to do everything, he does nothing. He is full of purpose, but void of that quality of mind which accomplishes purpose.[28]

It should be added here that Coleridge seems to give Hamlet no credit for what ordinarily might be considered bona fide examples of action. For instance, besides belittling the prince's reasons for sparing the king at prayer—he adopts Richardson's theory of rationalization[29]—he gives Hamlet no credit for attempting to carry out his purpose at the time Polonius is killed by mistake. What is more, he sees as of importance in the trip to England, the disgraceful feature of Hamlet's allowing himself to be sent at all, ignoring the plain meaning of the script that he was compelled to go, under custody. Moreover, he does not see the significance of the triumphant return after successfully eluding the pirates and arranging the dispatch of Rosencrantz and Guildenstern. For Coleridge the prince is finally impelled to action by either chance or passion.[30]

To catch for these pages the full quality of the Coleridgean Hamlet, it will be necessary to examine the record still more closely. It is an arresting and delightful task. In the data before us the critic offers both the line by line analysis already described, and generalizations drawn from such a method. Ordered exposition is rendered more difficult through the fact that the method is half poetic. Even the generalizations are tinged with a color, an intangible half-appeal to the emotions. Above all, let me insist again, this Hamlet has clinging to him if not an histrionic, at least a dramatic quality. It is often difficult to catch the exact word or phrase that conveys this impression. All one can say is that the final imprint left by all the marginalia, lecture notes and other remains is of such a Prince of Denmark. Where this quality appears more specifically I shall point out the items that contribute toward such a sum total of impression.

28. *Ibid.*, II, 197.
29. *Ibid.*, 195-6.
30. *Ibid.*, I, 35; II, 209-10, and 273.

In a number of instances we catch a glimpse of the "Hamlet within." By an act of sympathy, we too, through Coleridge's words, look out on the world as Hamlet sees it:

He is a man whose ideal and internal images are so vivid that all real objects are faint and dead to him.[31]

A person, in whose view the external world, and all its incidents and objects, were comparatively dim, and of no interest in themselves, and which began to interest only, when they were reflected in the mirror of his mind. Hamlet beheld external things in the same way that a man of vivid imagination, who shuts his eyes, sees what has previously made an impression on his organs.[32]

His thoughts, images, and fancy [being] far more vivid than his perceptions.[33]

Of course, for one who has his eye on Shakespeare's script, Coleridge's interpretation seems possible only to a reader, not a spectator of the play; and even then is really plausible only if he interprets the soliloquies in isolation, and ignores the evidence that supports Hamlet's more normal qualities and actions. Of such a prince, one might say that, paradoxically what for us would be the normal subjective world is for him the objective world, and what is objective for us is subjective for him!

It is our good fortune that Coleridge plays again and again with the problem of Hamlet's character, holding his subject up for scrutiny in various lights and half-lights. One great passage gives an interpretation of the prince's strange subjectivity in terms of the Kantian sublime:

His mind, unseated from its healthy balance is forever occupied with the world within him, and abstracted from external things; his words give a substance to shadows, and he is dissatisfied with commonplace realities. It is the nature of thought to be indefinite, while definiteness belongs to reality. The sense of sublimity arises, not from the sight of an outward object, but from the reflection upon it; not from the impression, but from the idea. Few have seen a celebrated waterfall without feeling something of disappointment: it is only subsequently, by reflection, that the idea of the waterfall comes full into the mind, and brings with it a train of sublime associations. Hamlet felt this: in him we see a mind that keeps itself in a state of abstraction, and beholds external objects as hieroglyphics. His soliloquy, "Oh that this too, too solid flesh would melt," arises from a craving after the indefinite: a disposition or temper which most easily besets men of genius; a morbid craving for that which is not.[34]

What removes this passage from the class of mere closet criticism,—in other words, what gives it a certain relevance as dramatic criticism is the

31. *Ibid.*, II, 209-10.
32. *Ibid.*, p. 192.
33. *Ibid.*, I, 37.
34. *Ibid.*, II, 273. For the relevant passage in Kant, see *Critique of Aesthetic Judgment*, J. C. Meredith, ed. (Oxford, 1911), pp. 94, ff; especially p. 104. I am indebted to Mr. Raysor's discussion for drawing this to my attention.

fact that the inwardness of the interpretation is given a most plausible outwardness by Hamlet's activity at the moment—the speech. A skillful actor reading what Coleridge says might gather clues for expression, manner, and gesture. Such an assignment calls for a Garrick who is able to depict a "progress of impassioned sensation" that is unusual indeed. Upon his face he must bear the marks of a dynamic abstraction, an abstraction that conceals behind it as behind a veil, a world of no ordinary proportions; and his words must "give a substance" to these sublime shadows. This face must thus give evidence to the fact that the sensation it depicts is fed largely from within. Outward objects make no impact analogous to that provided in normal sensory reaction. They are merely hieroglyphics, cues that help to release activity in that other world which for Hamlet is reality. This explains why his words in soliloquy represent a desire to retreat from what we call external reality. His yearning is pathological and insatiable.

Of Coleridge's many attempts to set forth Hamlet, what I consider the most striking is a good-sized bit of marginalia commenting upon the "wassail music" speech, and the dramatic situation of which it is a part. Here we find the critic making a simple observation that may be considered inherently sound, but then immediately going *beyond* this observation to a lengthy explanation that gives a picture of the more extreme Coleridgean prince. This more extended elaboration is not so convincing as the shorter one, but, phrased as it is in Coleridge's half-poetic wording, one must keep his critical sense of values sharply at hand, or he will accept the extended analysis rather than the simpler one.

In the extended passage, the prince appears in a situation that forces the critic to show his relation to an outside world thrusting itself upon him. Hamlet himself has no desire to deny or retreat from *this* external reality. He is waiting and eager for it. However, even at this arresting moment when he is just about to meet the ghost, for a space he must retreat again into the abstractions that fill his mind on hearing the sounds of the revelry within the palace. Then, as the ghost appears, he again fixes his attention on this world of the here-and-now, to attend to the business at hand. Thus, in this bit of criticism, Coleridge presents three worlds, and does it within a dramatic framework: the visitor from beyond the grave appearing in the here-and-now; and Hamlet, who steps from the world of his own abstraction to meet the visitor.

Coleridge opens his comment with the notation: "apropos of the wassail music speech," and then adds the comment, "predominant idealism" and "ratiocinative meditativeness." He then proceeds:

It has the advantage of giving nature and probability to the impassioned continuity of the speech instantly directed to the Ghost. The momentum had been given to his mental activity, the full current of the thoughts and words had set in, and the very forgetfulness, in the fervor of his argumentation, of the purpose for which he was there, aided in preventing the appearance from benumbing the mind. Consequently, it acted as a new impulse, a sudden stroke which increased the velocity of the body already in motion, while it altered the direction. The co-presence of Horatio, Marcellus, and Bernardo is most judiciously contrived, for it renders the courage of Hamlet and his impetuous eloquence perfectly intelligible. The knowledge, the *unthought* of consciousness, the *sensation*, of human auditors, of flesh and blood sympathists, acts as a support, a stimulation *a tergo*, while the *front* of the mind, the whole consciousness of the speaker, is filled by the solemn apparition. Add, too, that the apparition itself has by its frequent previous appearances been brought nearer to a thing of this world. This accrescence of objectivity in a ghost that yet retains all its ghostly attributes and fearful subjectivity, is truly wonderful.[35]

To set forth clearly what Coleridge has said here, and to place his extended interpretation carefully into focus, one must say several things:

The preliminary phrasal comments, "predominant idealism" and "ratiocinative meditativeness" undoubtedly represent the more valid analysis of the wassail speech. But, considering what follows, one must label the critic's method contradictory and dualistic here. First, he gives a simple explanation of Hamlet's psychology, and then goes on to a further analysis that does not agree logically with what he has first said. Hamlet is waiting for the ghost to appear. As he waits, he fills in the moments with casual conversation as any of us would, and the cue to this casual talk is furnished to him by the drunken revelry, within.[36] Thus we can say that Coleridge's descriptive phrases taken in their simpler meaning, imply that Hamlet has not forgotten "the purpose for which he was there." He is merely filling in the anxious moments at hand by accepting the incidental subject for thought and speech that comes most easily to him. If Coleridge had stopped here, he would have been a sounder critic, but a less interesting one. Instead, he proceeds to the less sound, but appealing interpretation that follows in the long excerpt I have given. Here he abandons his initial sound evaluation to go further and in contradictory terms, set forth again his characteristic "deep prince," whose mental activities were perpetually at war with the demands of action. For better or worse, it is the latter picture that we must accept as Coleridge's considered contribution to *Hamlet* criticism.

Two other smaller passages are so relevant and illuminating as to demand inclusion here. Like the excerpt just quoted these two also, etch for us the relation between the unfathomably "deep Hamlet" and the out-

35. *Raysor*, I, 25.
36. See E. E. Stoll, *Shakespeare and Other Masters*, p. 140.

ward sign through which his character is registered histrionically. Of his words to the king. "A little more than kin, and less than kind," the critic here says:

No one can have heard quarrels among the vulgar but must have noticed the close connection of punning with angry contempt. Add to what is highly characteristic of superfluous activity of mind, a sort of playing with a thread or watch chain or snuff box.[37]

Thus in masterly fashion, Coleridge motivates Hamlet's aside by making it spring both from his sharpened emotion of the moment and from his razor-like intellect.

The second of the two comments is on the words of the prince to his mother, starting, "Seems, madam? Nay, it is; I know not 'seems.' " Here again, the critic sets forth his subjective prince with genuine plausibility, implying the very cast of countenance and trace of emotion that should be registered by the actor:

The aversion to externals, the betrayed habit of brooding over the world within him, and the prodigality of beautiful words, which are, as it were, the half embodyings of thoughts, that make them more than thoughts, give them an outness, a reality *sui generis,* and yet retain their correspondence and shadowy approach to the images and movements within.[38]

Indeed, one may pick up Coleridge's own words here, and say in general of his portrayal of Hamlet that it represents a brave and at least partially successful attempt to give a histrionic "outness, a reality *sui generis"* to that which by its very nature would seem to resist any such dramatic realization.

Concerning Hamlet's intellectual prowess there are several final items of interest that should not be overlooked. He is penetrating and quick in his detection of the hidden intentions of Ophelia, Polonius or the king.[39] On the other hand, he can analyse himself equally well, for he is "deeply acquainted with his own feelings"; he has, Coleridge says, "a perfect knowledge of his own character."[40]

The last item of evidence that bears on Coleridge's conception of the intellectual prince is his arresting account of Hamlet's mental workings, set forth in the *Essay on Method.* He possesses, says the critic, a mind of the highest generalizing and constructive power. Through a "methodizing mind" like Hamlet's,

Things the most remote and diverse in time, place, and outward circumstance,

37. *Raysor,* I, p. 38.
38. *Ibid.*
39. *Ibid.,* I, 30; II, 352.
40. *Ibid.,* II, 194-5.

are brought into mental contiguity and succession, the more striking as the less expected.[41]

That Hamlet has such power in superb degree is manifested by his words to Horatio, those in which he describes his fingering of the packet, and the subsequent events (V, ii, 4 ff). In an acute analysis Coleridge shows how even here an almost pathological mentality appears:

Here the events, with the circumstances of time and place, are all stated with equal compression and rapidity, not one introduced which could have been omitted without injury to the intelligibility of the whole process. If any tendency is discoverable, as far as the mere facts are in question, it is the tendency to omission: and, accordingly, the reader will observe, that the attention of the narrator is afterwards called back to one material circumstance, which he was hurrying by, by a direct question from the friend to whom the story is communicated, "How was this sealed?" But by a trait which is indeed peculiarly characteristic of Hamlet's mind, ever disposed to generalize, and meditative to excess (but which, with due abatement and reduction, is distinctive of every powerful and methodizing intellect), all the digressions and enlargements consist of reflections, truths, and principles of general and permanent interest, either directly expressed or disguised in playful satire.[42]

From the whole account of which this excerpt is a part, one may gather that Hamlet had a mind that was too quick. Like a superb dynamo that shakes to pieces its physical moorings, this man's mind used almost to the point of its own destruction all of the data which past and present experience presented it; and as it worked itself ever into some new excess, it got farther and farther from any relevant relationship with present environment. Thus at last we see the prince spinning his intellectual cobwebs over the open grave of Ophelia. Coleridge does not add the fact that one material item to be remembered in judging Hamlet there is that he does not know at the moment that the grave has been dug for Ophelia. It is only by ignoring matters of dramatic relevance such as this that Coleridge can make his telling interpretation of the romantic prince.

But, in spite of all this, here as in so many other places, the notable thing about the *Hamlet* criticism of Coleridge is that it possesses real, almost vivid plausibility.[43]

41. *Ibid.*, II, 340.
42. *Ibid.*, II, 337-8.
43. I am not prepared at the moment to trace the origin of Coleridge's ideas on "Method." However, I suspect that part of his treatment goes back ultimately to Kantian epistemology. Take for example this statement from the essay:
> Method . . . must result from the due mean or balance between our passive impressions and the mind's own reaction on the same. (Whether this reaction does not suppose or imply a primary act positively *originating* in the mind itself, and prior to the object in order of nature, though co-instantaneous in its manifestation, will be hereafter discussed.) *Raysor*, II, 338.
Coleridge does not fulfill his promise,—at least not in the same essay.

The "deep Hamlet" I have just set forth has several other characteristics that make him distinctly less freakish, more human than the central interpretation implies. He is noble, princely, and generous.[44] He is capable of quick and intense flashes of passionate anger, either against others or against himself.[45] His love for Ophelia is deep and abiding. At times this love acts as one psychological ingredient in a self-tormenting irony, visible, for example in his brutal jibe at Ophelia:

> Ha, ha! are you honest?

His wild mental stress at this moment, Coleridge says, is only partially feigned madness, for by cunning subtlety he is here pretending to act something which in reality he almost *is*.[46] One gains the impression, however, that when these gusts of wild passion and agony pass, the generalizing prince again retreats into his own world of sublime shadows.

In spite of the fact that Coleridge through the subtlety and power of his interpretation shows us the subjective prince "in action," it is nevertheless true that he wishes to emphasize the presence in him of depths for which the outward dramatic sign may be termed inadequate indeed,—just as the ripple may play over a pool of unfathomable depth. In one place[47] Coleridge calls to his aid a quotation from *The Borderers* of Wordsworth. Without exaggeration or misrepresentation, we can accept his suggestion, and apply the excerpt in its full sense to the Coleridgean Hamlet:

> Action is transitory—a step, a blow,
> The motion of a muscle—this way or that—
> 'T is done, and in the after-vacancy
> We wonder at ourselves like men betrayed:
> Suffering is permanent, obscure and dark,
> And shares the nature of infinity.
>
> (III, v, 405-10)

One modern commentator has said of Coleridge as critic:

His highest achievements are in his penetrating analyses of Shakespearean characters and in his profoundly imaginative re-creations of the full impression which Shakespeare may make in a mind more sensitive, more just and experienced, and more intelligent than the minds of normal men.[48]

To accept this statement at its full value might be perilous for one who wishes to be an objective historian of *Hamlet* criticism. However this seems to be true: One reason a critic such as Coleridge can extract from *Hamlet* his amazingly subtle interpretation is that in this play even more

44. *Ibid.*, I, 36-7.
45. *Ibid.*, I, 39-40; II, 194-5.
46. *Ibid.*, I, 39-40. This suggestion has its original source, of course, in Richardson.
47. *Ibid.*, I, 37.
48. *Ibid.*, I. xlviii.

than in others, Shakespeare created a character whose rich personality removes him violently and at times almost completely from the dramatic action in which he is placed. As the critic just quoted says in another part of his remarks, Shakespeare had "a profound interest in individual personality, over and above the needs of the action and sometimes at the expense of the action."[49]

It may be remembered that the man who wrote the *Remarks* of 1736 had a considerable inkling of this truth.[50] Coleridge however, almost a hundred years later, with his lack of historical perspective concerning sources, and thus of the real architecture of the play, and with his romantic bias,—with these handicaps, I say, could not see Hamlet's real relation to the plot in which he moves. The "excess meaning" in *Hamlet* offered to Coleridge a heady wine that intoxicated him. Thus he proceeded to create out of Shakespeare's rich and superfluous bounty his own psychological interpretation.

It is easy to see why, as far as *Hamlet* was concerned Coleridge should turn away from the stage, as indeed he turned from the Shakespearian stage in general.[51] Let me concede the availability of an actor to take the role,—no, go further and concede even a more debatable point: that the stage, involving though it does a medium-in-time, may catch many or most of the subtleties that Coleridge saw in Hamlet's character. Conceding, if one may, even these points, he must still say that this "deep Hamlet" could be realized histrionically only before an audience made up of a group of Coleridges.

Can one believe that Shakespeare himself, schooled as he was in writing down to the popular level of aesthetic appreciation, intended such a Hamlet? If such a prince is in the script, must it not be by some miracle of unconscious craftsmanship?

Possibly the only safe course for the present chronicler to take is resolutely to shake off the magic influence of Coleridge's critical and poetic subtlety; and affirm his belief that even if the above mentioned hypothetical Coleridges should leave their studies (under protest!) and go to the theatre, it is quite probable that the script of *Hamlet* might reassert its inalienable right to become, histrionically, its old self. If it did so, it would compel these super-subtle critics to adopt the simpler and more naïve psychology that is natural for theatre-goers. If this happened there would again emerge for them from Shakespeare's lines as brought to life on the stage, the traditional prince heroic and active, who would speak all the words that Coleridge quotes, and yet who would bear in his heart

49. *Ibid.*, I, xli.
50. *Supra*, pp. 54-5.
51. *Supra*, p. 119.

and mind none of the frightful weight of tormented subtlety that that critic found there.

HAZLITT

William Hazlitt, the last of the great romantic critics of these years, had most decidedly an individual approach to *Hamlet*. Unlike Lamb and Coleridge he presents the anomaly of being both theatrical and closet critic. He is much more derivative than either of the other two. However, his roving intellectual acquisitiveness was driven by a romantic gusto for experience that made even extensive borrowings seem his own. Even where these ideas of others strike the reader with painful obviousness, the text itself seems to make them the property of Hazlitt.

I have already touched upon this critic's analyses of the performances of Kemble and Kean.[52] It is clear that, different as his reaction to the interpretations of each actor is, he was critical of them for the same underlying reason. Neither one gave him the Hamlet he desired, for he saw the prince in romantic closet terms, in terms that had so little dramatic relevance as quite obviously to make the play impossible of adequate histrionic realization.[53]

In objecting to Kemble's "mannered Hamlet" and to Kean's active and "splenetic" prince, Hazlitt was caught within the meshes of a dilemma of which he was not conscious. As concerns Kemble, he was rejecting one of the more possible methods of satisfying the theatre-goer with romantic leanings. As concerns Kean, he was in reality objecting to the intrinsic nature of the Shakespearian script that Kean was interpreting with considerable emphasis on its older, fuller accents. Hazlitt himself wished neither interpretation. But his own is as impossible of stage realization as is the Hamlet in *Wilhelm Meister*.

Hazlitt's conception of the prince grew most unequivocally out of a philosophy of interpretation that is much like that expressed by Lamb in his essay of 1811. In fact much of his thought seems reminiscent of that critic:

It is only the *pantomime* part of tragedy, the exhibition of immediate and physical distress, that which gives the greatest opportunity for 'inexpressible dumb-show and noise,' which is sure to tell, and tell completely on the stage. All the rest, all that appeals to our profounder feelings, to reflection and imagination, all that affects us most deeply in our closets, and in fact constitutes the glory of Shakespear, is little else than an interruption and a drag on the business of the stage.
. . . Those parts of the play on which the reader dwells the longest, and with

52. *Supra*, pp. 121 and 124-5.
53. This is true in spite of his remark that if Kean should study the Shakespearian text carefully he would find that "Hamlet is a fine character in the closet, and might be made so on the stage, *by being understood.*" (*Works*, VIII, 518.)

the highest relish in the perusal, are hurried through in the performance, while the most trifling and exceptionable are obtruded on his notice, and occupy as much time as the most important. We do not mean to say that there is less knowledge or display of mere stage-effect in Shakespear than in other writers, but that there is a much greater knowledge and display of other things, which divide the attention with it, and to which it is not possible to give an equal force in the representation. Hence it is, that the reader of the plays of Shakespear is almost always disappointed in seeing them acted; and, for our own parts, we should never go to see them acted, if we could help it.⁵⁴

In short, Hazlitt's real enjoyment of Shakespeare came to him in the capacity of a reader. And in spite of his own experience as a theatrical critic, he read Shakespeare using principles of interpretation not legitimate for the critic who keeps in mind the full integrity of the script in his hands.

It is here that Hazlitt differed from Coleridge. The latter, in some of his *Hamlet* criticism at least, dealt with dramatic relevances. In his typical speech-by-speech and line-by-line analyses, he set forth an unfathomably deep Hamlet in inevitable contact with an outside world; and he showed the manner in which this contact is registered dramatically. Hazlitt, on the other hand, like Lamb was willing to abandon the stage as an aesthetic instrument incapable of registering the most valuable part of the play.⁵⁵

Thus this critic, like Lamb, cast himself loose from any technique of interpretation that might force him to respect the script before him. Indeed, in one of his finest passages, Hazlitt uses his freedom to indulge in pure poetic rhapsody. Here he sets forth Hamlet's universality,—the intimate association he has with our remembered past. He is "That Hamlet the Dane, whom we read of in our youth, and whom we may be said almost to remember in our after-years. . . ." As a consequence of such possession of the play, he says, "we hardly know how to criticize it any more than we should know how to describe our own faces." However, he finally overcomes this handicap and gives us his conception of the prince.

The Hamlet here outlined is a character in whom intellectual and sentimental qualities are combined. For the former, Hazlitt must have gone straight to Coleridge. For the latter, to the line of romantic critics that started with Richardson. In this prince, however, the Coleridgean element has the priority. It forms the fundamental bias of Hamlet's nature:

54. From *A View of the Stage*, first printed as "Mr. Kean's Richard II," in *Examiner*, March 19, 1815 (*Works*, VIII, 221-2).

55. He is not wholly consistent. At times he seems to accord full recognition to the script as *drama*; and at least implies that a critic would ignore these dramatic values at his own peril. See "On Shakespeare and Milton," *Works*, V, 48-9.

His ruling passion is to think, not to act; and any vague pretext that flatters this propensity instantly diverts him from his previous purposes.[56]

Again Hazlitt says:

The character of Hamlet stands quite by itself. It is not a character marked by strength of will or even of passion, but by refinement of thought and sentiment. Hamlet is as little of the hero as a man can well be: but he is a young and princely novice, full of high enthusiasm and quick sensibility—the sport of circumstances, questioning with fortune and refining on his own feelings, and forced from the natural bias of his disposition by the strangeness of his situation. He seems incapable of deliberate action, and is only hurried into extremities on the spur of the occasion, when he has no time to reflect. . . . At other times, when he is most bound to act, he remains puzzled, undecided, and sceptical, dallies with his purposes, till the occasion is lost, and finds out some pretense to relapse into indolence and thoughtfulness again.[57]

By "refinement of sentiment" as he uses it above, Hazlitt evidently meant the emotional sensitivity with which Hamlet reacted to the helpless situation into which he had been led through his over-refining intellect. The resulting emotional predicament is extreme indeed, and may be said to complete the paralysis started by the extreme activity of his mind. Kemble, Hazlitt says, failed in the role, "from a want . . . of that quick sensibility which yields to every motive, and is borne away with every breath of fancy. . . .There is a perpetual undulation of feeling in the character of Hamlet. . . ."[58]

But in spite of his great emotional capacity, this Hamlet is intellectual in dominant bias of character. He is not, however, a prince whose mental workings illustrate any Kantian sublime, nor the beauties of Method. He has self-knowledge, but what he perceives within himself is not an inner world, but weakness and paralysis. He thinks, but his thought must ever be colored with sentiment. In this respect, Hazlitt's prince seems quite unlike that of Coleridge. His procrastination is an intellectual-emotional compound in which rationalization, Machiavellian refinements of purpose, and a sort of vicarious imaginative fulfillment mingle. Such seems to be what Hazlitt must mean by saying that Hamlet's "ruling passion is to think, not to act." To illustrate these various strands in Hazlitt's thinking, the following passage is illuminating:

He refuses to kill the King . . . and by a refinement in malice, which is in truth only an excuse for his own want of resolution, defers his revenge. . . .
He is the prince of philosophical speculators; and because he cannot have his revenge perfect, according to the most refined idea his wish can form, he de-

56. From "Hamlet" in *Characters of Shakespear's Plays* (*Works*, I, 235).
57. *Ibid.*, p. 233.
58. From "Mr. Kemble's Retirement," *Times*, June 25, 1817 (*Works*, VIII, 377).

clines it altogether. So he scruples to trust the suggestions of the ghost, contrives the scene of the play to have surer proof of his uncle's guilt, and then rests satisfied with this confirmation of his suspicions, and the success of his experiment, instead of acting upon it. Yet he is sensible of his own weakness, taxes himself with it, and tries to reason himself out of it. . . .

Still he does nothing; and this very speculation on his own infirmity only affords him another occasion for indulging it. It is not from any want of attachment to his father or of abhorrence of his murder that Hamlet is thus dilatory, but it is more to his taste to indulge his imagination in reflecting upon the enormity of the crime and refining on his schemes of vengeance, than to put them into immediate practice.[59]

It is difficult to draw into any real unity all that Hazlitt says concerning the character of Hamlet. The dominant coloring of the remarks I have just quoted is of a prince not altogether pleasing in character. In the same essay this critic goes on to add: "He is full of weakness and melancholy, but there is no harshness in his nature. He is the most amiable of misanthropes."[60]

As can be seen, the dominant note of Hazlitt's critical method with *Hamlet* is impressionism. Taking his central cue from Coleridge he combined it with a number of other suggestions all of the same romantic cast. Better than either one of the other two great critics he illustrates a quality that seems typically romantic: his inspiration bloweth where it listeth. He was as wedded to "free conceptions" as Lamb, but was less original. His Prince of Denmark is far less attractive than the deeply appealing and poetic figure drawn by Coleridge. In another way his is unlike the Coleridgean Hamlet: His lacks the convincing dramatic relevance which that prince possesses. And finally, as would be expected from Hazlitt's method of synthesis rather than sharp critical analysis, his Hamlet lacks the individuality of the other two.

THE MINOR CRITICS: 1817-1821

Five critical contributions falling in the last five years of the period covered by this book deserve brief mention here. Aside from any question of intrinsic value, they offer additional evidence for the historian in his attempt to make accurate and valid generalizations.

Nathan Drake's large account of *Shakespeare and His Times* devotes a number of pages to *Hamlet*. This critic's position may be termed a synthesis of the tendencies of fifty years. He starts with a prince in whom the intellectual quality was most pronounced. Then, as in Hazlitt, this tendency is combined with all the sentimental, tender attributes which roman-

59. "Hamlet" *op. cit.*, pp. 234-5.
60. *Ibid.*, p. 237.

tic critics from Richardson on down had given Hamlet. The relationship
between intellectual and sentimental character-ingredients is fixed thus:

His powers of action are paralysed in the first instance, by the unconquerable
tendency of his mind to explore, to their utmost ramification, all the bearings
and contingencies of the meditated deed; and in the second, by that tenderness
of his nature which leads him to shrink from the means which are necessary to
carry it into execution.[61]

Surprisingly enough, for his description of Hamlet's intellectual tendency, as quoted above, Drake seems to go to A. W. Schlegel rather than to
Coleridge.[62]

Of the many other critical suggestions made by Drake, only one is
worthy of note here. Hamlet's mental state is described as so close to actual insanity that it is hard to make the distinction. The appearance of
the ghost "unhinges a mind already partially thrown off its bias, and fills
it with indelible apprehension, suspicion, and dismay."[63] Odd to say,
however, Hamlet knows he is unbalanced, and decides (as one might imagine only a sane man could decide) to counterfeit mental disorder.[64]

Oxberry's Hamlet of 1818 may be called the first appearance of the
prince as a fully developed "romantic genius."[65] This sentimental interpretation is couched in such terms as to seem almost contemporary. One
wonders whether Irving Babbitt may not have read Oxberry with approval:

His imagination is stronger than his understanding; he is always busied in satisfying the cravings of a romantic fancy, picturing to himself what he will do,
and thus losing the time for action in thinking upon its effects . . . . never indeed does he appear so happy as when, by some subtlety of excuse, he can de-
ceive himself and escape from the reality of deeds . . . . the intention . . . fades;
it is a cloud sailing on the winds of evening and changing with the winds . . . .

61. (London, 1817), II, 392.
62. See Schlegel, *Sämmtliche Werke* (Leipzig, 1846), VI, 248, starting: "Das Ganze
zweckt. . . ."
63. *Op. cit.*, p. 393.
64. *Ibid.*, p. 394. Drake is of course not original here. However he seems to imply a
state of mind much closer to actual insanity than that pictured by such others as
Richardson and Coleridge.
By the close of the period I am dealing with, the question of whether Hamlet was
really insane or not assumed serious proportions. Akinside, himself a physician, gave
such a position his name in the Eighteenth Century. In the second decade of the
Nineteenth, two "medical critics" took up the problem. Dr. Alderson deals at least
obliquely with it in his discussion of the objectivity of the ghost. (See "Essays on
Apparitions" annexed to the 4th edition of *Rhus Toxicodendron*, 1811.) And in 1813,
Dr. John Ferriar in *An Essay towards a Theory of Apparitions* (London) said that
Hamlet's character could be interpreted in terms of "latent lunacy."
65. Although the term "genius" had been applied to Hamlet before Oxberry, he was
the first critic to give the word the denotation set forth in the quotation above.

he seems like some lovely flower . . . half broken by a tempest, and looks even lovelier in its fall; . . . he is brave, pious, learned, affectionate, full of fervour and fancy; all his ideas are those of an uncommon genius, that perhaps loves too much to dwell in the kingdom of the imagination . . .[66]

Three other portraits from the pens of minor critics still lie before us: one is the "deep Hamlet" drawn on Coleridgean lines by a critic signing himself "T.C.," and published in *Blackwoods*, 1818;[67] another is Boswell's lines added to the last pages of the *Variorum Hamlet* of 1821; the last is a surprisingly interesting bit from the pen of a now forgotten writer in a theatrical journal.

It would be gratifying if one might record the fact that the *Variorum* notes represent a fine and discriminating choice of the most acute things said about Hamlet for over two hundred years. It is hardly so. The reader drops this volume, concluded by Boswell's own note, with weariness. It is difficult to find any guiding principle of selection beyond that evinced by a mere collector. And Boswell's own description of Hamlet is sentimental, and sentimental only. As far as this writer is concerned, Coleridge had added nothing of value on the subject. Goethe, on the other hand, received generous notice. A good sized paragraph from *Wilhelm Meister* is inserted in the notes.

Hamlet, like Charles I, says Boswell, was an example of a man born in the wrong period. Such an estimate may pass muster with the reader, but what shall we say of the direction Boswell takes later: he ends his critique with a eulogy of the late lamented George III, who achieved a measure of success that must be denied to both Charles I and Hamlet. With this inglorious note, the *Variorum* all but brings English criticism through 1821 to a close.

One critical item, dated December 1821, remains. Its point of departure is Hamlet's madness:

Of the general madness of *Hamlet* the proof is not clear. If his actions are often such as no man in his senses would commit, his words are such as no lunatic could utter. All the circumstantial evidence is on the side of his predominant rationality. He professes to adopt frenzy as a disguise: from the wildest ramblings of the mind, he suddenly rises into the loftiest philosophy, and there seems to rest upon the wing with the delight of a spirit escaped from a lower world of dissembling and emptiness. But the great dramatist was too deep in the secrets of Nature to have left him altogether untouched by the turmoil of the mind. He is in the midst of contagion; the atmosphere is coloured with an unusual light, and he must have worn its hue. He stands on the rocking of a

66. *Hamlet* (London), pp. xv, ff.
67. See Vol. II, 504 ff. The identification by Furness of "T.C." as Thomas Campbell is questionable. A. L. Strout attributes this essay to John Wilson. See "A Note on Shakespearean Criticism." *PQ*, 11, 91-3.

moral earthquake, and he must rock with it. All around him is fierce, strange, portentous, a whirl of parricide, conspiracy, and usurpation. He stands in the glare of a tyrant's royalty and his crimes. He is in the center of a dance of death; his night and day are surrounded with visions: his visitants are from the grave. Ambition and Love, the two great ministers of youthful hope, have sunk into the earth before his grasp. He feels his life devoted to one act of terrible justice, and is forced to clasp up his glowing genius and his generous heart in a cold and iron determination of murder. With a man harassed by such trials, perfect sanity of mind must be impossible. He is embarked in a storm, and must heave with the surge. Even the habitual disguise of madness would disturb the brain.[68]

Considering the general quality of the minor criticism that I have been recording, especially that from the *Variorum,* the passage quoted above seems amazingly acute. In fact it is good enough to honor the pen of a critic with more renown than "Mr. Dalby" achieved. These are the most sensible and balanced words on Hamlet that I have encountered in English criticism of the years 1800-1821.

CONCLUSION

To summarize: From the vantage point of the year 1821, what is the impression to be gained from a glance backward over nineteenth-century English criticism of *Hamlet?*

The romantic position has been matured and strengthened. The study rather than the theatre is now the generally accepted workshop for critics of this play. Coleridge's great and influential contribution has been made. The sentimental prince still appears, at times in pure isolation, and at other times in combination with the newer intellectual Hamlet. Hazlitt's prince is a notable example of the latter method.

The growth and full development of the romantic Hamlet were motivated partly by the inner preferences of the times; and partly by the fact that no adequate historical point of view had yet grown up to influence and shape the judgment of critics. Furthermore, what assistance English critics received from abroad,—from a Goethe or a Schlegel, for example, merely intensified them in their romantic leanings.

Of the minor critics little is to be said, beyond the fact that they often show how soon and how thoroughly the ideas of the greater critics were accepted. The last five men whose ideas I have described furnish proof that by 1821 the intellectual Hamlet must have been generally known and partially accepted. Oxberry's prince is an excellent simplification of the sentimental position set forth in phraseology that is, oddly enough,

68. From "The Dramatic Reflector" . . . by J. W. Dalby, in *The Drama—or Theatrical Pocket Magazine,* 2, 21.

relevant even now. Boswell's weak prince gives an indication of what from now on, one may expect from much English criticism: it had all but forgotten the existence of the heroic Hamlet. All the more refreshing it is, then, to discover in these years, so dominated by other points of view, an obscure critic who could pen words of illuminating sense about Hamlet's madness,—indeed, who could see him generally in terms that brush aside more than one of the critical absurdities of the time.

And finally,—as to the manner in which romantic criticism influenced the stage during these twenty-one years: No doubt the actors were obliged to accommodate themselves to new tastes, and in doing so produced a prince who differed from that of Garrick. He assumed Kemble's "manner" or displayed Kean's "splenetic energy." At times contemporary theatrical critics manifest a point of view colored by closet study, and thus saw in him certain "soft" characteristics. However, we have no real evidence that the histrionic tradition itself (as carried on by the actors themselves, or as interpreted by any considerable number of spectators) had changed in any marked way.

Viewed historically, it could hardly have changed. As witness for such a conclusion we have the interpretations of actors later in the century, actors who offer an heroic Hamlet that would be well-nigh an artistic anomaly unless their art had been fed from a traditional source offering them inspiration and guidance from a fairly immediate past. Such evidence, however, comes to us from a period that lies beyond the limits of this book.

9

French and German Criticism: 1800-1821

IT BECOMES quickly obvious to a student who examines foreign criticism of *Hamlet* in the Nineteenth Century, that the framework of twenty-one years which is so meaningful a category for this criticism in England is arbitrary indeed as a descriptive limit here. A much larger perspective of years would be necessary in order to show either French or German criticism in its true light. Since, however, such an extended treatment is impracticable for this volume, an effort is made here at least to sketch the larger critical picture of which these years form a part.

FRENCH CRITICISM

Concerning the histrionic tradition, these years offer little that has not already been recorded. No breath of real change had as yet blown through the French theatre.

The *Hamlet* of Ducis still reigned supreme, with the great actor Talma as the contemporary favorite in the leading role. For the sake of accuracy it may be well to give some attention to this actor's prince as reported by Madame De Staël, for in spite of the strictures that have been passed on the Ducis *Hamlet* earlier in this study, Talma's performance in its strange Gallic dress seems to have possessed some authentic spark of the Shakespearian spirit. At least he was able to register on his face some of the "progress of impassioned sensation" for which Garrick was so famous. Madame De Staël speaks of the manner in which the sight of the ghost in the coulisse was reflected in the actor's face for his audience, and of how impressive it was for them. And of the "to be" soliloquy she says:

Talma ne faisait pas un geste, quelquefois seulement il remuait la tête, pour questionner la terre et le ciel sur ce que c'est que la mort. Immobile, la dignité de la méditation absorbait tout son être. L'on voyait un homme, au milieu de deux mille hommes en silence, interroger la pensée sur le sort des mortels! Dans peu d'années tout ce qui était là n'existera plus, mais d'autres hommes assisteront à leur tour aux mêmes incertitudes, et se plongeront de même dans l'abîme, sans en connaître la profondeur.[1]

This prince is one that a follower of the English tradition might recognize. But Madame De Staël soon shows that, notwithstanding, he is

1. From "De la déclamation," in *De l'Allemagne*, 1810 (Paris, 1852), p. 335.

French. Her description of Hamlet's action before his mother is both Gallic and sentimental,—and the latter as it could appear only on the French stage:

Alors Hamlet tire le poignard que son père lui commande d'enfoncer dans le sein maternel; mais au moment de frapper, la tendresse et la pitié l'emportent, et, se retournant vers l'ombre de son père, il s'écrie: *Grâce,* grâce mon père! avec un accent où toutes les émotions de la nature semblent à la fais s'échapper du coeur, et, se jetant aux pieds de sa mère évanouie, il lui dit ces deux vers qui renferment une inépuisable pitié:

> Votre crime est horrible, exécrable, odieux;
> Mais il n'est pas plus grand que la bonté des cieux.[2]

Apart from Ducis, the histrionic tradition for these years is a melancholy story. Shakespeare generally, including *Hamlet,* furnished the material for opera, pantomime and circus performance.[3] In 1822, a year after the limit set for this study, the break came. *Hamlet* and other Shakespearian plays were acted publicly in English in a French theatre. After the opening efforts had been hissed off the stage, private performances still persisted before an enlightened few. And not many years afterwards both Charles Kemble and Edmund Kean gave their portrayals of the Danish prince in Paris.

FORMAL CRITICISM

In spite of the significant events that had been taking place in French political and social life, the standard of cultivated taste, or at least that standard in so far as it concerns classical tragedy, seems to have changed very little. We have already seen how conservative and slow to accept change the stage was. The same is true of all French criticism at that time. A deeply rooted aesthetic conservatism gave way only after many years; and even then the French kept their own Gallic point of view.

In the opening years of the century, some shift in attitude toward Shakespeare is evident in Madame De Staël and in Chateaubriand. While they did not abandon the French distaste for Shakespeare's "crudities" and "improprieties," they at the same time realized that his tragedies contained a force not to be found in French classical tragedy. Chateaubriand evidently sensed in French aesthetic opinion an increasing acceptance of Shakespeare, for he warned his countrymen that there was a danger in "returning to a love for the monstrous." He looked upon such a tendency as hazardous: "Chez les Anglais il n'y a qu'ignorance; chez

2. *Ibid.,* pp. 335-6. It must have been in 1809 that Madame De Staël first saw Talma act this Hamlet. See her letter to Talma quoted in Baldensperger, *op. cit.,* pp. 190-1.
3. Jusserand, *op. cit.,* pp. 450, ff.

nous il y a dépravation."[4] This critic could not forget that he was a Frenchman, and that therefore Shakespeare contained what for him was impossible of acceptance. He says: "Celui qui aime la laideur n'est pas fort loin d'aimer le vice: quiconque est insensible à la beauté peut bien méconnaître la vertu."[5]

Voltaire himself would have approved of Chateaubriand's sturdy aesthetic conservatism. Madame De Staël was more liberal. Writing first a year after Chateaubriand, she went further than he in admitting Shakespeare's superiority along certain lines. She had the same Gallic prejudice against "crudities," but she at the same time admitted Shakespeare's ability to portray tragic isolation in all its awful vividness.[6] Ten years later she came to the conclusion that it might be salutary if a dramatist could do what Talma had done on the stage: effect an union of Shakespeare and Racine.[7] A few years later, the critic N. L. Lemercier carried further still the process of French aesthetic liberalization. He seems to have reached the stage of the average neo-classical critic of the preceding century in England, the critic who was attracted to Shakespeare in spite of the fact that he broke the sacred rules. He admires his "art suprême à dessiner largement les physionomies historiques et passionnées dans tous les genres." For this critic, the "triste Hamlet" has his place in "l'immense galerie de ce poète michelangesque."[8] Later in the same work his words again take on an earlier-century tinge when he quotes Hamlet's words to the players as an illustration for his discourse on "Déclamation Dramatique."[9]

Against this general background of aesthetic opinion, one or two critical items of a more specific nature may be placed. Madame De Staël's most direct verdict is found in her volume of 1800. Here she sees the prince as at the center of one of the finest dramatic situations to be found in the theatre. She had of course read the play in its Shakespearian form; but her interpretation is obviously influenced by her familiarity with and admiration for the version of Ducis. She pays heavy attention to the soliloquies. Her prince is one of pure and virtuous spirit, but terribly bewildered and altered by the revelations of the ghost. He thinks of killing himself more often than of achieving his deed of vengeance (à la Ducis!). Furthermore, and paradoxically enough, his spirit was so

---

4. From *Mélanges Litteraires* (1801), in *Mélanges Politiques et Littéraires* (Paris, 1868), p. 377.
5. *Ibid.*
6. *De La Littérature* (Paris, 1800), pp. 162-3.
7. *De l'Allemagne*, p. 337.
8. *Cours Analytique de Littérature Générale* (Paris, 1817), I, 396.
9. *Ibid.*, IV, 80-1.

touched by the evil around him that he himself felt an anguish and mental stress that would befit a criminal, and this in spite of the fact that it was he who should be taking vengeance for crime.[10]

Madame De Staël's Hamlet as outlined above seems to have been the product of at least two streams of suggestion. In so far as she was not thinking of Ducis, she was using her own interpretation as formed in the study; and in the latter her mental process is similar to that used by such critics as Richardson and Goethe. That is, it tended to part company with histrionic tradition. At the time of her first words on Hamlet she did not make explicit the full implications of her position. She did this, however, ten years later. Her criticism was practically contemporary with similar utterances from the pens of Lamb and Goethe. Possibly her approach is a bit different. She says that Shakespeare is often too philosophical for the theatre, that his ideas were often lost in histrionic representation, and that there "sous ce rapport, il vaut mieux lire ses pièces que de les voir." She goes on to say, "il possède encore plus la connaissance du cœur humain que celle du théâtre."[11] It is unfortunate that we do not have an estimate of Hamlet's character written after Madame De Staël had articulated these views. Even her prince of 1800, however, shows himself akin to other ultra sensitive (or speculative) Hamlets that will be found in increasing number on the pages of nineteenth-century criticism.

Besides Madame De Staël there is only one other critic to mention. Intrinsically J. L. Geoffroy's comment of 1819 deserves little attention. But because of the very meagreness of the record, he merits a few words. What is more, the negative quality of his criticism helps to bear out my earlier statement that these twenty-one years of French criticism add little of notable interest for this volume.

Geoffroy had read both Shakespeare and Ducis. His essay consists of a three-way comparison of Sophocles, Shakespeare and Ducis,—to the advantage first of Sophocles, and second, as between Shakespeare and Ducis, of Shakespeare. *Hamlet* is taken by this critic as the typical representative of all modern revenge tragedies that display a hero quite different from Orestes. Such a hero, in comparison with the latter and his single-minded drive toward revenge, is weak: "C'est cette affreuse fermeté du fanatique qui Sophocle a voulu représenter comme vraiment tragique, et non pas les angoisses de l'homme faible, se débattant contre la volonté des dieux."[12]

10. *De La Littérature*, pp. 161-2.
11. *De l'Allemagne*, p. 189.
12. From "On Ducis' Hamlet" in *Cours de Littérature Dramatique* (Paris, 1819), III, p. 296.

So much for what seems to be the central idea of Geoffroy. The rest of his material is confusing and ununified. For example he confuses Shakespeare and Ducis on one important point. It is Ducis, not Shakespeare, who has Hamlet tell his mother that the goodness of heaven is equal to any crime. What is more, this critic insists that Hamlet is mad, and yet he does not reconcile such a condition with the hero's seemingly sane moments. Then with Gallic inevitability, Geoffroy emphasizes the absurdity of Hamlet's taking Polonius for a rat, and exhibits his words while the king is at prayer as "idées . . . burlesques et bouffonnes." In spite of such strictures, he sees Shakespeare as preferable to Ducis:

"Ce qu'il y a de très-certain, c'est que l'Hamlet de Shakespeare occupe toujours, et attache quelquefois, tandis que celui de Ducis fait bâiller à le représentation, et qu'on n'en peut pas soutenir la lecture."[13]

Slight as is the story of French criticism of *Hamlet* for these years, it contains at least suggestions of several tendencies or ideas found in contemporary English or German criticism. One idea is missing: There is no suggestion of an "intellectual prince." But thanks to Ducis and to Madame De Staël, the sentimental, "tender" Hamlet is there. The latter gives us also the almost inevitable complement of such a prince, her version of the Lamb-Goethe doctrine of "reading rather than seeing." Then thanks to Geoffroy, the mad Hamlet appears. There is nothing, however, that would lead one to forecast for the future in France such a plunge into subjectivity as showed itself inevitable in Germany even before the close of the Eighteenth Century. After all, it is not easy for the French to be like that. The Gallic temperament must ever keep some sense of reality. Restricted as it is, it cannot easily commit the romantic excesses of the Germans.

Up to 1821, indeed, it was not easy for the French critic to get more than partial glimpses beyond the narrow aesthetic enclosure in which his prejudices had kept him restricted. Even the privilege of being subjective is one that freedom alone can give. As I have pointed out, on the other hand, the French had been feeling a sense of increasing liberty. Soon *Hamlet* in English was to be playing in Paris, and most Frenchmen would be able to forget about even the baffling "gros rat." Like the critics, they were to take their place quite unequivocally in the international current of ideas that eddied around the figure of Shakespeare's prince of Denmark.

GERMAN CRITICISM: 1800-1821

During and even beyond the early years of the Nineteenth Century covered by this survey there was a contest for survival on the German

13. *Ibid.,* p. 302.

stage between the older Schröder version and that of Schlegel.[14] Although the Schröder version finally lost out, it did so only after a vigorous battle. The older play appeared in provincial theatres as late as the decade 1830-40. What is more, the translation of Schlegel itself had to undergo a number of revisions in the course of its early stage history, some of them in the form of compromises that damaged its validity as "real Shakespeare."[15]

It seems also a fact that the final victory of Schlegel was won at a price. With all of its weaknesses when considered as a valid representation of Shakespeare's play, the Schröder version had possessed a meaning for the German people. It suited the popular aesthetic taste that demanded a "family tragedy," or a more "classical play" than Shakespeare offered. On the other hand, as regards Schlegel's play, there is no evidence that it awoke any such degree of interest from the public as the earlier "verwässerte" versions. And this in spite of the fact that there was no scarcity of able and energetic actors to take the leading role. For example, Widmann records the fact that Pius Alexander Wolff, a fine actor, played the role in Berlin only nineteen times over a period of eleven years. When the man who is called the best product of Goethe's tutelage had only this modest record in the part, we may surmise that the aesthetic response to the Schlegel play must have had a highbrow rather than a popular quality.

There is ample reason for this, a reason that lies in the very nature of Schlegel's achievement, in the very validity of his success. No great masterpiece can be translated into a foreign tongue, least of all the Elizabethan Shakespeare into late eighteenth-century German. Schlegel produced something remarkably close to *Hamlet,* but in trying to reproduce the richness and metaphorical brilliance of Shakespeare, he had to press his native language into something at times un-German or even obscure. These very qualities, however, bear witness to the scrupulous effort he made to be true to his original.[16]

In getting a fairly complete idea of what happened to *Hamlet* on the German stage during these years, there is one other consideration to take account of. If it is true that the Schlegel play had to recruit its patrons from the upper level of the German populace, one can see that the potential audience was the same as that from which came the readers of the Shakespearian criticism increasing in volume with every year. And

14. Widmann, *op. cit.,* pp. 186, ff.

15. For example, the first version of Schreyvogel's adaptation (1825), omitted the graveyard scene (*Widmann,* p. 187); and in 1815, Klingmann inserted a chorus of young men and maidens into the graveyard scene (*Widmann,* pp. 191-2).

16. See comment of R. Pascal, *Shakespeare in Germany* (Cambridge, 1937), pp. 28-9.

one tendency in this criticism was the articulation of an attitude almost parallel with that set forth by those contemporary English critics, and Madame De Staël in France, who said that Shakespeare was unfit for the stage. In Germany the most famous mouthpiece for this position was Goethe. The main appeal in Shakespeare, he says, in words strikingly like Lamb's,[17] is not one that can be registered on the stage:

Shakespeare nun spricht durchaus an unsern innern Sinn; durch diesen belebt sich zugleich die Bilderwelt der Einbildungskraft, und so entspringt eine vollständige Wirkung, von der wir uns keine Rechenschaft zu geben wissen; denn hier liegt eben der Grund von jener Täuschung, als begebe sich alles vor unsern Augen. Betrachtet man aber die Shakespeare'schen Stücke genau, so enthalten sie viel weniger sinnliche That als geistiges Wort. Er läszt geschehen, was sich leicht imaginiren läszt, ja was besser imaginirt als gesehen wird. Hamlets Geist, Macbeths Hexen, manche Grausamkeiten erhalten ihren Werth erst durch die Einbildungskraft, und die vielfältigen kleinen Zwischenscenen sind blosz auf sie berechnet. All solche Dinge gehen bei'm Lesen leicht und gehörig an uns vorbei, da sie bei der Vorstellung lasten und störend, ja widerlich erscheinen.[18]

Goethe, as is well known, put into practice on the Weimar stage his belief that Shakespeare unaltered was unactable. As concerns *Hamlet,* indeed, he had experience to substantiate his views, for the Schlegel play presented at Weimar under his direction in 1809 could win only three performances.[19] Quite characteristically the last evidence connecting Goethe as theatrical manager with *Hamlet,* is the information that in 1812 he was contemplating a production in which Claudius was to take the place of Polonius behind the arras, and be killed by Hamlet![20]

But Goethe never produced such a version of the play. A more authentic *Hamlet* was gaining favor. True, the old lusty days of the "Hamlet fever" were over. Nevertheless the play was still an active force on the German stage; and because of the more genuine form in which it was now appearing it may be said that for the first time a hero whom Shakespeare might recognize as his, spoke the lines.

FORMAL CRITICISM

When one turns from the stage itself to examine formal criticism, he finds that these two decades offer only a modest harvest. There was one critic of importance: A. W. Schlegel. The names of three others may be included, also, and their contributions evaluated. Herder in one of his

17. Lamb's ideas were set forth two years earlier than Goethe's.
18. *Werke,* I Abteilung, XLI, 54 (from "Shakespeare und Kein Ende," 1813 section).
19. Widmann, *op. cit.,* p. 188. One cannot be surprised at Goethe's failure here. How could the creator of Wilhelm Meister's Hamlet be successful in producing the play from a fully Shakespearian script?
20. Pascal, *op. cit.,* p. 20.

last pieces used the play and its hero to illustrate his interpretation of the doctrine of tragic fate. F. W. Ziegler is of interest because of the critical method he pursued; and C. A. H. Clodius set forth a line of thought that illustrates one phase of the climate of opinion in Germany at the time. Although of slight intrinsic importance when compared with A. W. Schlegel, each has a certain interest for us, nevertheless, if one wishes a complete record for the period.

Herder's final ideas on Hamlet were included in his *Adrastea* of 1801.[21] His main object in the rather cryptic remarks here seems to be to use the prince as a modern example of his thesis that either in Greek or Modern tragedy, character is fate. It will be remembered that Herder had already characterized Hamlet as a "pathetic good fellow," with the implication that he was hardly capable of a stern and active task.[22] The critic has now changed his ground somewhat, but in final substance all he accomplishes is the presentation of a confused and paradoxical interpretation.

Herder first puts a question concerning the prince, who has just had the revelation from the ghost: "Warum fährt Hamlet nicht zu, und ermordet den Mörder?" He adds: "An Willen fehlte es ihm nicht, und gewisz nicht an Kraft, wie sein Schlag auf Polonius, sein Kampf mit Laërtes, und so mancher Monolog beweisen."

The critic then goes on to solve the problem he has presented, and his solution is strange indeed. Odd to say, this Hamlet of his, who had "strength" and "will," had also other qualities that nullified the former. He turns out after all to be a Goethean prince with a speculative cast that has been accentuated by a sojourn at Wittenberg. And of that sojourn Herder rhapsodizes: "Glückliche Idee, die dem Dichter von unserm Wittenberg, vom Hange der Deutschen zur Metaphysik anhing!"

At moments it is the speculative cast of this Hamlet that seems to determine his action, at times his sentimental, or "soft" side, for his "Seele ist eben so zartfühlend als nachdenkend." He suspected the ghost because of metaphysical and conscientious scruples. He does not kill the king at prayer, Herder says, because his own "geistiges Gefühl" and Shakespeare's "zärteres Gefühl" (for his own creation) forbade it.

How then was vengeance finally accomplished? No matter what his creator may say to the contrary, it is obvious that Herder's soft and speculative prince could not do the task! Destiny then stepped in, and the guilty ones really committed suicide by drinking the poison: "So ist von diesem Orestes der Mord des Vaters rein und Schuldlos gerächt. . . .

21. *Sämmtliche Werke*, XXIII, 362-5. It is possible that Herder's criticism appeared a year earlier. Furness in his *Variorum Hamlet*, II, 276, dates the passage as 1800.
22. *Supra*, pp. 100-101.

Den guten Hamlet konnte Trotz aller Vorschritte, selbst seines Vaters
Geist aus seinem Charakter nicht treiben."

Such is Herder's final picture of Hamlet. In spite of the fact that the
critic explicitly gives the prince a bill of health here to free him from
any imputation of lack of will or courage, he turns out to be a "paralyzed" hero who quite fittingly is a companion for the Hamlets of either
Goethe or Friedrich Schlegel. Even the Tragic Fate which Herder evokes
here to aid his helpless "hero" can hardly give the drama a convincing
dénouement.

F. W. Ziegler came next. One's first impression of him is that he is
absurd. Himself an actor and a stage Hamlet, he set forth an interpretation that has little to do with any authentic (or unauthentic) script he
could have possessed. But considering the direction that German criticism was to take, Ziegler has some importance. He set forth ideas and
displayed critical tendencies that were prophetic of such critics as Tieck,
Klein and Werder.

One major obstacle, Ziegler thought, in the way of Hamlet's carrying
through his revenge was external. He was avid for revenge, but the king
was too well guarded. After the revelations of the ghost and Hamlet's resulting storm of emotion had subsided, his situation is described thus:

Nun kommt er zu sich—er sieht, dasz es Nacht ist; er erinnert sich, dasz eine
Mauer von Garden den Mörder umgibt. Er schiebt das Schwerdt also unwillig
in die Scheide; aber der Mensch, der sich an dem Objekt selbst nicht rächen
kann, musz für seine Rache doch etwas thun. Er musz sie äuszern und Hamlet
hängt seinen Onkel *in effigie* in seiner Schreibtafel auf. Dieser Zug ist sehr wahr
und schön.[23]

However, the whole desperate situation of the prince was more serious
than mere external difficulty. The dramatist evidently knew what he was
doing in making it impossible for Hamlet to proceed at once, for such
an activity would have been destructive to both the hero's character and
to the subtleties of the play:

Könnte Hamlet ein Heer ins Feld stellen, er würde ohne Zweifel rascher zu
Werke gehen und nicht zagen; aber so musz er gegen sein Temperament; gegen
seine Erziehung und Geburt das Strafamt selbst verrichten und an wem?—An
einem Onkel, dem Gemahl seiner Mutter—an einem, von seiner Nation gewähl-
ten König.[24]

As Ziegler proceeds, it is evident that he interprets Hamlet as realizing
that he must not kill the king until his guilt is clear, and also, by special
injunction from his father, until his mother will not be damaged nor

23. *Hamlets Charakter nach psychologischen und physiologischen Grundsätzen* . . .
zergliedert (Vienna, 1803), p. 48.
24. *Ibid.*, pp. 53-4.

compromised by the deed. All these ideas are clearly prophetic of later German critics. Adopting Schröder's arrangement of the "to be" soliloquy, which placed it immediately after the instructions to the players, Ziegler goes ahead to describe Hamlet's mind at the time of that soliloquy:

Nun erst ist er fähig, zu überlegen, wie die von ihm geschriebene Komödie oder die eingeschobenen Scenen auf den König wirken, und welche gefährliche Folge sie für ihn haben müssen und auch wirklich haben.[25]

This critic goes on to say that if the king betrays his guilt, Hamlet feels that he must at once put him to the sword; but even then the prince will not have properly fulfilled his tragic task. Merely killing the king will not serve the subtleties of the situation:

Hauen ihm des König's Anhänger und die Garden nicht zusammen, was er fürchten musz: so musz er doch vor ein förmliches Gericht, den Königs Mord [*sic*] vertheidigen; . . . Er setzt seine Mutter, die ihm der Vater befohlen hat zu schonen, in eine schreckliche Lage; denn sie klagt sich selbst an, wenn sie den Sohn vertheidigen will und er hat auch alles von ihrer Selbsterhaltung zu fürchten. Die rabenschwarze Ungewiszheit breitet ihre bleierne Fittige über ihn und eine peinliche Unruhe lagert sich über seine so unentschlossene Seele. . . . Die Folgen des Schauspiels stehen in ihrer ganzen fürchterlichen Gestalt vor seiner Seele—er sieht die Freunde und Garden mit geschliffenen raschen Schwertern; oder den Richter mit kalter Miene über den Königs Mörder [*sic*] sein Urtheil sprechen. . . . In dieser gefährlichen Lage fängt er das verzweifelte Grübeln über Leben und Tod an; . . .[26]

In such a manner as this Ziegler in 1803 gave German critics a prophetic blueprint for their later activities. Could they go much further in the process of reading what they wished into the dramatic situation or into the hero's psychology? Or in a spawning of subtleties that could not find a place within a dramatic framework? It would hardly seem possible.

Leaving Ziegler, let us turn to a far greater critic, indeed to the first unequivocal champion in Germany of the "thoughtful Hamlet." I refer to A. W. Schlegel, and his criticism in the Vienna lectures of 1809-11. His interpretation had already been hinted at by his brother, Friedrich, and, during the same years covered by his lectures, was being developed in England by Coleridge.[27]

25. *Ibid.*, p. 75.
26. *Ibid.*, pp. 75-8.
27. The question of whether Schlegel or Coleridge deserves priority in credit for developing the "thoughtful Hamlet" will probably never be finally answered. The testimony of at least two witnesses, J. P. Collier and Henry Crabb Robinson gives the priority to Coleridge. Robinson at least would seem a reputable witness. This much is surely true: Coleridge developed this interpretation independently of Schlegel. And the important fact remains that anyway, from the point of view of real substance and quality,—or even of quantity, Coleridge's criticism is vastly superior to that of Schlegel. (See Raysor, *op. cit.*, I, lii-liii.)

Schlegel starts with a paradox that might well have caused him to pause further before setting forth his prince whose,

native hue of resolution
Is sicklied o'er with the pale cast of thought

He phrases the paradox thus: "Am meisten musz es in Erstaunen setzen, dasz bei so versteckten Absichten, bei einer in unerforschte Tiefen hinabgebauten Grundlage, das Ganze sich auf den ersten Anblick äuszerst volksmäszig darstellt."[28] Like many another critic of *Hamlet*, however, Schlegel did not see the full nature of the baffling dualism to which his paradox leads—a play for the stage and one for the study,—two separate entities with little or no relation to each other.

Schlegel's Hamlet is, then, this second prince, not the "volksmäszig" one of the stage. The critic puts Hamlet's major characteristic in a few words when he says: "Das Ganze zweckt ja dahin ab, zu zeigen, wie eine Ueberlegung, welche alle Beziehungen und möglichen Folgen einer That bis an die Gränzen der menschlichen Voraussicht erschöpfen will, die Thatkraft lähmt; . . ."[29] He then proceeds to describe a prince for whom, on the whole, he can have only an unfavorable reaction. In spite of Hamlet's high qualities, he cannot praise him as Goethe does. He proceeds: "Aber bei seinen so oft gefaszten und immer unausgeführten Vorsätzen ist die Schwäche seines Willens offenbar: . . ."[30]

Besides these undesirable qualities centering around a weakness in volition, this prince has a romantic propensity toward absorption in his own emotional processes:

Am meisten ist er verklagt worden wegen der Härte, womit er Ophelias von ihm selbst veranlaszte Liebe zurückstöszt, und wegen seiner Fühllosigkeit bei ihrem wiewohl unwillkürlich verschuldeten Tode. Aber er ist zu sehr in seinen eignen Gram versunken, um Mitleiden für Andre übrig zu haben: seine Gleichgültigkeit giebt uns den Maszstab seiner innern Zerrüttung.[31]

Schlegel noted also a quality that is akin to the "cruelty" which had bothered so many critics in connection with Hamlet:

Dagegen spürt man unläugbar in ihm eine tückische Schadenfreude, wenn es ihm gelungen ist, mehr durch Noth und Zufall, die ihn allein zu raschen Streichen treiben können, als durch das Verdienst seines Muthes, seine Feinde aus dem Wege zu räumen; so äuszert er sich nach Ermordung des Polonius und über Rosenkranz und Güldenstern.[32]

28. "Vorlesungen uber Dramatische Kunst und Literatur," *Sämmtliche Werke* (Leipzig, 1846), VI, 247.
29. *Ibid.*, p. 248.
30. *Ibid.*, p. 249.
31. *Ibid.*, pp. 249-50.
32. *Ibid.*, p. 250.

And finally, this "hero" offers an example of extreme skepticism:

Hamlet hat keinen festen Glauben, weder an sich noch an irgend etwas: von Aeuszerungen religiöser Zuversicht geht er zu skeptischen Grübeleien über; er glaubt an das Gespenst seines Vaters, wenn er es sieht, und sobald es verschwunden, wird es ihm beinahe zur Täuschung . . . der Dichter verliert sich mit ihm in den Irrgängen des Gedankens, worin man weder Ende noch Anfang findet. Und auch die Gestirne geben durch den Lauf der Begebenheiten keine Antwort auf die so dringend vorgelegten Fragen. . . . Das Schicksal der Menschheit steht da wie eine riesenhafte Sphinx, die jeden, der ihr furchtbares Räthsel nicht zu lösen vermag, in den Abgrund des Zweifels hinabzustürzen droht.[33]

Of the various motifs of character stressed by Schlegel in the passages quoted, the one definitely new so far as German criticism is concerned is his emphasis on the intellectual. The other motifs are for the most part commonplaces that Schlegel might have gathered almost anywhere on the pages of earlier critics.

Schlegel's prince is not a great nor an arresting figure. Much as German Shakespearian criticism owes to Schlegel in general, here he cannot be awarded distinction nor high influence. In influence, his fellow German, Goethe, must receive priority over him. What is more, entirely aside from the moot question of originality, it is the Coleridgean intellectual prince who must be accorded acclaim in the annals of *Hamlet* criticism. By their very nature the critical formulas of all three—Goethe, Coleridge, and Schlegel, are, from the histrionic and historical points of view, misreadings of the script; they are romantic exaggerations. The secret of the power and influence of Goethe and Coleridge lies in the fact that with rare and complete sympathy they infused into their interpretations a portion of their own poetic spirits. Their criticisms therefore are almost poetry. Schlegel, although himself a poet like the other two, did not do this. His words are unsympathetic, objective and rationalistic. They do not fire the imagination nor touch the heart.

After Schlegel there is only one other piece of criticism that falls within the chronological limits set for this study. Goethe's *Shakespeare und Kein Ende* has already been discussed, at least in so far as it has relevance here. The other piece is a fairly long discussion of the play by C. A. H. Clodius, dated 1820.[34] The content and tone of this essay show that its author had fallen under the influence of the romantic ideas developed after 1800 by such critics as Schelling and Friedrich Schlegel. These critics came to see tragedy in the light of a religious significance. Friedrich

33. *Ibid.*, pp. 250-1.
34. "Ueber Shakespeare's Philosophie, besonders im Hamlet," in *Urania, Taschenbuch auf das Jahr 1820*, Leipzig.

Schlegel was struck with the gloom and pessimism of Shakespeare, and thought of that dramatist's skeptical genius as lacking the Christian qualities of Calderón.[35] He speaks of him as "the most dolorous and tragic of all ancient or modern dramatists,"[36] and specifically mentions in this connection Hamlet's skeptical views that "invest him with a strange mysteriousness."[37] In another illuminating passage, Schlegel says of Shakespeare: "Im Innersten seiner Gefühls—und Behandlungsweise ist Shakspeare mehr ein alter, wenn auch gerade kein griechischer, sondern vielmehr ein altnordischer Dichter, als ein christlicher."[38]

It was in harmony with ideas such as these that Clodius set forth his views on Hamlet. On the whole his is an un-Christian prince who can "drink hot blood," and who lived in a world over which Hell itself had spread its torment and blight. This world was one in which the Old Testament principle of vengeance,—an eye for an eye and a tooth for a tooth prevailed. Hamlet himself, who is of a somewhat soft and gloomy nature, possesses an "etwas weichliches und schwermüthiges gefühl," a character "der seine Feindschaft mehr in Worten, als in Thaten an den Tag zu legen vermag." He had picked up at his father's court and at Wittenberg a profound skepticism. He believes neither in life nor in a higher intelligence. His studies are unfinished, for he has not added to his belief in man's corruption, the saving factor of Augustinian grace. Added to all this comes the terrible crime involving his father, to plunge him into a nightmare of skeptical negation: "Das aus seiner Verborgenheit hervorgezogene Verbrechen hat mit kaltem Hauche in Hamlets Innerm fast jeden Funken von Liebe und Glauben erstickt, ..."[39]

There is one final touch to crown the horror. Hamlet's assumed madness becomes real. The feeling by which he was driven became too strong. Clodius describes the process of deterioration:

So endlich Hamlets geistiger Stolz aus Geniestolz, Tugendstolz, Philosophenstolz, Rangstolz und Ehrgeiz zusammengesetzt, wird, durch die Erscheinung des väterlichen Dämons, zur heftigsten Rachsucht dann zum Rande des anfangs nur nachgeahmten, späterhin, gleichsam aus Strafe fast natürlich gewordenen Wahnwitzes, hingerissen, wenigstens zu einem melancholischen Tiefsinne, der die Phantasie bis zum Spott über Alles hinaufschraubt, und jede natürliche Ansicht,

35. "Shakspeare hat den entgegengesetzten Fehler, dasz er uns das Räthsel des Daseins, wie ein skeptischer Dichter, allzu oft nur als Räthsel in seiner ganzen verwirrung und Verwicklung vor Augen stehen läszt, ohne die Auflösung hinzuzufügen." (*Sämmtliche Werke,* II, 131).

36. *Ibid.,* p. 137.

37. It is probably no accident that A. W. Schlegel in his contemporary lectures at Vienna was also stressing Hamlet's skepticism. (See *supra,* p. 163).

38. *Op. cit.,* p. 131.

39. For this and the preceding excerpts from Clodius, see *op. cit.,* pp. 293-7.

jedes Ebenmaasz der Dinge verrückt. Hierin hätten wir eine wahre innere Handlung, das wahre Tragische des Stücks.[40]

It is such a tortured and maddened seeker of revenge as this who finally
sinks with the guilty to ruin, at the end of the play. Paradoxically, however, the unfortunate madman has a humour and philosophical depth
that keep Clodius interested in him.

Taking all into consideration, it is not difficult to see why Clodius felt
that he must disagree with Horatio's final eulogy: "Izt bricht ein edel
Herz. Schlaf wohl, mein süszer Prinz."

Here Clodius calls the English Steevens to his support. Whatever else
be its fate beyond the grave, this critic feels that Hamlet's spirit cannot find
a "Christian" peace. There is in the play, he says, just a hint of such a
higher philosophy, a hint and no more.[41] On the whole the play and its
mad hero are part of "das Zeitalter der romantischen Barbarei."

With Clodius we come to the end of German criticism, in so far as
this book can set it forth. It is obviously impossible to find in the positions of these several critics any single unifying principle,—unless it be
the romantic tendency that in its various manifestations seems to color
each. German criticism of *Hamlet* has its own physiognomy, in part con-
ditioned by the fact that, like French criticism it must approach the play
from without. Its intellectual and imaginative bias is individual to a
marked degree. It is subjective in its own heavy-handed Teutonic way,
the net result of which is in one fashion or another to rob the play of
its integrity as a histrionic entity. German criticism can be experienced
more easily than described; and this exposition is indeed a failure if it
does not offer the concentrated materials for such an evaluation.

Within the next few years in Germany, critic after critic was to add
his contribution to what was becoming even in 1821 a truly formidable
and amazing body of material, centered as it was around a foreign masterpiece in another language and belonging to another people. One
critical complexity in particular loomed immediately ahead. The He-
gelians must soon have their day!

40. *Ibid.*, p. 301.
41. See the words of Marcellus, I, i, 157, ff.

A Final Word

WITH the year 1821 this volume has reached its point of terminus. In England the greater critics, with Coleridge at their head, had fixed a romantic point of view as the reigning philosophy of interpretation. The stage kept alive, with a somewhat lessened potency, the older heroic tradition.

French criticism of *Hamlet* was still largely a continuation of eighteenth-century tendencies; and no really Shakespearian prince had yet appeared on the stage.

German criticism had already gone to extremes in subjective interpretation,—extremes that it was to surpass in later years. On their stage the Germans had seen and were seeing (perhaps unwillingly!) Schlegel's authentic translation.

In final summary of the material in this volume, these points may be made:

There is the continuity of the histrionic tradition: No other English play has had as vital, or as consistent, or as honorable a tradition on the stage as has *Hamlet*.

Of formal criticism itself, from its first meager beginnings in the early Seventeenth Century to its confusing abundance in the first quarter of the Nineteenth, one may note the simplicity of its genesis and the complexity of its final many cross-currents; how with increasing inevitability, the play and the character of Hamlet himself, drew the primary attention of Shakespearian critics.

Then there is the manner in which *Hamlet* criticism gathered body and meaning as critics of varying degrees of analytical acuteness gave it their attention. What is more, this criticism furnishes an amazingly interesting commentary on the different climates of opinion that are registered in the very coloration and point of view seen in the ideas themselves.

There is also the sharp dualism that develops and becomes ever more accentuated as the Eighteenth Century progresses, between the acted tradition and a closet criticism that sets forth the romantic Hamlet in his several aspects.

One may see, furthermore, the slow working out of the principles of historical criticism, starting with such men as Hanmer, and gaining impetus in the work of scholars like Malone. Almost obliterated from consideration by the romantic critics, it will again gain force in later *Hamlet* criticism, but not reach maturity before modern times.

The cosmopolitan nature of *Hamlet* criticism is built securely on the foundations of French and German criticism, starting in the Eighteenth Century. Each of these countries saw the prince through the lenses of its own national bias and prepossession. Neither contributed any wholly new factor to the sum total of the critical canon. We may, however, see in these two bodies of foreign criticism what happens when the interpreter is either classic or romantic to the extreme. No Englishman could outdo Voltaire in the former; and possibly even Coleridge, although more original and powerful, is not more extreme in his romantic bias than is Goethe. Today, *Hamlet* criticism is truly international. In this field the French and the Germans were the pioneers.

Two hundred and twenty years have been covered by this survey. Somewhat over a hundred lie ahead for the chronicler who may wish to bring the record down to the present. It is doubtful whether the years ahead of 1821 can be gathered into two volumes of this size, for *Hamlet* scholarship finally becomes a literary deluge. These confusing seas should be charted, for they will no doubt produce new facets of interest for those who find absorbing the career of Shakespeare's prince. Luckily though, for those who wish to keep some sense of reality through it all, there exists today a sound historical criticism. But more important still, the stage still produces gifted actors who carry on the tradition established by Burbage, Betterton, and Garrick. An heroic, active prince still walks the boards,—from Burbage to Evans, the splendid continuity holds. And after Evans there will be others, we can be sure of that. Without a knowledge of this fact, we might well tremble for the fate of Hamlet at the hands of the critics.

Index